Under the editorship of

DAYTON D. McKEAN

University of Colorado

OTHER TITLES IN THE SERIES

The Government of Republican Italy
JOHN CLARKE ADAMS and PAOLO BARILE

British Parliamentary Democracy
SYDNEY D. BAILEY

The Federal Government of Switzerland
GEORGE A. CODDING, JR.

Government and Politics in Israel
OSCAR KRAINES

Contemporary Government of Japan
THEODORE McNELLY

The Indian Political System
NORMAN D. PALMER

Contemporary Government of Germany
ELMER PLISCHKE

Norwegian Democracy
JAMES A. STORING

South Vietnam:

Nation

Under Stress

ROBERT SCIGLIANO

MICHIGAN STATE UNIVERSITY

HOUGHTON MIFFLIN COMPANY · BOSTON

CONTENTS

FOR JUNE

PREFACE

This book deals with South Vietnam since independence. For practical purposes, Vietnamese independence was achieved in July, 1954. In that month, at Geneva, Switzerland, France reached a political settlement to the Indochina War which recognized Communist authority over all of the northern half of Vietnam. In that month, also, Ngo Dinh Diem formally acceded to power in the southern part of the country. These two actions decisively marked the end of the colonial period in Vietnam's history and the beginning of its modern period of independence.

This is not a history of modern Vietnam, but rather an analysis and assessment of major developments in South Vietnam during its brief experience as an independent state. Material relating to the colonial and earlier periods has been introduced where this has been essential for understanding recent developments. My approach to the subject has been essentially political, although I have treated economic and military developments in addition to more strictly political developments. Perhaps it is sufficient justification to say that in Vietnam, at least, all important developments are related to and ultimately dependent upon the political equation.

I have had to grapple with problems of fact and interpretation that beset anyone who attempts to deal seriously with recent Vietnamese events, and I am not sure that I have overcome all of them. I do know that I have been very considerably aided by the willingness of others to read and criticize the manuscript for this book. I must first thank those who read and commented upon major portions of the manuscript: Professors Wesley R. Fishel, Guy H. Fox, and Lloyd D. Musolf, of Michigan State University; Professor John D. Montgomery, of Boston University (whose own study of *The Politics of Foreign Aid* was helpful in two chapters of this book by providing information and a check upon my own data); Mr. Douglas Pike, of the U.S. Information Agency; Mr. Hoang Van Chi, of Paris, France; Mr. C. Richard Spurgin, of the U.S. Foreign Service; and Mr. Nguyen Thai, of Cambridge, Massachusetts. The following persons were kind enough to read and comment upon certain parts of the manuscript: Professors John D. Donoghue and Milton C. Taylor, of Michigan State University; Professor Frank C. Child, of the University of California at Davis; Mr. Roger Hilsman, Assistant Secretary of State for Far Eastern Affairs; Mr. Robert H. Johnson, of the Policy Planning Council, U.S.

State Department; and Mr. Dang Van Sung, of Saigon, Vietnam. In expressing my indebtedness to these people, I must at the same time exonerate them from any responsibility for the final product.

I must acknowledge too the help which was extended to me in the course of my Vietnamese research by Mr. Leonard Maynard, of the U.S. Agency for International Development; and Messrs. Pham Xuan An and Dang Duc Khoi, of Saigon, Vietnam.

My scholarly interest in Vietnam developed during the two years I spent in that country, from 1957 to 1959, as a member of the Michigan State University Vietnam Advisory Group. Grants from the Rockefeller and Ford Foundations, the latter given to me through the International Programs Office of Michigan State University, enabled me to return to Vietnam in 1961 and to obtain the time and assistance for writing this book. My colleague Ralph H. Smuckler, Associate Dean of International Programs, assisted the execution of my project in much more than the obvious way of providing financial means.

Finally, I must thank Mrs. Hilda Jaffe, of the Bureau of Social and Political Research, and Mr. Richard N. Clark, of the Houghton Mifflin Company, for their editorial assistance; Miss Barbara Rall, Mrs. Janet Brooks, and Mr. Michael Devaney for their research assistance; and Mrs. Dorothy Young for her various secretarial services.

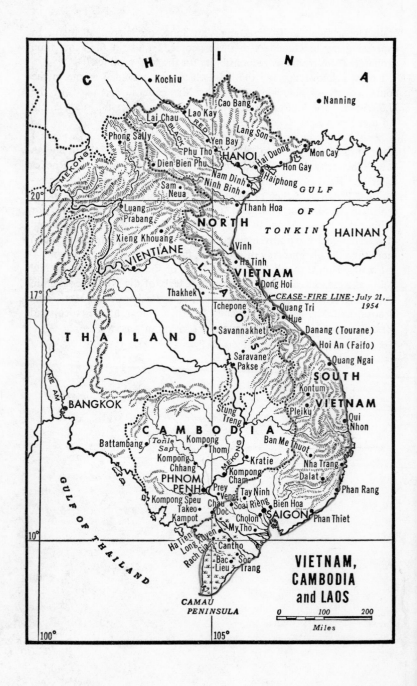

VIETNAM,
CAMBODIA
and LAOS

1

Introduction

Land and People

Vietnam forms an elongated figure S at the southeastern end of the Asian mainland. It faces China to the north, Laos and Cambodia to the west, and the South China Sea to the south and east. The seaward side of the S curves over a distance of 1,100 miles from the Chinese frontier to the point of the Camau Peninsula, and then turns northward about 150 miles to join Cambodia. Because it juts out into the sea, Vietnam has been called Southeast Asia's Balcony on the Pacific. Because of its shape, it resembles two baskets of rice supported from the ends of the shoulder-pole that Vietnamese peasants use to carry loads.

The second analogy is particularly apt. In the northern part of Vietnam, called Tonkin when it was a French protectorate, is the rice-growing delta of the Red River. The delta's extent is confined by the hills and mountains which rise on all sides except for a gateway leading south. At its widest, from coastal Haiphong to the border Vietnam shares with China and Laos in the northwest, the northern region penetrates inland a distance of about 280 miles. South of the Red River delta, in the upper part of what used to be the French Protectorate of Annam, Vietnam becomes a narrow funnel; it is less than twenty miles wide just south of the line of partition which separates Communist from non-Communist Vietnam. Mountainous terrain fringes the western side of this region.

About one hundred miles south of the partition line, Vietnam broadens once more, to an average width of about 100 miles down to the Camau Peninsula. But mountains and high plateaux, often heavily forested, cover the southern part of Central Vietnam. The lowlands here are along the coast, at some places cutting fairly deeply into the interior as the mountains fall back and at others walled in by high hills which press directly against the sea. The high terrain quickly descends into foothills about fifty miles northeast of Saigon; then begin

1

the great alluvial plains of Southern Vietnam, formerly the prized French Colony of Cochinchina. The Mekong River in its several branches traverses this other great rice basket of Vietnam.

The people of Vietnam have adapted themselves to the shape of their land. Over 90 per cent of the country's approximately 32 million people[1] live in the deltas of the North and South or along the lowland rim of Central Vietnam. The tropical climate, the flat land, and the abundant moisture of the skies and rivers have made rice cultivation a natural means of livelihood for the great majority of them. The cycle of preparing and seeding the rice fields, of transplanting the young plants, and, some six or seven months later, of harvesting the mature crop sets the rhythm of the peasant's life. The rice calendar is coordinated with the rain and with the rise and fall of the rivers. An intricate system of canals and irrigation ditches captures, diverts, and releases the precious water as it is needed. The peasant is attached to the land which provides his sustenance. He is one with the cycle of the rain and the rice, which dictate the time and the tempo of his work. And he depends on the bounty of nature, whose caprice he must constantly seek to control.

Because they live on the edge of a great sea swarming with marine life, many Vietnamese seek their livelihood from fishing. This is particularly true along the long Central Vietnamese coastline, where fishing is frequently combined with farming. But the South China Sea is not the only source of fish. Vietnam's rivers and canals, its many thousands of small family ponds, even the rice fields during the rainy season, provide large quantities of fish and crustaceans for the Vietnamese diet.

Until recently the highlands regions of Vietnam were rarely entered by the Vietnamese. Their principal occupants are a diversity of tribal peoples whose binding elements are an ethnic and cultural apartness from the Vietnamese and a low level of civilization. The many hundreds of highlands tribes include the prehistoric settlers of Vietnam, peoples of Indonesian stock who came from southwestern China or perhaps from overseas, some of whom intermixed with still earlier Austro-Melanesian arrivals in Indochina. They include also later Mongolian immigrants, among whom people of Thai stock figure prominently; this second broad wave began to move into Vietnam less

---

[1] The population of South Vietnam was about 14.4 million in 1961, according to U.S. Operations Mission to Vietnam, *Annual Statistical Bulletin, Data through 1961* (Saigon, July, 1962), p. 4. This figure is a projection of a South Vietnamese government estimate of 14.1 million for 1960 (*ibid.*), and I have extended the projection through July, 1963. The North Vietnamese government's census of population in 1960 revealed 15.9 inhabitants, and I have likewise projected this figure through mid-1963.

than 3,000 years ago, and today accounts for most of the tribal groups of North Vietnam. The tribal peoples, particularly those of Central Vietnam, tend to live in small isolated villages, and their economy is based on hunting, some raising of animals, and shifting agriculture. Since 1954, both the North and the South Vietnamese governments have extended their authority over these areas and — particularly the Southern government — have transplanted there large numbers of Vietnamese settlers.

The subject of this study is the part of Vietnam which lies south of the seventeenth parallel. This is the Republic of Vietnam, now politically separate from the Democratic Republic of Vietnam whose rule extends over all Vietnamese territory to the north of the parallel. These two regimes will be usually referred to, following common usage, as South Vietnam and North Vietnam, and the Southern regime will sometimes be called simply Vietnam where there is no question of possible confusion.

South Vietnam embraces two regions: the lower half of Central Vietnam (the former Protectorate of Annam) and all of Southern Vietnam (the former Colony of Cochinchina). It is interesting that the term Central Vietnam remains in common usage, despite the political division of the country. No one in the Republic of Vietnam ever refers to the city of Hue as being in the northern part of his country, and no one in the Democratic Republic of Vietnam ever locates the city of Dong Hoi in the southern part of his country. As much as anything else, this geographical concept of Vietnam as a single nation testifies to the artificial and tentative character of the dual states created on Vietnamese soil in 1954.

The Geneva partition gave South Vietnam control over 66,000 — slightly more than half — of Vietnam's 127,000 square miles. The North, however, has the greater population, about 17 million people to the South's 15.2 million. To use an American comparison, South Vietnam is almost exactly the size of New England but has nearly one-third again as many people, most of whom, in sharp contrast to the inhabitants of New England, live in rural areas. According to South Vietnamese estimates, three-fourths of the civilian work force makes its living from agriculture; commerce, the second most important occupation, employs only one-twentieth as many persons.[2] Most of Vietnam's people are heavily concentrated in the southern delta. Here the population density is 371 persons to a square mile, more than ten times that of the Central highlands. The city of Saigon alone has 1.5 million inhabitants.

The most important ethnic minorities in South Vietnam are the

[2] USOM, *Annual Statistical Bulletin, 1961*, p. 9.

highlands tribes and the peoples of Cambodian and Chinese extraction. The tribal people number perhaps 700,000, though any estimate must be a guess.[3] They are set apart from the dominant Vietnamese both physically and culturally. Their semi-nomadic existence, their primitive living patterns, and their dire poverty pose severe problems for the Vietnamese government. Officially the tribal peoples are Vietnamese citizens and are called brothers; in practice, most Vietnamese cannot overcome an ingrained feeling of superiority to them and call them *moi*, or savages. The attitude of the tribesmen toward the Vietnamese varies from one area to another, but there is in general a suspicion combined with dislike of the Vietnamese. These attitudes have been intensified by the settlement of large numbers of Vietnamese in highland development centers since 1954. The tribal groups are particularly resentful of this "theft" of their land. The Vietnamese government has wished to soften the shocks of modernization as it develops the highlands and seeks to modify the living patterns of the original inhabitants of the region, but the problems confronting these people do not lend themselves to easy solution.

The Cambodians in South Vietnam number about 400,000,[4] nearly all of whom are engaged in agriculture. Concentrated in the southwestern provinces of the country, the Cambodians were absorbed by the expanding Vietnamese empire during the eighteenth century. They are not sharply set off from the Vietnamese, though their cultural background is the Indianized Buddhism of Cambodia. Most of them speak both Cambodian and Vietnamese and have in other ways bridged the differences between the two societies. In general, Vietnam's Cambodian residents have been fairly well integrated into the dominant Vietnamese pattern, although the Cambodian government has never quite reconciled itself to the loss of the Mekong delta and from time to time accuses South Vietnam of cultural oppression against its Cambodian minority.

The Chinese are probably the most numerous minority in Vietnam; they are certainly the most important to the functioning of the economy. The Vietnamese government listed its Chinese population in 1960 as a mere 15,000, but an unpublished report of the American Embassy in Saigon estimated the number of Chinese in Vietnam in

[3] This estimate is a 1963 projection of data given *ibid.*, p. 5.

[4] Official Vietnamese estimates, reproduced *ibid.*, p. 5, and projected into 1963, place the combined Cambodian and Laotian population in South Vietnam at 195,000. A more accurate estimate is the 400,000 Cambodians given by Joseph Buttinger, "The Ethnic Minorities in the Republic of Vietnam," in Wesley R. Fishel (editor), *Problems of Freedom* (Glencoe, Ill.: The Free Press; and East Lansing, Mich.: Bureau of Social and Political Research, 1961), p. 99.

1956 at 830,000.[5] The discrepancy is accounted for by the Vietnamese government's policy of Vietnamizing its Chinese residents. In August, 1956, it decreed that all Chinese born on Vietnamese soil (an estimated 600,000) were Vietnamese citizens, and the following month it excluded foreign nationals from eleven professions, all of which were Chinese-dominated. After an interval of resistance and intense bad feeling, most Chinese complied with the citizenship formalities. Under the government's assimilation program, all Chinese-operated schools must teach Vietnamese, and Chinese cannot be offered even as a major foreign language. But the Chinese community in Vietnam has probably gained more than it has lost. It has by token acceptance of Vietnamese citizenship been able to maintain its powerful position in Vietnam's economy, while at the same time it has found ample means for perpetuating its cultural identity.

Over 500,000 of South Vietnam's Chinese live in Cholon, once a separate city but now administratively part of Saigon. Other large concentrations are to be found in Gia Dinh, a Saigon suburb, and in the delta cities of Rach Gia, Soc Trang, and Bac Lieu. The Chinese control most of the rice trade from the purchasing of paddy[6] to the final milling. They control most of the retail trade in Saigon and in many smaller cities, and are very influential also in transport, textile manufacturing, sugar milling, real estate, and banking. It is, in fact, hard to name an area of business or commerce where Chinese participation is not heavy. Only in the government are Chinese almost totally absent. Despite their eligibility for military conscription, the Vietnamese government has not sought its armed manpower from the Chinese community, and because they were until very recently aliens, few Chinese are in civil government employment. Even the police and other services of Cholon are entirely staffed by Vietnamese.

Thus South Vietnam contains, in addition to several smaller minorities, three large ethnic minorities, each bearing the marks of a different culture. The Vietnamese themselves are the result of the mixing of Mongolian and other races in South China or the Red River delta some time after the tenth century B.C. They have been from the very beginning of their written history deeply influenced by Chinese civilization, and they have quite freely intermarried with the different groups they have encountered. French policy in Vietnam denied the very existence of the Vietnamese nation. There were, for the French, only

[5] USOM, *Annual Statistical Bulletin, 1961*, p. 5; American Embassy, Saigon, *Background Report on Overseas Chinese in Vietnam* (Typewritten, unclassified, November 9, 1956.)

[6] "Paddy" is commonly used to refer to the unmilled rice as well as to the field in which it is grown.

the Tonkinese, the Annamese, and the Cochinchinese, and these "separate" peoples were combined with the Laotians and the Cambodians to form the five parts of the French Indochinese Union.

It would, however, be a serious mistake not to recognize the fundamental unity underlying the apparent diversity within Vietnam. Unlike many of the newly independent nations, Vietnam existed as in integrated state before the French began their conquest of the country in 1858. Indeed, the Vietnamese can trace their independent nationality back to the Kingdom of Nam Viet, a Sinized state created several centuries before Christ and occupying what is now North Vietnam and part of southeastern China. The Kingdom of Nam Viet was overrun by the Chinese in 111 B.C. and became a Chinese province. The Vietnamese willingly adopted superior Chinese cultural, religious, and economic practices, but never accepted Chinese rule. In 939 A.D., they succeeded in regaining their independence and defended it against new Chinese attempts at conquest in the thirteenth and fifteenth centuries; one of the Chinese invasions which withdrew in defeat was that of the armies of the mighty Kublai Khan. Thereafter China recognized Vietnamese independence, and the Vietnamese acknowledged a vague suzerainty of China over Vietnam and paid regular tribute to the Chinese emperor.

No sooner had the Vietnamese regained their independence in the tenth century than they began their long southward movement. The major obstacle to expansion was the Empire of Champa, an Indianized civilization extending over practically all of present-day Central Vietnam. A series of wars ensued in which the Vietnamese constantly pressed forward into Cham territory. Cham power was decisively broken in the fifteenth century, and the Vietnamese two centuries later completed their absorption of the small principalities into which this once integrated civilization had degenerated. Only archeological traces of this people can be found today. The destruction of the Chams brought the Vietnamese to the frontiers of another Indianized civilization, that of the Khmers or, as they are called today, Cambodians. Once the greatest empire on the Southeast Asian mainland, the Khmers were in a serious state of decline by the seventeenth century. They were compelled to place themselves under Vietnamese suzerainty in 1658 and, by the end of the eighteenth century, to cede what today are the fertile plains of the southern region of Vietnam.

The rapid extension of Vietnamese territory probably accounts in major part for the political division of Vietnam in 1620. While the Le emperors maintained their nominal authority, two rival families in fact ruled separate parts of a country partitioned just north of Dong Hoi in present-day North Vietnam. Some South Vietnamese today derive comfort from the circumstance that this earlier division was healed by the victory of the South. It took until 1802, however, for reunification to be achieved, and it had to be won by military means. Further, the period of a reunified Vietnam was short: the French arrived less than 60 years later. By 1867 they had created their Colony of Cochinchina; by 1884 they had reduced the Central and Northern parts of Vietnam to protectorate status; and by 1887 they had added Cambodia and Laos and had imposed their Indochinese Union upon all three once-independent states. The Vietnamese at the time of the French conquest were not, despite nearly 200 years of division and intermittent war, a people with only a dim sense of national consciousness. On the contrary, as one of the French officers who participated in the conquest said of his experience, "We found ourselves, from an ethnic as well as a political and social viewpoint, in the presence of the most unified people one could imagine."[7]

The Anciens Régimes

Between the expulsion of the Chinese in the tenth century and the coming of the French in the eighteenth, Vietnam evolved a highly developed administrative system. Its dominant feature was a strong central government (except during the two centuries of divided rule), modeled on that of China, operating through mandarins selected through competitive examinations. These examinations were made compulsory as early as 1075, and a fixed hierarchy of civil and military officials, in which the civil mandarins were accorded a much higher status, was established soon after. There was not at this time or later an hereditary nobility in the full sense of that term, though the emperors themselves succeeded to the throne through heredity.

Vietnam could boast in the eleventh century a postal system, military conscription drawing upon the entire population, and a road network which connected the main cities of the country. By the fifteenth century, according to one scholar, it had become the strongest and most advanced of the Indochinese states, and its monarchs were in many respects ahead of their royal European contemporaries.[8] Emperor Gia Long, who reunited Vietnam at the beginning of the nineteenth century, re-established the machinery of a centralized state under his absolute power. The central government was at this time organized in six ministries whose heads developed, under Gia Long's

---

[7] Charles Gosselin, *L'empire d'Annam* (Paris: Librairie Académique Didier, 1904), p. 7.

[8] Joseph Buttinger, *The Smaller Dragon; A Political History of Vietnam* (New York: Praeger, 1958), p. 145.

successor, Minh Mang, into an imperial cabinet. Competitive examinations open to all were re-established in the early 1800s, given every three years.[9]

The administrative structure of traditional Vietnam stopped short of the villages, behind whose bamboo hedges the overwhelming majority of the Vietnamese people lived a fairly autonomous life. They were ruled by village heads selected, after the fifteenth century, by the villagers themselves, and by councils of notables whose members were chosen from among the distinguished members of the locality. Through their officials the villages were responsible to the provincial administration for those obligations essential to the state: collecting taxes for the imperial treasury, filling quotas for the army, and providing free labor for road construction, canal digging, and other public works. The Vietnamese saying that imperial law bowed before village custom may exaggerate the relationship between the central government and its people, but it does convey the deference accorded village self-government in pre-colonial times. Great deference was also accorded by the people to their rulers and, above all, to the Emperor. As one French historian put it, in traditional Vietnam "the authority of the Emperor partakes of that of the father of a family."[10] Strong (and by modern Western standards sometimes brutal) sanctions enforced obedience to the imperial will.

Nearly a century of French colonialism drastically altered the Vietnamese governmental apparatus. The imperial government was excluded entirely from southern Vietnam, which, as the Colony of Cochinchina, fell under direct French rule. A French governor administered the Colony, supported by a French administration down to the provincial level and sometimes farther, which applied French colonial law adjudicated in French-created courts. Vietnamese were allowed only into the lower ranks of the French civil service, where they constituted, according to one authority, a smaller proportion of the bureaucracy than nationals in the British and even the Dutch colonial regimes of Southeast Asia.[11] In Saigon even such modest positions as policeman and postman were filled by French civil servants, and in the provinces the highest office to which a Vietnamese could aspire was that of district chief.

Imperial rule did not fare much better in northern Vietnam, which, as the French Protectorate of Tonkin, theoretically retained its in-

[9] Le Thanh Khoi, *Le Viet-Nam, histoire et civilisation* (Paris: Éditions de Minuit, 1955), pp. 324–28.

[10] Henri Gourdon, *L'Indochine* (Paris: Librairie Larousse, 1951), p. 77.

[11] D. G. E. Hall, *A History of South-East Asia* (New York: St. Martin's Press, 1955), p. 643.

digenous administration. The authority of the Imperial government, located at Hue, was transferred to a French Superior Resident at Hanoi, who was assisted by French administrative services, and the provincial mandarins, matched by French residents and their staffs, were permitted to retain little more than the honorific functions of their office. Only in Central Vietnam, which became the Protectorate of Annam, did the traditional mechanisms continue to operate, but here too French influence made itself strongly felt. The Emperor's advisory council was superseded by one whose members were all doubled by French civil servants. It was presided over by the French Superior Resident who was for practical purposes the real head of the government. The provincial mandarins retained the ceremonial forms of their office more fully in Annam than in Tonkin, but they too were doubled by French residents. In both Annam and Tonkin, French courts operating under French codes existed side by side with the traditional courts and assumed much of the latter's jurisdiction. Vietnamese sovereignty was so far eclipsed that the imperial treasury lost its control over taxes and was forced to depend on the colonial dole in order to sustain the royal family, the court, and the shadow Vietnamese administration.

The real ruler of Vietnam was a French Governor-General who headed the Indochinese Union (composed of the three divisions of Vietnam and of Cambodia and Laos in addition). The Governor-General was vested with vast civil and military powers under the supervision of the Ministry of Colonies in France. The French officials in the five parts of the Union were integrated into a single Civil Service; there was an Indochinese budget superimposed on those of the individual states, maintained by customs duties, land and poll taxes, and state monopolies over alcohol, opium, and salt; and the general government established administrative departments for customs and excises, public works, agriculture and commerce, and postal and telegraphic communications.

The pre-colonial Vietnamese administration had been oriented to a rural society based on irrigated agriculture, a society which had become stagnant by the time of the French intrusion. The colonial administration was oriented to the economic exploitation of Vietnam for the benefit of French interests, for Indochina was the prize of French possessions, and Vietnam the brightest jewel. Prior to World War II, the area was the world's third largest rice exporter, and it exported large amounts of other agricultural products, rubber, coal, and iron. French administration thus concentrated on developing those aspects of Vietnamese society necessary to the sustenance of a colonial economy and the control of the subject population. French rule did not include training in the intricacies of representative self-government. The two most important institutions in Indochina were the Grand Council of Economic and Financial Interests and the Colonial Council of Indochina. The first body was not elected but was an advisory council on budgetary matters dominated by major French business interests. The second body, which also played an advisory role to the Cochinchinese administration, had an electorate of about 12,000 and a division of seats between Vietnamese and French representatives that guaranteed the domination of the latter. The popular representative chambers established for the Vietnamese living in the protectorates were also purely consultative, and of even less significance in the government scheme.

It is often thought that the colonial administration did not affect the lives of the rural masses of Vietnam. This is true only in that the villages continued to be ruled by their own councils. But these councils were given many new tasks which brought them under the modernizing influence of the colonial system: they had to keep regular registers of births and deaths in order to provide more accurate tax rolls, and they were responsible for collecting taxes, recruiting labor, and preventing the destruction of telegraphic lines and other colonial facilities. To ensure the proper performance of their new duties, tight controls were established over the councils, and the French authorities substituted election for co-optation in the period following World War I as a means of selecting their members (an innovation which the Pétain regime did away with, apparently considering it to smack too much of democracy).[12] Thus, the villages maintained their autonomy under the French, but at the price of placing their governing bodies at the disposal of the colonial power, and nearly all Vietnamese felt, if only indirectly, the impact of colonial rule.

The death knell for France in Indochina sounded in 1940, when the French were forced to accept Japanese military occupation of the area. In March, 1945, the Japanese removed the French from their positions of administrative authority and permitted the weak Vietnamese imperial authority of the Protectorate of Annam to assert Vietnam's independence. In September of that year, on the heels of the general Japanese collapse, the Communist-led Viet Minh movement proclaimed a republic in Vietnam, and Emperor Bao Dai quickly abdicated in its favor. French military forces reoccupied the southern half of Vietnam in the fall of 1945 and, after an uneasy truce with the Viet Minh, wrested control of most of the northern half from the

[12] Paul Mus, "The Role of the Village in Vietnamese Politics," *Pacific Affairs,* 22 (September, 1949), 266–67, says that the elective councils were abolished because of the sullen opposition of local rural leaders.

Viet Minh a little over a year later. It was at this time, in December, 1946, that the protracted guerrilla war between the French and Viet Minh started; it was to culminate in the staggering defeat of French Union forces at Dien Bien Phu, in May, 1954, and then two months later to terminate in a negotiated settlement reached at Geneva, Switzerland.

It is ironic that France's need to rally popular support in its war against the Viet Minh should have forced it to take a step that guaranteed, win or lose, the end of French sovereignty in Vietnam. In 1949 it created the Associate State of Vietnam with Bao Dai as its hereditary Chief of State, and it began the transfer of administrative services to the new government. By the middle of 1954 this transfer had been nearly completed, except in the military realm and in key political controls. The Associate State of Vietnam thus inherited from France an administrative system equipped to perform many of the functions of a modern state. This administrative system was also patterned on that of France in its organization, its civil service practices, and its legal procedures. The most significant departure from French administrative policy was the regional decentralization of the public bureaucracy; the post-1949 Vietnamese governors of Tonkin, Annam, and Cochinchina, perpetuating the colonial divisions of Vietnam, governed their administrative regions with considerable freedom from Saigon. They had their own budgets generated from self-sustaining revenues and considerable control over central government operations within their spheres. At all levels of the civil service, Vietnamese bureaucrats inherited the disposition of their French teachers to subordinate the ends of public policy to proper, and time-consuming, legal procedure, and to view the public as *les administrés* rather than as the served.

The French inheritance contained other deficiencies. For one thing, many administrative practices were antiquated. For example, Vietnam's fingerprint systems (two different systems were used there) had long ago been replaced in France, and its comprehensive financial procedures had not been overhauled since they were promulgated in 1912. In fact the whole body of law and regulations needed revision, for it had been established for a colonial regime. More serious still was the lack of technicians and trained high and middle level administrators in the government. These positions had been filled almost entirely by Frenchmen, and those Vietnamese who moved into them by and large lacked the qualifications and experience for their jobs; for the most part overshadowed by French "advisors," they also lacked initiative and the inclination to accept responsibility. Finally, most of the able and scrupulous nationalists refused to serve in a government which, even after 1949, was regarded as French-dominated, and those Vietnamese who became civil servants carried the mark, and often the mentality, of French colonial collaborators.

Except for national independence, the most insistent cry of Vietnamese nationalists during the pre-Geneva phase of the Bao Dai period was for constitutional government, especially an elected national legislature. Bao Dai had promised a popularly chosen constituent assembly "when possible" when he resumed office in mid-1949. An unofficial congress of nationalist groups, meeting in Saigon in September, 1953, added an elected national assembly to its demand for unconditional independence; and even the Bao Dai-packed congress which met the following month supported this position. The nationalist surge was so great that Bao Dai's Premier, Nguyen Van Tam, a French citizen and hitherto a loyal friend of the French, was impelled to join the chorus for national elections in late 1953, just before his fall from power. The only national institution which was produced by the Bao Dai regime between 1949 and 1954, however, was an appointive Provisional National Council, established in July, 1952, to perform an advisory role on budgetary matters similar to that formerly performed by the Colonial Grand Council of Economic and Financial Interests. An attempt was made in 1953 to create a national assembly through the election of municipal and village councils which would designate members to provincial councils, which would in turn select deputies to the national institution. Due to Viet Minh influence in the countryside, elections were held only in a small portion of rural Vietnam. The whole affair was attended by widespread lack of interest, and the institution-building never proceeded beyond the provincial level where it was more a form than a reality.[13]

The effective champions of representative government were not, unhappily for the nationalist cause, the various governments established by the French and Bao Dai after World War II, but the Communist-led Viet Minh. No sooner had Ho Chi Minh, the Moscow-trained leader of the Viet Minh, taken office as President of the Democratic Republic of Vietnam on September 2, 1945, than he announced general elections under universal suffrage. These elections were held on January 6, 1946, in North and in North Central Vietnam, the regions under Viet Minh authority, and also clandestinely in numerous parts of the French zone in the South. There was much wrong with these elections: through a political deal with leaders of two nationalist parties, 70 of the 350 seats in the new National Assembly

[13] The 1953 elections are discussed by Bernard B. Fall, "Representative Government in the State of Vietnam," *Far Eastern Survey*, 23 (August, 1954), pp. 122–25.

were reserved to nationalist competitors of the Viet Minh. The voting, moreover, was hardly secret, nor was there much choice among candidates. But these were the first elections ever held in Vietnam in which the population as a whole was permitted to participate, and the response was enthusiastic. The Viet Minh also set up village councils based on universal suffrage and vested with many decision-making functions in their jurisdictions. Succeeding nationalist governments could ignore these Communist-sponsored innovations only at their peril. Unfortunately for the subsequent course of Vietnamese history, they did.

Diem au Pouvoir

Two events during the months of July, 1954, marked the re-emergence of Vietnam to independence. The first was the conclusion of a series of agreements at Geneva, on July 21, which ended the Indochina War and eighty years of French domination in Vietnam. France recognized the Communist Democratic Republic of Vietnam as the lawful authority over the northern half of Vietnam and resigned itself to the loss of the remainder of the country by agreeing to the reunification of the divided nation through elections to be held within a period of two years. It was commonly expected that the Communists, having led the resistance movement against the French, would easily win these elections. In making its settlement at Geneva, France recognized also the failure of its "Bao Dai experiment" — its effort to undercut the Viet Minh appeal by placing the former Emperor at the head of a rival government.

The man responsible for disentangling France from her Indochinese burden was Pierre Mendès-France, who had been invested as Premier by the French National Assembly on June 18, scarcely a month before the final settlement at Geneva. By coincidence, the second major event of July had its beginning, also in Paris, within hours of Mendès-France's investiture. There, on June 18, Ngo Dinh Diem announced that he had accepted Bao Dai's invitation to take over the premiership of the Associate State of Vietnam and hurried home to form his government. This government formally assumed power on July 7, and with it began the existence of an independent state in South Vietnam. Diem had in the past vowed to accept office only if the French were willing to accord Vietnam dominion status similar to those of India and Pakistan, and now France was willing to accept even Vietnam's departure from the French Union. In fact, French hopes extended no further than to protect French economic interests and to maintain as much cultural influence and liaison as possible with whatever government should emerge victorious in Vietnam. Diem had also demanded and obtained from Bao Dai the delegation of full civil and military power.[14] Under his leadership, the southern part of Vietnam was to eliminate the remaining political influences exerted by the French authorities and by Bao Dai himself.

With the possible exception of his native Central Vietnam, Ngo Dinh Diem was not known to the mass of the Vietnamese people before he assumed the premiership, but there is contemporary evidence of his renown in more limited circles. The French writer, Philippe Devillers, in a book published in 1952, says that as early as 1933 Diem was "reputed for his perfect integrity, his competence, and his intelligence"; that in 1943 he was a "well-known Catholic leader" in Central Vietnam; and that he was the nearly unanimous choice of persons whom Bao Dai consulted in March, 1945 when he was looking for a premier.[15] Le Thanh Khoi, a pro-Viet Minh Vietnamese historian, in a book written before July, 1954, says that Diem was "well-known for his competence and integrity" in 1933.[16] Likewise, the American scholar, Ellen J. Hammer, writing in 1954, qualifies Diem as being "already widely respected for his honesty and ability" in 1933, as being "popular among the Vietnamese" in 1945, as "speaking for the nationalist majority who refused to commit themselves either to Bao Dai or Ho Chi Minh" in 1949, and as the "most prominent" of the nationalist leaders in 1953.[17] However future events have affected his renown, Ngo Dinh Diem was in 1954 the most respected of a relatively small number of political leaders in the non-Communist camp.

On what was Diem's fame based? Certainly not on his actions after 1933, when he resigned from the Imperial government of Vietnam, for he had neither participated in governmental affairs nor taken an aggressive role in the struggle against French colonialism. Like a number

[14] This stipulation, verified by the author from confidential sources, has been given recent published corroboration by an intimate of Diem's during this period. See Wesley R. Fishel, "Problems of Democratic Growth in Free Vietnam," in Fishel (editor), *Problems of Freedom,* p. 16. There seems to be no corroborating evidence, however, for Fishel's statement (*ibid.*) that Diem also extracted authority to establish a national assembly and to determine Vietnam's future status, including the deposition of Bao Dai, limited only by a pledge to Bao Dai that he, Diem, would not depose the Chief of State by arbitrary means.

[15] Philippe Devillers, *Histoire du Viet-Nam de 1940 à 1952* (Paris: Éditions du Seuil, 1952), pp. 63, 93, and 126.

[16] Khoi, *Le Viet-Nam,* p. 446. It is quite possible that Khoi borrowed Devillers' judgment of Diem.

[17] Ellen J. Hammer, *The Struggle for Indochina* (Stanford: Stanford University Press, 1954), pp. 86, 48, 245, and 286. It should be noted that Hammer had had contact with Diem and was at this time well disposed toward him.

of other Vietnamese nationalists he maintained contacts with the Kempeitai, the Japanese military police, during World War II and, like other nationalists, he was provided protection by his Japanese friends when it appeared that the French authorities were about to round him up.[18] Like a number of other nationalists, he declined Ho Chi Minh's invitation in February, 1946, to join a national union government which, as Ho intended, would have made the nationalist collaborators share responsibility for the Viet Minh decisions to permit French troops to land in the North and to accept, for the time being, full French control of the South.[19]

And, again like other nationalists, he did not respond to the proposal by the French High Commissioner of Indochina in January, 1947, that the traditional monarchy should be restored to Vietnam; it was widely suspected that the French were seeking to acquire another counter with which to negotiate with the Viet Minh.[20] But Diem was, along with others, ready to support Bao Dai if this would achieve nationalist ends.[21] What distinguished Diem from most of the other nationalists is that he avoided any involvement, either with the French, the Viet Minh, or the restored Bao Dai regime prior to 1954. He lived abroad after 1950 in self-imposed exile in the United States, Belgium, and France. Most of this time was spent in religious solitude with Catholic orders, until about the end of 1953 when he began actively to promote his cause among French and Vietnamese circles in Paris.

How then did Diem gain his renown? The answer, briefly, is: through a patriotic gesture in 1933 which was nourished thereafter by an uncompromising position toward the colonial power. In May, 1933, Bao Dai, who had become emperor the previous year, replaced most

[18] Devillers, *Histoire du Viet-Nam de 1940 à 1952*, p. 93.

[19] A minor legend has sprung up concerning this 1946 encounter between Ngo Dinh Diem and Ho Chi Minh, according to which Diem flatly defied Ho or, as one *Time* story has told it, "Angrily, Diem turned on his heel and walked out." (August 4, 1961, p. 26.) However, according to Hammer's account (*Struggle for Indochina,* p. 150), which is based on a pre-Geneva interview with Diem, Diem refused to join Ho's government "without far more information on Viet Minh activities and plans than he had yet been given," and was finally permitted to return home. Neither version mentions the motive behind Ho's offer nor the refusal of other nationalists to swallow the bait.

The Communist side of the story, for what it may be worth, simply mentions that Diem had been arrested after the August, 1945, revolution and had been released "thanks only to President Ho Chi Minh's clemency." (*Some Press Evidence on the Ngo Dinh Diem Regime in South Vietnam* [Hanoi: Foreign Languages Publishing House, 1955], p. 3.)

[20] Devillers, *Histoire du Viet-Nam de 1940 à 1952*, pp. 367–68.

[21] Hammer, *The Struggle for Indochina,* p. 211.

of his aged ministers with young mandarins and offered the Ministry of Interior to Ngo Dinh Diem, who was then, at 32 years of age, the governor of Phan Thiet province. Diem's quick rise in the Annamese administrative hierarchy was apparently due at least in part to the patronage of a relative, Nguyen Huu Bai, the former Interior minister.[22] The French Superior Resident at Hue had himself assumed the functions of prime minister, making the Interior minister the key Vietnamese official in the Imperial government. Diem was also made head of the secretariat of the Commission of Reforms, which, composed of high French and Vietnamese officials, was supposed to implement the administrative and other reforms which Bao Dai had promised in September, 1932. When he found his efforts checked by the combined opposition of traditional court circles and, especially, officials of the French Protectorate, Diem brusquely resigned from his post in September, 1933, and went into retirement.[23] This behavior made Diem a symbol of firm and unsullied opposition to colonialism, and the symbol grew brighter as after 1945 he repeatedly refused overtures to head various Vietnamese governments unless the minimum of dominion status were accorded his country. He never received Bao Dai's telegram inviting him to head the government established on the heels of the Japanese *coup* of March, 1945, probably because the Japanese, distrusting his intransigent nationalism despite his friendliness towards them, prevented its delivery.[24] He refused to head the provisional central government created in mid-1948 or to serve as Bao Dai's prime minister when the latter returned to power as Chief of State in April, 1949, but so too did other nationalists hold themselves aloof from participation in French-controlled governments. However, by 1954 most of the nationalist politicians had taken sides. Some cast their lot early with the Viet Minh, others rallied early to the support of the French, and still others moved behind Bao Dai after his return to power in 1949. A number of anti-Viet Minh leaders, who were frequently anti-French as well, ended up victims of Viet Minh assassination. Those who chose to work with the French or with Bao Dai, which, in the eyes of most people, amounted to the same thing, found their reputations strongly tainted by the association, even when they avoided the pecuniary and other temptations of office. Ngo Dinh Diem was the best known and most respected representative of the

[22] Nguyen Thai, "The Government of Men in the Republic of Vietnam" (East Lansing, Michigan: private mimeographing, June, 1962), p. 100.

[23] See, for example, his "Statement of June 16, 1949," reprinted in *Major Policy Speeches of President Ngo Dinh Diem* (Saigon: Presidential Press Office, Republic of Vietnam, 1956). Some of Diem's Vietnamese critics maintain he was forced to resign by his Court rival, Pham Quynh.

[24] See Hammer, *The Struggle for Indochina*, p. 48.

dwindling group which had committed itself neither to the Viet Minh nor to Bao Dai. His early government career had stamped him as an able administrator, his resignation in 1933 gave him credentials as a principled nationalist, and his subsequent behavior emphasized that he was a man who would not compromise his principles for political gain.[25]

It may be true, as some people have claimed, that Diem's arrival to power in mid-1954 was due to official American pressure, to American or European Catholic diplomacy, or to Bao Dai's desire to install a premier who would command support from the United States, which he saw as replacing French influence in Vietnam. It is quite possible that Bao Dai hoped to finish off Diem politically by giving him power at such a difficult juncture. But in view of the depleted leadership resources in South Vietnam in June, 1954, and the drift of Vietnamese politics to the position which Diem, better than anyone else, symbolized, his investiture as premier at that time seems in retrospect altogether natural.

Diem's predecessors in office had been preoccupied with the task of coping with the Viet Minh threat while trying to extract greater independence from the French. Neither France nor the Viet Minh constituted a major problem for Diem during his first two years in power. Two weeks after Diem took office, French and Viet Minh delegates brought an end to the Indochina War and, over the futile objections of the new nationalist government, divided Vietnam at the seventeenth parallel. The Viet Minh forces relinquished Southern territory under their control in early 1955, in compliance with the cease-fire arrangements, and attempted no serious interference with the operations of the Southern government during its initial years in power. Ho Chi Minh and his collaborators apparently expected to gain the South through the reunification elections which the Geneva Agreements had stipulated for no later than July, 1956, and they may have hoped that the fledgling Diem regime would fall from internal conflict before then. French maneuvers against the Diem government were, as we shall see, somewhat more substantial, but they did not include the witholding of full sovereignty from Vietnam. France reached agreements with the three former Indochinese states in September and December, 1954, in which full control over national economies was passed to the Vietnamese, Cambodian, and Laotian governments, and Vietnam obtained administrative control of its armed forces the following February.

[25] But Diem apparently was willing to line up support for the premiership after late 1953, when he saw that the crisis in Vietnam was entering a new phase.

The serious threats to the Ngo Dinh Diem regime arose from nationalist, not Communist or foreign, quarters. Diem met these threats one at a time as he moved to consolidate his power over the truncated nation. First, he faced dissidence within the armed forces, provoked by sharp disagreements with his chief of staff, General Nguyen Van Hinh. Hinh flouted the orders of his superior, including one issued in early September sending him off to France but, although Hinh commanded the support of most of the army, he made no move to depose Diem, for the United States had come to the Premier's aid. Hinh was warned that all American aid to Vietnam would be cut if he unseated the Premier,[26] and General J. Lawton Collins, President Eisenhower's special ambassador to Vietnam, made this point starkly clear to Hinh's army backers on November 17 shortly after his arrival in Vietnam.[27] Hinh left Vietnam two days later, on a summons from Bao Dai, and once safely out of the way was dismissed from office.

A more formidable menace to the regime was presented by the private armies of the Binh Xuyen, a group which had once been engaged in brigandage, and the Cao Dai and Hoa Hao reformist Buddhist sects.[28] The Cao Dai had perhaps two million believers (some estimates range much lower) spread throughout the country in a number of competing branches. The greatest concentration was in the area running northwest of Saigon to the Cambodian border, and the headquarters of its principal branch was located in the border province of Tay Ninh. The Hoa Hao, because of its later formation, had developed a less cohesive organization and it broke into jostling factions after its leader, Huynh Phu So, was murdered by the Viet Minh in April, 1947. The great bulk of the one and a half million (or fewer) Hoa Hao adherents were clustered in the Bassac provinces of An Giang, Vinh Long, and Phong Dinh in southwestern Vietnam. Although they began as purely religious institutions, the strength of Vietnamese nationalism was such that both the Cao Dai and the Hoa Hao quickly took on political coloration. They mixed anti-colonialism with religious tenets, cooperated with the Japanese during the wartime occupation in order to obtain protection from the French, and joined

26 See Peter Schmid, "Free Indochina Fights against Time," *Commentary,* January, 1955, p. 28; also Donald Lancaster, *The Emancipation of French Indochina* (London: Oxford University Press, 1961), p. 350.

27 *New York Times,* November 17, 1954, p. 14.

28 Detailed accounts of the origins and pre-1954 activities of the Binh Xuyen and the sects can be found in A. M. Savani, *Visage et Images du Sud Viet-Nam* (Saigon: Imprimerie Française d'Outre-Mer, 1955), "Les Féodalités et autres groupements armés," pp. 71–105; and Bernard B. Fall, "The Political-Religious Sects of Vietnam," *Pacific Affairs,* 28 (September, 1955), 235–53.

with the Viet Minh in resisting the return of French troops to Cochin-china at the war's end. The sects soon found that alignment with the Viet Minh posed a more direct threat to their existence than living with the French, and by 1947 most of the Cao Dai and Hoa Hao factions, caught between two fires, had decided to rally to the French in return for arms and other assistance. In the zones of their greatest concentration Cao Dai and Hoa Hao troops maintained security in the rural areas lying outside of the French-garrisoned district towns. The association of the sects with the French was thus an opportunistic one, and some sect forces never did come to terms with France, or alternated between support and opposition as a means of extracting more aid. One force, led by the Cao Dai General Trinh Minh The, went into permanent opposition in 1951. Also, despite their cooperation with the French, Cao Dai and Hoa Hao representatives, meeting in Hue with delegates of a smaller group in January, 1948, firmly opposed the French maneuver to separate Cochinchina from the rest of Vietnam. In what a French writer has called "a bold new program," they demanded as much for their country as did any other Vietnamese political group, including the Viet Minh: full dominion status, political independence, control of foreign relations and all internal economic matters, and a national army.[29]

It was inevitable that the sects should become major forces in nationalist politics during the Indochina War. They were the only political groups outside of the Viet Minh which had any kind of a popular base, and it was only natural, considering the poor educational background of most of their spiritual leaders, that they should attract a number of nationalist politicians without parties who could advise them and represent them in Saigon politics. It was perhaps also inevitable, considering the disintegration of normal governmental authority, that the sects should develop states within states, a trend which was occurring in North Vietnam under the Catholic bishops of Phat Diem and Bui Chu, and in the area running southeast from Saigon to the China Sea, under the Binh Xuyen. The Binh Xuyen had developed power from a different source than the sects — banditry and the control of some of the commerce entering Cholon, the Chinese city attached to Saigon. But they too were caught up in or joined the nationalist surge — one writer even described them as having "a nationalist spirit pushed to the extreme,"[30] and they too, after a bitter and, for them, nearly disastrous alliance with the Viet Minh, rallied to

[29] See Philippe Devillers, "Vietnamese Nationalism and French Policies," in William L. Holland (editor), *Asian Nationalism and the West* (New York: Macmillan, 1953), p. 222.

[30] Savani, *Visage et Images du Sud Viet-Nam*, p. 101.

the French in order to receive support against their early cohorts. All three groups controlled important segments of rural Vietnam, and — the Cao Dai and Hoa Hao especially — imposed levies on their local populations and ran the local administrations. The Binh Xuyen was more concerned with commercial activities and, by 1954, was operating lucrative gambling and prostitution establishments in Saigon in addition to its control of the opium trade, a good segment of the fish and charcoal trade, and some hotels and rubber plantations. It did not have to worry about police interference in its illicit businesses after 1953, for it was then given control of the national police and security services of the country, from which vantage point it was able to run the city of Saigon-Cholon as its personal preserve.

By 1954 the sects had become deeply involved in Saigon politicking — every Bao Dai cabinet, for instance, normally had Cao Dai and Hoa Hao representatives in it. They had also become as much interested in preserving their territorial autonomy, with all its quasi-feudal perquisites, against the exertions of the central government and against each other, as in furthering the cause of Vietnamese nationalism. They had, in short, been transformed by events into reactionary forces seeking to prevent the establishment of national authority throughout all of Vietnam. In the case of the Binh Xuyen, there never had been much of a conception of public service, and the vague nationalism which it did develop after World War II was quickly dissipated amid the fruits of its economic operations. Earlier government efforts to bring the two sects and the Binh Xuyen under control had failed, but the situation in mid-1954 differed significantly from the past. The Ngo Dinh Diem government was known to be ill-disposed toward the three groups and bent on extending its authority over all territory left to it by the Geneva partition. France could not be relied upon to intervene on behalf of its former allies and, indeed, was preparing, now that the war was over, to end its subsidies to them. This prospect, which came to pass in February, 1955, spelled the dissolution of the Cao Dai and Hoa Hao armies, which totaled perhaps 35,000 men, and at least extreme inconvenience to that of the Binh Xuyen which, besides being better heeled, had only about 2,500 men under arms.[31] Thus, quick action was essential if the three groups were to extract maximum advantage from their existing, but rapidly waning, power.

The Diem government followed a policy of separating the three

---

[31] In April 1955, when the showdown occurred between the feudal groups and the government, informed Saigon sources put their strength as follows: Cao Dai, 15,000–20,000; Hoa Hao, 10,000–15,000; Binh Xuyen, 2,000–2,500. These figures may be low. (*New York Times,* April 21, 1955, p. 8.)

groups, which was not too hard to do considering the rivalries which ran between and within them, and of dealing with them one at a time. The government policy owes much to Nguyen Ngoc Tho, a member of Diem's cabinet and later his Vice-President, who had a thorough knowledge of the internal politics of the sects and Binh Xuyen. The general plan was to isolate the Binh Xuyen and eventually to destroy it, while bringing over most of the sect leaders through persuasion, through promises of political position and the incorporation of sect troops into the national army, and through outright bribery. In the first move, the united front formed by the three groups in early September, 1954, was broken when Diem brought four Cao Dai and four Hoa Hao leaders into his Cabinet, later that same month. This maneuver gave Diem time to dispose of his dissident army chief of staff. In January, 1955, two important sect military commanders, Nguyen Van Hue of the Hoa Hao and Trinh Minh The of the Cao Dai, rallied to the government with their troops, another Hoa Hao commander, Nguyen Giac Ngo, followed suit the following month. In January, also, the government felt itself strong enough to close the Binh Xuyen gambling concessions in the Saigon area, thereby depriving the Binh Xuyen of a major source of revenue. The three dissident groups reunited in early March, but by then it was too late. Some of their own leaders were firmly in the government camp, and the remaining private troops, many of whom were now payless, were showing signs of strong discontent.

The fragmented sects withdrew their ministers from the Diem cabinet in late March when the premier refused to comply with an ultimatum demanding drastic reorganization of the government, but this action merely sealed their fate. Acting against French and American advice which urged him to patch up his differences with the dissidents, who now called themselves the United Front of Nationalist Forces, Diem decided to provoke a showdown.[32] During the evening of March 29–30, fighting broke out between government and Binh Xuyen forces in Saigon and, although a precarious truce was arranged by the French High Command, it merely postponed the inevitable settlement by arms. On April 28, after the government had lured over further sect elements, government and Binh Xuyen troops in Saigon resumed fighting, and the latter were quickly driven from the city and forced to retreat in disorder to the swamplands near the mouth of the Saigon river. There they were bottled up until September, when the national army moved in to crush the last remnant of Binh Xuyen

[32] Ngo Dinh Nhu has told the author that the Vietnamese government deliberately pushed the United Front into armed combat against government forces. (Personal interview, November 25, 1962.)

power. Hoa Hao resistance quickly crumbled in the Mekong delta under the double assault of government troops and special emissaries from Saigon carrying bribes and other inducements to Hoa Hao leaders. The few Cao Dai forces which had not already deserted to the government were peacefully disarmed in October. Ba Cut was the only dissident leader who continued his armed resistance, and he was finally captured in April, 1956, and subsequently executed. Some dissident leaders like Le Van Vien, the Binh Xuyen chief, fled, with French assistance, to France or, like the Cao Dai Pope, Pham Cong Tac, crossed the frontier into Cambodia; others, such as the Hoa Hao general, Tran Van Soai, made belated amends to the government. Trinh Minh The, perhaps the most able of the sect officers, was killed by a bullet while directing the expulsion of the Binh Xuyen from Saigon in early May, 1955.

The most notable and surprising feature of the struggle of the feudal groups was how quickly their power melted when pitted against that of the national forces, since foreign observers had thought them a match for the government. Not only were the sects running out of money, but they were anachronisms in a country which, having just recovered its independence, was in a surge of nationalist feeling. The serious danger to the Diem government did not come from the Cao Dai, Hoa Hao, and Binh Xuyen, but rather from its Western allies. The French in particular wanted to replace Diem, and in April, 1955, they had apparently convinced General Collins of the necessity of such an action,[33] but the joint recommendation of Collins and the French High Commissioner, General Ely, to this effect was not accepted in Washington. The French also prevented the national government from wiping out the Binh Xuyen in the initial fighting of late March by withholding fuel and other necessary military supplies, and some French elements, probably without official sanction, aided the Binh Xuyen during the later fighting. In disregarding American and French advice Diem had to face the disapprobation of his main supporters, but he was able to present them with a *fait accompli* — and one which met with broad popular approval.

Bao Dai's fate was sealed with that of the Binh Xuyen and the sects, for his power was based upon them. From his remote position in France, he attempted to check Diem's routing of the dissident groups. In early March he was instrumental in bringing the regime's opponents together in a united front. During April he attempted to appoint his own man, General Nguyen Van Vy, as chief of the armed forces,

[33] See C. L. Sulzberger in the *New York Times,* April 18, 1955, p. 22.

with full military powers, and to draw his premier to France for "consultations" and, it was presumed, sacking; but Diem rebuffed both gambits. At the end of April, a Popular Revolutionary Committee called together under government auspices set the stage for Vietnam's metamorphosis from a monarchy to a republic. It urged the removal of Bao Dai and the dissolution of the Bao Dai government, and the establishment of a provisional government under Ngo Dinh Diem charged with several missions, the most important of which was organizing general elections for the establishment of a National Assembly.[34]

The action of the Popular Revolutionary Committee gave Diem authority of a sort to act against Bao Dai,[35] and, once the Binh Xuyen and the sects had been quelled, he used it. In a referendum held October 23, 1955, the Vietnamese people voted the deposition of Bao Dai and the ending of the monarchy, and proclaimed Ngo Dinh Diem Vietnam's first President and entrusted him with establishing a republican form of government. Bao Dai remained in France during the referendum campaign and took no more notice of the proceedings at home than to declare them illegal and to issue a futile order dismissing Diem from office. Diem got 98.2 per cent of the vote and Bao Dai 1.1 per cent, with the remaining portion of the ballots declared invalid,[36] a margin of victory which, even considering Bao Dai's lack of popular strength, his absence from the country, and the employment of the public bureaucracy on behalf of his successful opponent, recalls elections in Communist states. On October 31 a special meeting of the Popular Revolutionary Committee, announcing that the goal of the organization had been accomplished with President Diem's convocation of a National Assembly, voted its own dissolution.[37] The Popular Revolutionary Committee had supported Diem in the referendum, but

[34] The manifesto is reproduced in Allan B. Cole and others (editors), *Conflict in Indochina and International Repercussions; A Documentary History, 1945–1955* (Ithaca: Cornell University Press, 1956), p. 223. The other recommendations of the Committee were that Diem put down the rebellion, gain full independence for the country, and request the complete withdrawal of the French Expeditionary Corps.

[35] According to one member of the Committee, Hoang Co Thuy, Diem, taken back by the sweep of the Committee's recommendations, asked its chairman, "Do you want me to make a *revolution?*" (Personal interview, June, 1959.)

[36] *New York Times,* October 26, 1955, p. 4.

[37] This news was communicated in a letter from the President of the Committee, Nguyen Bao Toan, who was soon to seek political refuge in Cambodia, to a "Comrade Van Ngo," dated November 10, 1955, copies of which were circulated around Saigon.

the President and his advisors, suspecting that elements within the Committee intended to use the organization for their own ends, with victory in hand, decided to disband it.[38]

For the first time since taking office in July, 1954, Ngo Dinh Diem was the undisputed master of the Vietnamese government. He was now able to turn his attention to building new institutions for Vietnam.

Conclusion

In this chapter, we have sketched the re-emergence to independence of that part of Vietnam which was saved from Communism by the Geneva Agreements. It is the story of what the Vietnamese government frequently calls the national revolution: the victory of nationalism over the forces of feudalism, Communism, and colonialism. The victory over feudalism refers to the destruction of the military and political power of the Binh Xuyen and the Cao Dai and Hoa Hao sects. Achieved during the course of 1955, this victory enabled the Ngo Dinh Diem leadership to establish its authority through the entire reach of South Vietnam. It was in tune with the strong unifying feeling of the people and was a signal achievement of the regime, though one easier to achieve than the Vietnamese leaders, or at least their foreign allies, believed possible.

The victory over colonialism was even easier to accomplish. The main effort in convincing France that its day in Vietnam was ended had already been made by Viet Minh arms. It is ironic that Vietnamese Communism, the deadly enemy today of Vietnamese nationalism, made possible the emergence of an independent nationalist government in the South. French intrigue continued in South Vietnam after July, 1954, but it was half-hearted, and the withdrawal of the French Expeditionary Corps, which symbolized the end of the French era, was done under terms set by the Viet Minh in Geneva, and not by the nationalists in Saigon. The chief embodiment of latter-day French colonialism, His Majesty Bao Dai, was swept from the scene in October, 1955; any possible influence he might possess had been earlier dissipated in the crushing of the sects and the cleaning out of pro-French and pro-Bao Dai elements in the army.

The victory over Communism was neither complete nor definitive, for the Geneva settlement consigned roughly half of Vietnam's territory and people to the Communist-run Democratic Republic of Viet-

[38] One observer who was in Saigon in late 1955 has commented that Diem's disbanding of the Committee "was a decision based on his need for political survival in a crisis period." John T. Dorsey, Jr., "South Vietnam in Perspective," *Far Eastern Survey*, 27 (December, 1958), 179.

nam. South Vietnam survived its first years in power not because it had vanquished its internal Communist movement but, rather, because it had refused to submit to the reunification elections agreed to in the Geneva settlement; the North's disinclination at that time to use military force against the South also helped. The victory is still at issue, with the resurgence of Communist activities now threatening to topple the non-Communist regime.

These victories over the sects, Communism, and colonialism were not only limited but were essentially negative. But there is more to the Vietnamese government's national revolution. In terms of basic institutions, it meant the development of a new constitution based on republican principles, the creation of new agencies of governance, and the infusion of a new spirit in the government and between the officials and the people. In the next chapter we shall examine the post-Geneva transformation of Vietnamese institutions and the relation of these institutions to the past. In short, we shall examine the extent to which the new regime in South Vietnam is truly new.

2

The New Regime: Institutions

The New Republic

The republican constitution which emerged after the Bao Dai referendum was basically an executive-drafted document. About one week before the referendum, it became known that government officials were preparing a draft constitution which, according to the original plan, was to be submitted to popular ratification.[1] The committee which was subsequently announced to the public included the President's Cabinet and a few private lawyers,[2] but the major work on the constitutional draft was apparently done by a handful of intimate advisors to President Diem, headed by his Secretary of State at the Presidency, Nguyen Huu Chau.

The idea of popular ratification gave way before the end of October, 1955, to one of limited participation by an elected National Assembly in the formation of a constitution; such an Assembly, consisting of 123 members selected from single-member districts, was chosen on March 4, 1956. The National Assembly was given forty-five days, later extended by one month to July 2, to study and discuss the presidential draft. It had the choice of approving the President's handiwork or of recommending changes which, if the President rejected them, would be resubmitted to it. In case of deadlock, the President was empowered to submit his draft to popular ratification.[3]

The presidential draft of the Constitution was not formally pre-

[1] *Tieng Mien Nam* (Saigon), reprinted in U.S. Operations Mission to Vietnam, *Saigon Daily News Round-Up,* October 18, 1955, p. 4.

[2] *La Gazette* (Saigon), reprinted *ibid.,* December 1, 1955, p. 2.

[3] The election, organization, and powers of the National Assembly were provided for in Presidential Ordinances 8 and 9, issued on January 23, 1956.

26

sented to the National Assembly. President Diem instead confined himself to a statement of general principles.[4] The purpose of this change in plan was probably to elevate the legislative body from the limited status of a ratifying convention to that of a constituent assembly. There was little risk that the Assembly would depart radically from the original executive draft, however, for not only was it overwhelmingly pro-regime in its composition, but the five leading members of its drafting committee had served on the special presidential committee. The only sharp divisions on the floor of the Assembly concerned an article directly affecting the interests of its members; on no other part of the legislative draft were there more than nine or ten deputies in opposition.[5] On July 2, its work concluded, the National Assembly presented its results to President Diem, and on October 15 it received his reactions. With several exceptions, the President's suggested changes, which extended to about half the articles of the legislative draft, were minor, and the deputies readily accepted all but about five of them.[6] The only important executive proposal rejected would have lowered the age qualification for President and Vice-President from 40 to 35, and the rejection did not reflect a conflict between the President and the National Assembly but between factions within the government. The President's position was supported by the 35-year-old Nguyen Huu Chau, the Secretary of State at the Presidency and chairman of the presidential drafting committee, and opposed by Mme Ngo Dinh Nhu, the President's sister-in-law. It appears that Chau hoped, under the terms of the Constitution, to be chosen by Diem as Vice-President of the Republic, and Mme Nhu, who was Chau's sister-in-law, was determined to prevent this possibility. In fact the only clear opposition to the President occurred on his recommendation that the majority of deputies required to approve declarations of war and treaties of peace be reduced from a two-thirds to a simple majority. This recommendation was approved by a vote of 46 to 31.

The President did not dispute the National Assembly's position on the questions remaining in issue, and the Constitution was promul-

[4] The Constitution, together with the statement of principles and other information, is contained in *The Constitution of the Republic of Vietnam* (Saigon: Secretariat of State for Information, [1956]).

[5] All Saigon newspapers, reprinted in USOM, *Saigon Daily News Round-Up,* June 21, 1957, pp. 4–5. The controversial provisions, which were approved by narrow votes, excluded deputies from executive posts and from bidding on government contracts.

[6] The Vietnamese press reports of most of these rejections are carried in *ibid.,* October 19, 1956, p. 1; October 20, 1956, p. 1; and October 22, 1956, p. 6.

gated on October 26, the first anniversary of the creation of the Republic. On December 29, the National Assembly, whose life had been extended three years by the Constitution, approved the nomination of Nguyen Ngoc Tho, Secretary of State for National Economy, as Vice-President. The Republic of Vietnam was now a going concern.

The institutions established by the 1956 Constitution can be briefly described as embodying the principle of separation of powers with a strong executive, a weak legislature, and an undefined judiciary. The framers of the Constitution were obviously inspired by the American example of a powerful President,[7] but they neglected the institutional checks of the American constitutional system and added executive powers which made the Vietnamese presidency a most imposing office.

Both the President and Vice-President, elected on the same ballot, and the National Assembly were to be chosen by universal direct suffrage. The presidential term of office was set at five years, with a limitation of three terms, and that of the deputies at three years. The National Assembly was given very little control over executive affairs. The appointment of civil, military, and practically all judicial officers was consigned exclusively to the President, and he was empowered to declare war, make peace, and conclude treaties with the support of a simple majority of the deputies.

The President, on the other hand, was granted considerable legislative power. In cases of emergency, he was authorized to rule by decree if the National Assembly was not in session, to suspend the laws anywhere or everywhere in the country whether the National Assembly was in session or not, and to receive from the legislative body broad grants of decree-making power for stipulated periods. His emergency decrees were to become statutory law unless subsequently rejected by the National Assembly. As if all this were not enough, the Constitution contained a temporary article permitting the President during the three-year life of the First National Assembly to suspend the constitutional guarantees of civil liberty. President Diem did not find it necessary to invoke this reserve power.

---

[7] For example, government sources informed the press that the draft being prepared within the executive branch would be based on the constitutions of the United States and the Philippines — the latter was itself modeled on the American document. (*Tieng Mien Nam* [Saigon], reprinted in *ibid.,* October 18, 1955, p. 4). The Minister of Information was also reported to have cited the American presidential system as a model, but then, probably piqued by nationalist sensibilities, generalized the parentage to be "a presidential system . . . not based on any model." (J. A. C. Grant, "The Vietnam Constitution of 1956," *American Political Science Review,* 52 (June, 1958), 440. The reader interested in a detailed examination of the Vietnamese Constitution is referred to this excellent source.

In ordinary lawmaking, the President was empowered to submit bills to the National Assembly and to veto in whole or in part all legislation passed by the legislature, and it required a three-fourths vote of the entire membership of the National Assembly — in contrast to a two-thirds majority of those voting in each house, in the American Congress — to override a presidential veto. Sessions of the National Assembly could not exceed six months in a year, divided into two three-month periods, and if the Assembly failed to vote upon the executive budget by December 31 of any year the President was enabled to make quarterly budgetary appropriations himself. The enactment of appropriations was the only lawmaking function specifically given to the National Assembly by the Constitution, but it was a function which provided little initiative for the deputies, due to a requirement that any expenditures originating with them must be balanced by proposed new revenues.

The judiciary was not included within the constitutional definition of separation of powers, with the presumption that it would continue to be attached to the executive power. The Constitution did promise an independent status to the courts, but it did not accord judges tenure during good behavior or guaranteed salaries. The organization of the courts was left to legislative enactment. The document also contained a series of "rights and duties of the citizen" too numerous to mention here beyond the observation that some provisions, such as the right and duty to work, were simply exemplary, and that others, such as the right to form trade unions and to strike, were made subject to legislative qualification. The emphasis throughout was on the social obligations attached to freedom, in contrast to the emphasis on individual rights found in the American Constitution, and the Vietnamese document explicitly declared any pro-Communist activities to be contrary to its principles. There was no mention of local government in the Constitution, and this vast area has in fact been organized by executive decree.

A written constitution does not, of course, by itself tell us how a political system functions. Much depends upon the society upon which it has been grafted — its traditions, its social and economic organization, and its aspirations, and upon the key decisions made by those in political control of that society. As we shall see, the direction which the Vietnamese political system has taken amply supports the assertion in Article 4 of the Constitution that "the President is vested with the leadership of the nation."

In certain important respects, the development of government institutions in South Vietnam since independence has been marked by a sharp break with colonial and pre-colonial tradition. The awesome

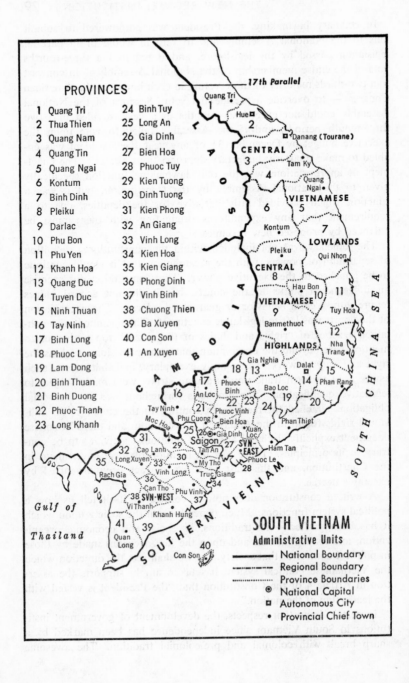

PROVINCES

1	Quang Tri	24	Binh Tuy
2	Thua Thien	25	Long An
3	Quang Nam	26	Gia Dinh
4	Quang Tin	27	Bien Hoa
5	Quang Ngai	28	Phuoc Tuy
6	Kontum	29	Kien Tuong
7	Binh Dinh	30	Dinh Tuong
8	Pleiku	31	Kien Phong
9	Darlac	32	An Giang
10	Phu Bon	33	Vinh Long
11	Phu Yen	34	Kien Hoa
12	Khanh Hoa	35	Kien Giang
13	Quang Duc	36	Phong Dinh
14	Tuyen Duc	37	Vinh Binh
15	Ninh Thuan	38	Chuong Thien
16	Tay Ninh	39	Ba Xuyen
17	Binh Long	40	Con Son
18	Phuoc Long	41	An Xuyen
19	Lam Dong		
20	Binh Thuan		
21	Binh Duong		
22	Phuoc Thanh		
23	Long Khanh		

17th Parallel

Quang Tri 1
Hue
Danang (Tourane)
CENTRAL
3
Tam Ky
4
Quang
Ngai
VIETNAMESE
6
5
Kontum
7
LOWLANDS
Pleiku
Qui Nhon
CENTRAL
8
Hau Bon
11
10
VIETNAMESE
9
Tuy Hoa
Banmethout
12
HIGHLANDS
Nha
Trang
Gia Nghia
Dalat
18
13
15
17
Phuoc
Binh
Bao Loc
An Loc
22 23
19
20
Phan Rang
21
24
Tay Ninh
Phuoc Vinh
Phu Cuong
Bien Hoa
Phan Thiet
Moc Hoa
25
26 Gia Dinh
Cao Lanh
Saigon
Xuan
Loc
31
29
Tan An
27
SVN-
Long Xuyen
30
EAST
Ham Tan
32
33
My Tho
Phuoc Le
35
36
Vinh Long
Truc Giang
28
Rach Gia
34
Can Tho
Phu Vinh
38 SVN-WEST
37
Vi Thanh
Khanh Hung
41
39
Quan
Long
40
Con Son

Gulf of

Thailand

L A O S

C A M B O D I A

S O U T H   C H I N A   S E A

SOUTHERN VIETNAM

SOUTH VIETNAM
Administrative Units

▬▬▬▬	National Boundary
▬ ▬ ▬	Regional Boundary
··········	Province Boundaries
◉	National Capital
◻	Autonomous City
•	Provincial Chief Town

power formerly reposed in an Emperor or, later, in a Governor-General has been divided between an elected President and National Assembly, both limited by a written Constitution. This Constitution has also brought into being institutions, already mentioned, which did not exist prior to the Republic. But more important than the changes wrought by constitutional action have been the administrative changes produced by executive decree. The uniform direction of these decrees has been the strengthening of presidential power over the agencies of the national government and the centralizing of national control over a burgeoning local administration.

A formidable obstacle to a unitary administration were the two regional administrations of Central and Southern Vietnam, and one of Diem's first acts, after becoming premier was to dismiss the governors of these areas and replace them with delegates responsible to him. He then, on August 4, 1954, abolished the legal autonomy of the regions and with it their independent budgets and control over local government, though full execution of this decision was deferred until early 1956. The number of government regions now stands at four. Southern Vietnam has been divided into eastern and western regions, and the Central highlands, which had been administered as a separate *Pays Montagnards du Sud* (PMS) under the French and as a Royal Domain under Bao Dai, was incorporated with the rest of the country in March, 1955. The regional delegates today exercise little more than ceremonial and some inspectional and advisory functions. The regions, created by the French as separate "countries," have disappeared as meaningful levels of government, and the threat which their rulers presented to central hegemony has been eliminated.[8]

The main administrative units of local government, with the sapping of regional power, have become the forty-one provinces into which South Vietnam is presently organized. (See map on p. 30.) The provincial administrations control the subordinate levels of government, the districts and villages, and channel the programs of central agencies to them. Considerable authority is vested in the province chiefs who, appointed by the President and directly responsible to him despite a chain of command which runs through the Department of Interior, possess great authority over all that happens within their domains, including the activities of police and security, and sometimes regular army, forces.

[8] Tran Van Lam, then the presidential delegate for southern Vietnam, told researchers of the Michigan State University Vietnam Advisory Group, on November 20, 1955, that one reason the regional representatives had to be reduced in status was that they posed a "potential danger" to the national government because of the powers which they had inherited from the past.

The Diem government has also fortified its direct control over district administration. Totaling around 233, the districts average six to a province, though one province, an island, has none, and a few of the heavily populated provinces have as many as eleven or twelve. The district chiefs have been made appointive by the central government, and the administrative services under their authority constitute the end point of most national government agencies operating in the field. The district is the intermediary between the province and the village, and it has assumed tremendous administrative burdens under the republican government. In a study of one district headquarters, it was found that, in addition to his many other duties, the district chief in the space of a single week received about one hundred instructions and other communications from the chief of the province and submitted a similar number of answers and reports to his superior.[9] To a considerable extent the district administration serves as a transmittal office for provincial communications to the villages. These communications, often retyped by district clerks in sufficient quantity, are then distributed, with district officials ensuring compliance, by village authorities. The district organization engages neither in the policy coordination and decisions of provincial government, nor the intimate relations of village officers with the local population.

Village autonomy quickly gave way before the centralizing thrust of the national government. Legally this came about through decrees which, in June and August, 1956, abolished elective village and municipal councils and replaced them with appointive officials.[10] The councils of South Vietnam's 2,560 villages came under the selection of the province chiefs, usually on the recommendation of the district chiefs, with the Department of Interior apparently reviewing and approving the choices. As an agency of the local population, village councils continue to draw up village budgets and regulate local revenues, such as those derived from the rental of communal lands, but their budgets have fallen under the review of provincial officials and, in the case of large budgets, the national government itself. Furthermore, village councils are now required to act as agents of the central government, collecting national and provincial taxes, disseminating government propaganda and controlling subversive activities, and

[9] Luther A. Allen and Pham Ngoc An, *A Vietnamese District Chief in Action* (Saigon: Michigan State University Vietnam Advisory Group; Republic of Vietnam, National Institute of Administration, May, 1961), p. 53.

[10] See Lam Le Trinh, "Village Councils — Yesterday and Today," *Viet-My* (Saigon: The Journal of the Vietnamese-American Association), Part I (August, 1958), pp. 36–44; Part II (September, 1958), pp. 59–70, for a historical discussion of the legal development of village government in Vietnam.

settling disputes arising under the government's land rent-limitation and other programs. A surprising amount of administration is carried on at the level of the village in spite of the small number of officials and the absence of public services. In addition to those functions mentioned, village officials register births, issue marriage certificates, collect rents and agricultural loans, approve requests of local inhabitants to leave the village, and sign and countersign numerous types of documents. Essentially, village administration is concerned with control and regulation, and the most consuming task of the village chief is settling the multifarious petty civil disputes which arise among the local population.[11]

Government administration does not end with the village council. Each village in South Vietnam is composed of a group of hamlets; there are about 16,000 hamlets in the country. Since the advent of the Republic, hamlet chiefs have been appointed by district chiefs, generally on the recommendation of the village chiefs. Like the village officials, hamlet chiefs are salaried officials, and their main duties are to maintain order within their jurisdictions and to carry out the instructions which have come from district, provincial, or, often, from Saigon agencies. Nor does the government's administrative reach stop with the hamlet chief, for the Diem regime, borrowing from Viet Minh practice, has, through the hamlet chief, organized peasant families into agglomerations (*khom*) each containing between 25 and 35 households and headed by an appointed agglomeration chief; and these agglomerations are further broken down into interfamily groups (*lien gia*), each containing about five families and headed by another appointed chief.[12] A similar system has been established in the urban areas, but has met with less success, especially in Saigon. The prefecture of Saigon and the cities of Dalat, Danang, and Hue, incidentally, are autonomous of provincial rule and are administered by mayors — a prefect in the case of Saigon — appointed by the central government.

With the abolition of village autonomy, the extension of central government controls into the villages, and the development of new government programs, the administrative system of the Republic of Vietnam has become more centralized than it ever was under the emperors or the French, and is surpassed only by the Communist

[11] The administration of a single village is examined in Truong Ngoc Giau and Lloyd Woodruff, *My Thuan: Administrative and Financial Aspects of a Village in South Vietnam* (Saigon: National Institute of Administration, Republic of Vietnam, in cooperation with the Michigan State University Vietnam Advisory Group, July, 1961).

[12] See the discussion in Roy Jumper, "The Communist Challenge to South Vietnam" *Far Eastern Survey,* 25 (November, 1956), 164–65.

bureaucracy created in North Vietnam. In Saigon, too, there has occurred a strengthening of central leadership, in the hands of the President. The President freely chooses and dismisses his top administrators and presides over the Cabinet Council where his voice is supreme. To assist his control over the executive departments, which at present number twelve, President Diem, in May, 1961, grouped them within three coordinating ministerial departments. This reform has not resulted thus far in any noticeable change in the direct relationship between the regular secretaries of state and the President, nor in the tendency of each department to go its own way except when under instructions from the Presidency. In fact, whatever coordination of executive agencies exists emanates from the Presidential Palace. The strongest department head is the Secretary of State at the Presidency, Nguyen Dinh Thuan, who has under his authority several important staff agencies including the general directorates of Planning, Civil Service, and Budget and Foreign Aid. Secretary Thuan is also the coordinating secretary of state for the departments of Interior and National Defense, as well as the Assistant Secretary of National Defense — the President himself holds the Defense secretaryship. As we shall see in the next chapter, these institutional arrangements, formidable enough, do not give the full picture of presidential domination of the executive branch or of the channels of authority which spread from the Presidential Independence Palace.

Continuity with the Past

The government changes which have been introduced since 1954 in South Vietnam show everywhere the influence of the past. It can be seen in the organization of government agencies, in the laws and decrees by which the country is governed, in the ways in which particular public institutions have developed. The general structure of the Vietnamese government is based on the French pattern. An administrative department, for example, is usually composed, in descending hierarchy, of general directorates, directorates, bureaus, and sections. A secretary of state of a department is assisted by his personally appointed cabinet and by one or more secretaries-general charged with coordinating departmental operations. Administrative practices throughout the government are governed mainly by pre-independence colonial regulations, and the civil service system, established in 1950, also follows that of France, with its classification of personnel by cadres, in contrast to American classification by positions, and with rare movement of an individual above his cadre level. Cadre classification is closely related to educational level, as is salary, except for the provision (following French practice) of family and other special allowances and supplements.[13]

French principles are even more strongly engrained in the judicial system, which has undergone less alteration or development since 1954 than the administrative system. Except for a small amount of patch-work, Vietnam still operates under the separate penal and civil codes which the colonial authority had promulgated separately for Tonkin, Annam, and Cochinchina. This situation is rendered more complex by the courts' following the "law of persons" in civil proceedings. If a court proceeding involves Northerners, the code of that region is applied, and if the parties to a dispute come from different parts of Vietnam, French international law is followed. Obvious gaps exist in codes which were developed long ago (the Cochinchinese code dates back to 1883, and those for the other two regions to the 1930s) and which reflect colonial legal concepts. Until the National Assembly can provide new codes, the Vietnamese courts are compelled to feel their way through this maze. Where the colonial code is silent on civil matters, such as the law of contracts, French civil law is used, and where French law is clearly inapplicable the courts must devise their own solutions. This has produced a small body of precedents similar to the judge-made or common law of the Anglo-Saxon world.

There are, as in France, separate court systems to handle civil and administrative disputes. The civil courts are based on the justices of the peace and justices of the peace of extended jurisdiction, who handle minor disputes, and the main trial courts, called Courts of First Instance, which operate, as in France, with multiple judges and no juries. The amount of litigation handled in these courts is not, by Western standards, very great; between 1954 and 1958, for example, the total number of criminal actions came to about 70,000 cases and the total number of civil actions to about 99,000 cases. It is worth mentioning that suits for debt constituted over half of all civil actions during this period, followed by housing and land disputes, and that divorce actions, which were unknown in pre-colonial Vietnam, made up about 2.4 per cent of the whole.[14] There are two courts of appeal, at Saigon and Hue; above the civil courts is the Court of Cassation, or Supreme Court, also at Saigon. The administrative courts, whose task

[13] A comprehensive study of Vietnamese public personnel policies has been made by Dale L. Rose, assisted by Vu Van Hoc, *The Vietnamese Civil Service System* (Saigon: Michigan State University Vietnam Advisory Group, April, 1961).

[14] These figures are taken from an undated mimeographed brochure entitled "The Record of Achievements in the Judiciary Field," issued by the Department of Justice, probably in October, 1958.

it is to resolve disputes between government agencies and private citizens, do not receive much litigation. They are located in Saigon and a few other main cities, and they culminate in the Council of State, a body which also renders legal opinions to the government on matters placed before it. The Vietnamese Constitution provides for several special courts: the Constitutional Court determines, at the request of other courts, the validity of laws and executive orders and regulations; the Special Court of Justice is invoked when the National Assembly brings charges of treason or other high crimes against the President and certain other high officials; and the High Council of the Judiciary controls the promotion and disciplining of judges and approves their designation by the Secretary of State for Justice.

In addition to the courts mentioned, special tribunals have been set up for settling labor disputes, disputes arising from land reform decrees (especially regulations which provide land tenure to tenants), and juvenile and military courts, the latter having jurisdiction over military personnel and certain political offenses. Appeals can be made from the decisions of these courts, but not from decisions of the special military tribunals created in 1959 to pass summary judgment, including the death penalty, with no right of appeal on acts of subversion.

The carry-over of the past can be seen not only in the organization and functioning of Vietnamese government institutions, but in their differential development as well. Vietnam, as we have noted, has had a long and strong administrative tradition. This tradition was disrupted by the colonial intrusion, but it was modernized as well. Although French influence was extensive throughout Vietnam, it was stronger in the South, which fell under direct colonial rule, than in the North, and it was least strong in the Center. The continued existence of an indigenous though far from independent administration at the Court of Hue accounts in part for the disproportionate number of government officials, in both the Ho Chi Minh and Ngo Dinh Diem governments, who are from Central Vietnam. Also, those officials who, like Diem, have served in the administration of Annam or who, like Ho, are the sons of Annamese public servants, probably reflect more of the traditional administrative system in their own behavior than do officials from other parts of the country. It is not by accident that President Diem frequently lectures foreign visitors on the administrative history of his country and of its relevance, in his eyes at least, for understanding present-day Vietnam. It is possible too that Vietnamese administrative tradition is more strongly present in those government activities, such as public works and most tax administration, which were important in pre-colonial Vietnam, than in such French-created services as public health, telephone and telegraphic communications, and labor relations. Finally, traditional practices are more deeply present in village administration which, as in the regulating of personal disputes, is heavily suffused with customary rules than in administration at the central and provincial levels.

In several respects, French administrative practice was congruent with traditional administrative practice. France has been described as having the Republic on top and the empire underneath, a reference to the establishment during the Napoleonic period of the basic organizations and legal codes of the French government which persisted with little change after the advent of republican institutions. Thus, French centralized administration through departments headed by nationally appointed prefects did not differ greatly from Vietnamese centralized administration through provinces headed by nationally appointed mandarins. Moreover, the mandarin system shared with the French civil service system an emphasis on intellectual attainment as a qualification for higher administrative office. In both systems, the well-educated man, interpreted as one well versed in literature, history, and philosophy, rather than the specialist, was the ideal sought for in recruitment examinations, and in both systems rank was closely correlated with intellectual achievement, with little possibility of passing from lower to higher ranks. Traditional Vietnamese administration, reflecting Confucian ideals, emphasized deference to authority, social harmony, and the avoidance of disagreement — what Westerners would call a lack of frankness — and a heavy paternalism. Individual initiative was not a characteristic of this system; the state was looked to as the originator of public action and, within the state, the Emperor himself. Protocol and concern for status pervaded the system from the lowest levels to the very highest. A revealing example of the fine grading of ranks and of diplomatic indirection was Emperor Minh Mang's response to the receipt of gifts from King Louis XVIII of France. Minh Mang realized that courtesy demanded reciprocity, but yet it would not do for him, an emperor, to elevate an ordinary king to his level. His solution was to send gifts of his own but to have his prime minister answer Louis' letter, on the pretext that the majesty of the Vietnamese throne forbade a letter signed by the imperial hand to travel on a merchant vessel.[15]

Two major administrative problems which faced the Vietnamese upon independence were staffing the upper levels of government agencies and adapting the governmental structure to new functions. It was rare during the colonial period for any Vietnamese to rise as high as bureau chief in the central agencies, with the result that high

[15] Georges Taboulet, *La geste française en Indochine,* Tome II (Paris: Adrien-Maisonneuve, 1956), p. 309.

government officials today are often ill-prepared to handle their recently acquired responsibilities. The government is seeking to overcome this lack of trained personnel through the National Institute of Administration; this Institute, created only in 1953, has been graduating about fifty candidates a year — recently more — for service in the government, a majority of whom have been assigned to provincial and district administration. Some of these officials are now working their way up to fairly responsible positions. Other avenues to higher government service are the Faculty of Law of the University of Saigon and civil service training abroad, mostly in the United States under programs sponsored by the United States economic aid mission. Many of the government's specialists have been recruited by the use of special contracts. The lack of qualified personnel will hamper government administration for some time to come, although, as will be seen later, the Vietnamese leadership has not made adequate use either of available talent or opportunities to train new administrators in large numbers.

Solution of the second major problem, that of adapting the administrative structure to new purposes, is also hindered by lack of qualified personnel, as well as by limited resources in general. At least equally detrimental are the mental habits of public officials carried over from the colonial past. Those Vietnamese who served their own or the colonial government during the period of French domination were trained to defer to the judgments of French officials. Very rarely did they attain decision-making positions. Moreover, administration was viewed as a mechanism for ensuring accountability of bureaucratic transactions and the control of both government officials and the subject population. This attitude is often referred to as the *fonctionnaire* spirit, the major manifestation of which is a dedication to procedural routine. Like the mandarin of old, the *fonctionnaire* is paid according to his cadre rank regardless of the job he holds, and the "ideal" *fonctionnaire* assiduously postpones decisions until the happy day of his retirement. Vietnam has since independence undertaken a number of social and economic development programs that require a positive orientation toward administration. The changes in attitude and behavior which this new orientation demands of government officials have been more than most of them have been able to make.

In general, the agencies which have been most adaptable to the new administrative needs have been the recently established ones like the General Directorate of Budget and Foreign Aid and the General Commissariat for Land Development. The old-line agencies, most clearly typified by the departments of Justice and Finance, have tended to perpetuate the inertia and concentration on form and procedure which is part of Vietnam's administrative heritage. The new agencies by and large have been more confronted with novel problems demanding imaginative responses. Since they were formed or underwent great expansion after independence, they have escaped to a considerable extent from the colonial mold, and were able to engage many of their higher personnel through special contracts, by-passing thereby the rigid status and salary rules of the civil service system. The new agencies are relatively dynamic, but they are also, because they are new, vulnerable to assaults from the entrenched sectors of the bureaucracy. The General Directorate of Civic Action, which had embarked on an ambitious community development program in 1955, found its activities sharply curtailed by the jealousies of several older agencies. More recently, the General Directorate of Budget and Foreign Aid, which had developed the most advanced budgetary system in all of Southeast Asia, fell victim to similar jealousies in its attempt to extend modern budget controls throughout the government.

Thus, the colonial heritage left Vietnam with modern governmental institutions, but institutions directed to the negative function of control and accountability. Further, the colonial monopoly of higher administrative positions left Vietnam with a severe shortage of persons qualified to assume these posts, and imbued those Vietnamese who had worked under the French with restrictive and legalistic notions of administration and a strong indisposition to assume initiative in the administrative process. Because the colonial administration was designed basically to serve colonial interests — specifically, to further the exploitation of certain primary resources like rubber, rice, and iron ore and to provide a market for French manufactured products — the Vietnamese have had to develop new administrative mechanisms to carry on new public objectives. The result has been strain and conflict within the administrative bureaucracy, and not a little confusion and duplication of effort.

The administrative branch, however inadequate its functioning, has been far more sturdy in post-independence Vietnam than non-administrative organs of the Vietnamese government. Administrative power has in fact dominated the rest of the government. Some non-administrative organs have been very slow in coming to life. The Constitutional Court and the National Economic Council, both provided for in the Constitution, were not created until March, 1961, and the latter did not begin functioning until nearly a year later. Similarly, the law creating the High Council of the Judiciary was only enacted in February, 1961.

The National Assembly furnishes an additional and more dramatic case of weak institutional development. It should be recalled that pre-colonial Vietnam had no representative institutions except for village councils, and that these bodies were largely chosen by informal co-optation. The French overlay of representative institutions was very thin: the various provincial, territorial, and Indochinese Union councils were based on limited suffrage, to the extent that they were not wholly or partly appointive, and were equipped with limited functions and dominated either by their French members or by the French administration. Various pressures made it inevitable that the Diem government should establish a National Assembly. Prior to independence, practically all urban nationalists, including Ngo Dinh Diem and his supporters, had demanded such an institution; a national assembly was regarded as a badge of sovereignty and modernity in South Vietnam's entry into the community of nations; and, if these reasons were not enough, North Vietnam had a National Assembly, and the South could not afford to offer less to its people. But while giving the country a national representative institution, President Diem at the same time took away the institutions of village self-government and also the weaker provincial bodies which had been established in 1953.

With certain important exceptions, the Vietnamese National Assembly closely resembles that of France under the Fourth Republic in its internal organization and procedures.[16] Each legislative body has a general bureau, with group representation based on numerical strength, responsible for general control of legislative activity; and each body has regular committees, also based on proportional representation, which, as in the United States Congress, consider legislation before it goes to the floor, thereby exercising, in theory anyway, strong discretionary control over subjects entrusted to them. Two formal divergencies from French parliamentary practice should be noted. First, to avoid the multi-party system of the French legislature, all deputies in the Vietnamese National Assembly must join one of two blocs, or else remain unaffiliated. In the second place, the executive in Vietnam is even more independent of legislative authority than in Gaullist France. The Vietnamese Cabinet is neither installed by vote of the National Assembly nor can it be overturned by it. On the other hand, the President of Vietnam cannot, as his French counterpart can, dissolve the National Assembly by calling new elections.

The mere act of creating a National Assembly and endowing it with constitutional powers did not, of course, assure it a meaningful role

[16] Compare the "Rules of the National Assembly," in Republic of Vietnam, National Assembly, *Constitution* (Saigon, 1956), and D. W. S. Lidderdale, *The Parliament of France* (London: The Hansard Society, 1951).

in government policy-making. After seven years of existence the National Assembly has not appreciably affected the concentration of power which had been lodged in executive hands. A good illustration of the imbalance of legislative and executive authority can be seen in the development of the Vietnamese budget, which has been the main occupation of the National Assembly.[17] The President has not yet found it necessary to disapprove any part of the budgets thus far presented to him, inasmuch as the deputies have made very few changes in his original requests, all of which probably had advance government sanction. The National Assembly has not changed the overall amount requested in any budget. Moreover, by a rationale which illustrates the importance of colonial precedents in the present-day operations of the Vietnamese government, the President is bound only by the total amount voted by the National Assembly, not by chapter or title totals, even though the budget is voted by chapters. Precedents for this exist in the comprehensive financial code established by the French government for its overseas territories in 1912, which gave territorial governors broad powers as fiscal managers of their budgets.[18] There were conflicting viewpoints within the government as to whether the colonial regulations gave the President the authority to transfer funds among budget chapters without preliminary approval of the legislative body; the President himself decided the question in the affirmative.[19] Further, under existing procedures, the President may transfer credits from the budget chapter of one department to that of another, and the Budget Directorate may authorize transfers and increases between major budgetary accounts within agency chapters. The budget approved by the National Assembly is treated in effect as a lump-sum appropriation, which has been made easier to do by the government's inability in most years to spend all the money which it requested and which the National Assembly has voted.

In short, the National Assembly does not exert an adequate review of executive budgetary policy. Administrative officials generally assume that approval of their budgets will be automatic; when it is not, they feel that they are being subtly undercut by the Presidency. The deputies themselves feel obliged to accept whatever the government proposes. Opposition to proposed expenditures is looked upon as

[17] For a detailed study of legislative-executive relationships in budget development, see the piece coauthored by the writer and Wayne W. Snyder, "The Budget Process in South Vietnam," *Pacific Affairs*, 33 (March, 1960), 48–60.

[18] France, *Juris-Classeur de la France d'Outre-Mer*, Décret sur le régime financier des territoires d'outre-mer, 30 décembre 1912.

[19] Personal interview with a high administrative official, November 11, 1958.

opposition to the President and an affront to his prestige. By and large, it is expected that the National Assembly will more or less freely discuss what is proposed and then vote as requested. Deliberations on the budget reflect this attitude. The deputies responsible for leading discussions of different parts of the budget consider themselves to be representatives of the administration and lean heavily on information fed to them by administration officials during floor debates. Debate is usually not very well informed nor do many deputies participate, and floor discussion often takes the form either of very specific questions, such as, "Why does Agency X want so much money for electricity?" or general suggestions as to how agencies should carry out or improve their programs. Very rarely are amendments proposed from the floor, though the Budget and Finance Committee has occasionally recommended transfers of sums.

Moreover, the National Assembly is excluded from meaningful action in certain important budget areas. Much of the government's expenditure for economic development is contained in the budgets of autonomous agencies or derives from the American aid program, neither of which comes under the scrutiny of the deputies. The latter program includes American aid to the defense budget, which has constituted about one-third of all government receipts since 1954. In fact, the deputies are given only the chapter figures for the military budget, with no explanation of the uses to which funds will be put. Then, too, there is the constitutional revenue-expenditure limitation, by which the National Assembly, but not the Executive, is required to match any proposed expenditure with new receipts. With this limitation the National Assembly cannot exercise initiative in budget-making without reducing what the President has requested. Finally, the National Assembly lacks the means to ensure administrative compliance with its appropriations. There is not yet any legislative machinery to check upon the expenditure of funds and, even if there were, the broad power of the executive to transfer funds would nullify any attempt at post-appropriation control.

The relationship between the legislative and executive branches in the budget process is typical of any situation in which the National Assembly has been called upon to exercise functions that brought it into direct contact with the massive power of the executive. On all such occasions the National Assembly has submitted to executive leadership. Never has it rejected or seriously changed any legislation the Presidency asked for, and never has it originated important legislation on its own initiative. Executive control of the legislature has been effected, first, through the election of an almost entirely pro-government chamber and, second, through control of Assembly activities. The leaders in the National Assembly have all been men willing to executive presidential wishes, which are transmitted by the President himself or, more commonly, by his brother or some other high officials. Ngo Dinh Nhu, incidentally, has been a member of the National Assembly since 1956, though he has rarely, if ever, attended its sessions. His influence in the deliberations of the deputies has thus been indirect, though pervasive. Nhu's wife is also a deputy, and though she seldom attends legislative sessions, she controls Assembly action in matters affecting women and, increasingly, in other areas as well. She has, on at least one occasion, had the National Assembly brought into session on her private demand.

The organization of deputies by blocs has not fulfilled its implied promise for the vigorous confrontation of viewpoints within the Assembly. In the first National Assembly, whose term extended from March, 1956, to October, 1959, there existed a Majority Bloc and a Minority Bloc. Both blocs, however, declared themselves to be in "complete agreement" on basic principles,[20] and about 13 of the 17 Minority Bloc members were actually pro-government deputies. Many deputies were evidently confused as to the purpose of the blocs at the time they were organized, as well they might have been.[21] In the second National Assembly, elected August 30, 1959, an attempt has been made to give the blocs meaningfully distinct names, and about eighty deputies have been formed into a Personalist Community Bloc (*Khoi Cong Dong Nhan Vi*) that is composed mainly of members of the main government party, and thirty-five deputies into a Socialist Union Bloc (*Khoi Lien Minh Xa Hoi*). (The term "Personalist" also appears in the title of Ngo Dinh Nhu's elite political party and is the name for the official philosophy of the Diem regime.) That nominal changes have made little difference in National Assembly behavior is evidenced by the choice of a leader of the Socialist Union Bloc as the President's campaign manager in the 1961 presidential election.

A further weakness of the National Assembly is that many policy matters do not even come before it for discussion, but are handled exclusively by administrative action. The scope of activity is reflected in the small amount of legislation enacted by the Assembly. In the three-year period, 1957 to 1959, for example, it passed only 63 measures. The principle that underlies administrative lawmaking seems to be that only the National Assembly can establish basic constitutional institutions, such as the National Economic Council and the

[20] USOM, *Saigon Daily News Round-Up,* December 17, 1956, p. 1.
[21] *Ibid.,* December 7, 1957, pp. 1–2.

Constitutional Court, or make basic revisions in colonial and Bao Dai legislation, as it did in the Family Code and in various tax measures, but that all other subjects can be regulated by the executive until the National Assembly chooses to act on them. Thus, except for numerous smaller adjustments made in legislation inherited from the past, the creation and abolition of cabinet departments have been done, as in France, by presidential decree, as have increases in the size of the armed forces and the transfer of about 210,000 people from the Central coastlands to new villages in the highlands region of Central Vietnam.[22] And, as has already been noted, the executive branch does not subject to review by the National Assembly the programs it undertakes with American assistance.

What initiative, then, is left to the National Assembly? The deputies have been left more or less free to develop legislation covering minor subjects, such as the regulation of pharmacists, rules governing the bar, and their own internal rules. They have also had some latitude in important measures in which the government is not directly involved or concerning which it has not taken a fixed position. Perhaps the strongest show of independence against the executive took place during the drawing up of the Constitution, when the Assembly disagreed with several presidential recommendations. Some deputies also resisted the comprehensive Family Code introduced by Mme Ngo Dinh Nhu in October, 1957. This legislation, which was finally enacted in June, 1958, and, after the acceptance of minor presidential changes, promulgated in January, 1959, made sweeping changes in Vietnamese domestic relations. Polygamy and divorce were outlawed; marital infidelity, which included being seen in public with a person of another sex, was made legally punishable, and women were given equal rights with their spouses in a variety of activities. If this bill did not produce, as one newspaper claimed, "the warmest discussions which have occurred since the National Assembly was established"[23] (an accolade which should be reserved to the discussions on the Constitution), it did mark the last affirmation of legislative independence from executive domination. The male deputies were clearly unsympathetic in their attitudes toward the bill, as their prolonged picking at its different provisions revealed, and at one time a motion was made to table it. A number of them even demanded that Mme Nhu apologize for unseemly remarks she addressed to her male col-

[22] For example, the President on May 28, 1961, established by unilateral action two Cabinet departments and three coordinating Cabinet departments, and transferred a number of agencies among departments. (Republic of Vietnam, *Official Journal*, Decrees 120–124-TTP.)

[23] *Nguoi Viet* (Saigon), June 6, 1958.

leagues, and, in a way, she did so.[24] But the important facts in this opposition are that the President was not himself especially interested in the legislation, and that when pressure was finally applied from the Presidency the legislation was speedily approved with only one deputy dissenting.

The National Assembly has thus played a restricted role in the governmental system. It does not dare oppose the executive on important legislation. It does occasionally modify his proposals, but it is questionable whether these modifications constitute spontaneous actions. The refusal of the Assembly to change the age qualification for President and Vice-President was, as we have seen, a dispute between factions around the President. Likewise, probably most, if not all, of the changes which the National Assembly has made in executive budgets have been engineered from the outside. The cuts made in the reconstruction and urbanism budget in 1958, which were accompanied by sharp legislative fault-finding, were inspired by the Presidency against the head of that agency, who was in disfavor. Likewise, the spirited attack on the Department of National Economy in December, 1960, in which that agency was charged with incapacity and with being a "nest of germs," preceded by a few months the fall of its leading official.[25] The deputies receive petitions from their constituents on local problems but, unless they stand in well with the main government party, they generally get no response from the executive agencies to which they forward these communications. Sometimes deputies make requests or give advice to provincial and district officials but, unless they are influential in the government, they are usually ignored. Some deputies make it a point to carry out charitable work in their constituencies, frequently at requests for help from local officials, but most of them have little contact with their electorates and almost all maintain permanent residences in Saigon.[26]

It should be observed that the deputies of the National Assembly

[24] Mme Nhu was accused of referring to her male colleagues as "very base" and suggesting that they resisted her legislation from a desire to keep concubines. According to some reports, she called the majority leader of the Assembly "a pig." Her denial of the first two charges appears in *Ngon Luan* (Saigon), January 22, 1958.

[25] What made this attack particularly interesting is the fact that the Secretary of State for National Economy was also the Vice-President of the Republic, Nguyen Ngoc Tho. See *Times of Vietnam,* December 31, 1960, for the attack and for Tho's defense of his agency.

[26] The district chief in Central Vietnam studied by Allen and An, *A Vietnamese District Chief in Action,* asked the two deputies from his district to provide rice to needy people in the area. The chief had never met the deputies prior to this request, which one of them fulfilled, nor had either ever visited any village in his district. (*Ibid.,* p. 99).

have learned how to operate legislative machinery, though little grist has been fed into it, and that some of them have attended seriously to their business. The executive branch, when it makes use of the Assembly, generally complies with the formalities of the legislative process. The trouble the government takes in preparing a legislative budget document, submitting it for discussion, and furnishing most of the information the deputies request gives some ground for hoping that the National Assembly may in time come to play a more meaningful part in the governmental system. Perhaps the National Assembly's most noteworthy achievements thus far, meager as they are, have been in reviewing the actions of administrative agencies. The agencies do not fear that the National Assembly will cut their budget requests on its own initiative, but they are somewhat concerned about being criticized, especially since criticism is reported in the press and may draw unfavorable presidential attention to them. The deputies, if they have not been free with legislative proposals, have been somewhat freer in finding fault with particular administrative operations, especially when they have been set on by members of the President's family. As a result, administrative agencies tend to cooperate with the Budget and Finance Committee and with ordinary deputies more than they otherwise would. This role of critic of administrative inefficiency and waste serves a useful purpose in helping the President know what goes on within his bureaucracy, and, so long as the deputies do not extend it to include the President or the basic aspects of his regime, it will probably be allowed to continue.

3

The New Regime: People

The New Men in Power

Outside of agriculture, government service is the main occupation in Vietnam. Of a population of some 15 million people, about 7,100,000 of whom are males, about 486,000 persons make their living from the state. This estimate does not include persons employed by publicly controlled economic enterprises. Put in another way, one out of every eight able-bodied men works for the government. The greater part of the 486,000 total is engaged in military service, distributed approximately as follows: the regular armed services, 210,000; the Civil Guard, a supplement to the army, 72,000; and the locally based Self-Defense Corps, 80,000. This leaves about 124,000 persons, the great majority of whom are men, employed by the civil bureaucracy.[1] A fair estimate of the relative importance of different civil activities of the Vietnamese government can be gained by comparing the employment levels of different agencies. In 1960, there were 25,100 persons working for the Department of Interior, most of whom were police and security agents; 17,700 persons, mostly school teachers, were under the Department of National Education; 12,100 were under the Department of Public Works; and 10,100 were under the Department of National Defense. In contrast, the Department of Agriculture employed only 2,900, a surprisingly low figure for a predominantly rural

[1] In 1960, about 13,000 women were employed by public agencies, according to Dale L. Rose, assisted by Vu Van Hoc, *The Vietnamese Civil Service System* (Saigon: Michigan State University Vietnam Advisory Group, April, 1961), p. 18.

47

country, the Department of National Economy 912, and the Department of Labor a paltry 382.[2]

There is no shortage of personnel in Vietnamese agencies. In fact, one of the features of many government offices is the surplus of clerks, typists, messengers, and other low-level civil servants, many of them engaged in unnecessary tasks. One reason for this oversupply of personnel was the necessity for the Diem government to absorb the large number of government employees who joined the refugee movement to the South after the Geneva Agreements. In addition, the unemployment resulting from the dismantling of the French war effort drew many people into the government through personal connections and political influence. Civil service regulations make it very difficult to eliminate even incompetent personnel, and private employment opportunities since independence have not been sufficient to encourage an exodus from the safety of government tenure. There is, however, a shortage of qualified personnel. In 1961, only 1,879 civil servants had a university education, and only about 4,000 civil servants a high school education.[3] In order to attract the college-educated from better-paying private employment at home and in France, the government has made liberal use of special contracts which permit hiring outside of civil service regulations. Nearly two-thirds of the university graduates have been hired in this way, many of them by the newer agencies.[4]

Whether educated at home or abroad, the higher level civil service is heavily permeated with Western values. Until recently, the whole Vietnamese educational system was organized along French lines; French was the main language, and students learned more about French history, literature, and philosophy than they did about their own. French influence remains strong in the Vietnamese school system, especially at the upper levels. The French Cultural Mission still provides about 300 teachers to instruct in the principal high schools, most high school and university teachers have been produced by the French educational system, either at home or in France, and, while French has been relegated to a secondary position in primary and secondary education, it is still employed by Vietnamese professors and their French colleagues in several faculties of the University of Saigon. The number of civil servants with American training is still small, though growing, and in most cases American education has been an overlay on a French mold.

[2] *Ibid.,* p. 17.

[3] *Vietnam Press* (English edition), March 17, 1961 (evening issue), p. H-10.

[4] The precise figures, as of December 31, 1961, which have been privately provided, are 818 contract employees of a total of 1,334 employees with university degrees.

The Western and specifically French orientation of the Vietnamese bureaucracy is even more pronounced when viewed in terms of length of service in the government. A Vietnamese government survey of 13,700 public employees in early 1959, found that 36 per cent had been at least ten years in government service.[5] In other words, over one-third of the bureaucracy serving the Republic had entered the government prior to the creation of the Bao Dai Associate State of Vietnam — that is, during the period when French civil servants still dominated middle and upper government positions and were extensively found in many lower ones as well. Indeed, eight of the present fourteen cabinet members, including the most important of the state secretaries, had served in the pre-1945 colonial or protectorate administration.[6] Although figures are not available, many more of those working for the government in 1959, enough to constitute a large majority of the total of civil servants when added to the pre-1959 group, must have obtained their jobs between 1949 and 1954, as the French turned more and more functions over to Vietnamese control. During this second period, it should be noted, French influence in the bureaucracy was still great, for not only did French officials retain key positions, but French was the official language in government oral and written discourse. Most of the general directors, directors, and bureau and service chiefs serving the Vietnamese government today probably served the French as well. It is interesting that the National Assembly should also be heavily populated with pre-1954 public officials. Of the 123 deputies elected to the first Assembly, for instance, at least 48, by the writer's count, were or had served in the government. Especially noticeable was the number of provincial and municipal council members who, their institutions having been abolished by the Diem government, made their way into the legislative branch.

The prevalence of French influence in the backgrounds of Vietnamese civil servants has strengthened the continuity, discussed in the last chapter, between the institutions and practices of the colonial

[5] John T. Dorsey, Jr., "Stresses and Strains in a Developing Administrative System," in Wesley R. Fishel (editor), *Problems of Freedom: South Vietnam since Independence* (Glencoe, Ill.: The Free Press; and East Lansing, Mich.: Bureau of Social and Political Research, Michigan State University, 1961), p. 152, fn. 4.

[6] Nguyen Thai, "The Government of Men in the Republic of Vietnam," (East Lansing, Michigan: private mimeograph, June, 1962), p. 56. The pre-1945 secretaries of state are Nguyen Ngoc Tho, Coordinator for Economic Development; Bui Van Luong, Interior; Nguyen Van Dinh, Public Works; Ngo Trong Hieu, Civic Action; Nguyen Luong, Finance; Nguyen Dinh Luong, Justice; and Vu Van Mau, Foreign Affairs. Tran Ngoc Lien, Commissioner General of Agricultural Credit, might be added to the list, inasmuch as he has the status of a state secretary.

regime and those of the present regime. It has, moreover, grafted to the great mass of the Vietnamese people a directing group varying widely from it in outlook and behavior. Since secondary and higher education has been the preserve of the well-off, the administrative class in Vietnam has been sharply distinguished socially and economically from the people. Many civil servants, even before the worsening of the security situation, have avoided assignment outside of Saigon, and many exhibit a surprising ignorance of the present condition and thinking of the Vietnamese people. Many administrators from the pre-1954 period were much more at home using French than Vietnamese and have had to learn the proper use of their own language since 1954. They moved into the middle and upper civil service positions because they were on hand when the French vacated these positions or when the Vietnamese government expanded its services after 1949, and often they lacked the administrative skills and the initiative required by their new jobs. The term "parachutists" has been derisively applied to those who landed in these choice slots.

A conflict has developed between this older, traditionally oriented, cautious, and not too competent generation of civil servants and the new, young, ambitious, and modern-educated men who have entered the government since 1954. The conflict is most noticeable between the old-line administrators and those who have been trained in American ways, but it extends also to the new French-educated and, to a lesser degree, the graduates of the University of Saigon and the National Institute of Administration. The new generation of administrators, as a whole more able, more imaginative, and more interested in using public administration as a means of achieving national development, has been frustrated by the heavy weight of tradition and inaction imposed on it in most agencies, and in some agencies where they have risen to responsible positions the young men have found themselves blocked by administrative rivals. This situation is changing as the old-time administrators retire and the number of new men in the government increases, but it is changing slowly.

Another problem which the Diem government inherited from the past has been the unwillingness of many bureaucrats, especially those from the South, to give their loyalty to the new regime. In part, this has been due to pro-French and pro-Bao Dai biases, but there is also a strong spirit of *attentisme,* which is the result of surviving various vicissitudes of politics, within the civil service.[7] *Attentisme,* of course, has not been confined to the bureaucracy. The refusal of Diem and

---

[7] On this point, see the discussion in Roy Jumper, "The Mandarin Bureaucracy and Politics in South Vietnam," *Pacific Affairs,* 30 (March, 1957), 47–58.

others in his present entourage to commit themselves prior to 1954 was a species of this wait-and-see attitude, as is the attitude of a number of persons who presently refuse to associate themselves with the Diem regime. The government's concern with the ideological attachment of its employees is reflected in questions contained in its performance rating and promotion forms. Civil service regulations prohibit any mention of an employee's political or philosophical opinions in his dossier; these two forms nonetheless do ask whether an employee believes in the republican regime and whether he has a "firm nationalist viewpoint."[8] A more important technique for cleansing the public service of disloyal or lukewarm thinking has been the program of study sessions inaugurated shortly after the Diem government came into office. Employees in all public agencies are required to meet regularly, usually once a week, to discuss subjects prepared by the General Directorate of Information, the main purpose of which, according to Ngo Dinh Nhu, is to "enable everyone to understand the government's general policy and to adapt his work to it."[9] The sessions, organized separately for higher and lower government employees, are heavily laden with political matter, much of it now related to the government's anti-Communist struggle, and they consist much less of open discussion than of the presentation of the government's line.

Another salient feature of the Vietnamese civil service is the minority position of Southerners in its middle and higher levels. President Diem's initial Cabinet apparently contained no Southerners; the first Cabinet created after the declaration of the Republic in October, 1955, had seven Southerners matched by four Northerners and three Centralists; and there are presently six Southerners, four Northerners, and four Centralists. Middle and higher positions below Cabinet rank have been still more heavily saturated with non-Southerners. A rough survey of 186 officials holding administrative posts down to that of service chief reveals 67 Southerners to be greatly outnumbered by the combination of 57 Northerners and 62 civil servants from the Center.[10] Not only have Northerners, practically all of whom are refugees, preempted many of the choice posts in the Diem government, but persons from Central Vietnam, which is only partly included within the territory of the Republic of Vietnam, hold government offices greatly out of proportion to the population of their area. In 1960 about five million people lived in the part of Central Vietnam, including the

8 Rose and Hoc, *The Vietnamese Civil Service System,* pp. 448, 455.

9 *Vietnam Press,* week ending December 13, 1959, p. 15.

10 This sample was made by the author, aided by several informed Vietnamese, on the basis of known regional backgrounds of officials whose names are contained in République du Vietnam, Présidence de la République, *Liste des Personnalités* (Saigon, 1961).

highlands, which is below the seventeenth parallel, in contrast to nine million people living in the Southern region.

Given the regional distinctions and rivalries which exist in Vietnam, it is not surprising that the dominance of Northerners and Centralists in the government should be resented by many Southerners. Regionalism has been a basis of internecine conflicts within government agencies, and certain agencies are identified in terms of regional influence. The departments of National Education and Foreign Affairs, the National Institute of Administration, and the Special Commissariat of Civic Action and General Directorate of Information are regarded by many in Saigon as "Northern agencies" because of their composition. All of these agencies were of recent origin in 1954 and underwent expansion in the period which followed the Geneva armistice, and they took in many Northern officials and other refugees who came South after partition.[11] Officials from Central Vietnam appear to be somewhat more evenly distributed among government agencies. Their concentration derives from place of origin in the Center. Two of the four Center members in the present Cabinet are from the city of Hue, and the rough tabulation of higher civil servant backgrounds, already referred to, indicates that 53 of the 62 officials from this region also come from Hue or its immediate environs. As the capital of Vietnam until 1945, Hue had developed a large number of families who had passed along from generation to generation a tradition of service in the Imperial government. But the Hue area is also the place of origin of Ngo Dinh Diem and many of his pre-1954 supporters, and the President, who relies heavily upon personal knowledge of his appointees and of their families as well, has clearly drawn disproportionately upon his fellow townsmen in filling responsible positions in his administration. The Communist government of North Vietnam likewise draws many of its top people from Central Vietnam — one source claims that "the [Workers] Party and the government are almost entirely run by Central Vietnamese";[12] but the element of nepotism found in Southern recruitment does not appear to be a significant factor in the Ho Chi Minh government.

The regional imbalance among the administrative personnel of the Republic of Vietnam poses serious problems for the government's

[11] The Northern influx also spread into American and other foreign agencies operating in Saigon. In the Michigan State University Vietnam Advisory Group, for instance, 60 of 99 national employees in 1959 were refugees. See this writer, "They Work for Americans: A Study of the National Staff of an American Overseas Agency," *American Sociological Review,* 25 (October, 1960), 696–97.

[12] *Far East American* (Hong Kong), April 28, 1961, p. 1.

relations with the peasantry. In the Southern region local officials frequently come from outside the area; this is particularly true of the information and civic action agents who serve as spearheads in the central government's effort to win the villagers to its side; almost all of them are Northerners. Writing of the relationship of one information chief to the inhabitants of a Southern delta village, a relationship which is duplicated throughout that region, two researchers reported, "His Northern or Central dialect . . . is a cause for ridicule and laughter, especially among the village children."[13] The shortage of Southerners in the civil service is due in part, as noted, to the sudden influx of job-seeking Northerners and to the President's predilection for persons from the Hue area. Of more fundamental importance is the colonial heritage which left the Southern region — the Colony of Cochinchina — with a dearth of administrators even at the middle levels. Further, some Southerners have been unwilling since 1954 to associate themselves with the Diem government, and the government has drawn its main support from that segment of the people which is most strongly anti-Communist: the refugees. At the same time, much of the internal non-Communist opposition to the regime has come from the refugees. A number of Saigon's critical intellectuals come from north of the seventeenth parallel, as did many of the paratroopers who tried to overthrow the regime in November, 1960.[14]

The overwhelming majority of the refugees have been Catholics; a smaller majority of the civil servant refugees have, too. The latter, added to Catholics who were already in the government or subsequently entered it, have given the regime a strong Catholic cast. In the whole of the Republic of Vietnam in 1960 there were about 1,014,000 Catholics, about 7 per cent of the population.[15] It is not known with any accuracy what the Catholic composition of the bureaucracy is. In a rough survey which the author made of the higher civil service, he was able to identify 34 civil servants as being Catholic and only 20 as being Buddhist, but this method was not too reliable inasmuch as it was easier to identify persons of Catholic persuasion. It is evident however that Catholics make up a much greater part of the bureaucracy than one would expect on the basis of their percentage of the

[13] John D. Donoghue and Vo Hong Phuc, *My Thuan: The Study of A Delta Village in South Vietnam* (Saigon: Michigan State University Vietnam Advisory Group, May, 1961), p. 29.

[14] The story of the paratrooper revolt is told in Chapter 7.

[15] Catholic authorities in 1960 estimated the Catholic population of North and South Vietnam at 1,807,784, with 793,000 members of the faith living above the seventeenth parallel. See *Vietnam Press,* week ending December 18, 1960, pp. 12–13.

general population. And private information concerning the 123 deputies in the first National Assembly indicates that at least 27, or 22 per cent of them, were Catholics.

Thus, the Diem regime has assumed the aspect of a carpetbag government in its disproportion of Northerners and Centralists, in the ease of access to high positions granted officials from the Hue area, and in its Catholicism. These imbalances have been a source of support for Diem and a foundation for a strong anti-Communist policy. The vehement anti-Communist programs of the government have been carried out by the Department of Information (later reduced to general directorate status), which is packed with Northern Catholics. The Southern people do not seem to share the anti-Communist vehemence of their Northern and Central compatriots, by whom they are sometimes referred to as unreliable in the Communist struggle.[16] Unlike many of their compatriots, the Southerners never tasted the general bitterness of Communist rule, but experienced only the patriotic tonic of a guerrilla movement which, not being powerful enough to establish itself securely, was on its best behavior.

The Vietnamese government devoted great energy and expended large sums of money, most of which was provided by American aid, to resettling the Catholic rural refugees who flooded the South after the Geneva partition. It would be difficult to determine whether it gave special treatment to the refugees as Catholics, though many Southerners apparently feel that it did. It would be equally difficult to say if the government was motivated by favoritism in certain of its reconstruction projects, like the high priority it gave to the rebuilding of the war-damaged railroad and highway connecting Saigon and Hue. Both schemes encountered American objections, and as a result the road program was reduced to a lower priority.[17] But national as well as regional considerations could have underlain the Vietnamese government's desire to link Central Vietnam with the capital. Religious favoritism has, however, been a clear component of government administration. This has been particularly noticeable in Central Vietnam, where Catholic influence within the administration is especially

[16] One concrete illustration, mentioned by Roy Jumper in "The Communist Challenge to South Vietnam," *Far Eastern Survey*, 25 (November, 1956), 165, is the conflict which broke out between Southerners and Northern refugees at the University of Saigon on the question whether the student organization of the University should support the government's anti-Communist crusade or remain apolitical.

[17] See Senate Committee on Foreign Relations, Subcommittee on State Department Organization and Public Affairs, *Situation in Vietnam, Hearings, December 7 and 8, 1959* (Washington, 1960), pp. 287–88; *ibid., Report, February 26, 1960*, pp. 28–29, 30–31.

active, but is reflected in actions of the central government as well. The land reform program, when it finally got underway, played no political favorites. Sizeable holdings belonging to the Vice-President and the Vietnamese ambassador to the United States were transferred along with other land. But there was religious favoritism: the 370,500 acres of land held by the Catholic Church were not transferred or even surveyed.[18] When Cardinal Agagianian visited Saigon in 1959, army engineers constructed a special monument and reviewing stands for the occasion, and government vehicles brought many thousands of Catholics into the city from neighboring provinces. When Bishop Ngo Dinh Thuc, the President's brother, was invested as archbishop of the Hue diocese in 1961, government planes flew a large number of clergy and officials to the ceremony. There have been numerous other instances of government assistance to the Church, including the repair of churches and, on at least one occasion, assistance to missionary efforts among the highlands people. While some of the Vietnamese Catholic bishops attempt to avoid a close identification with the regime, this has not been the general attitude. Some clergymen supported President Diem's re-election bid in 1961 to the extent of endorsing his candidacy in a specially distributed letter. The Church runs the special school at Dalat, formerly at Vinh Long, which indoctrinates civil servants into the official creed of Personalism, which is itself a compound of Catholic doctrines, and a Catholic cleric is rector of the public University of Hue. While priests in the refugee villages hold no formal government posts, they are generally the real rulers of their villages and serve as contacts with district and provincial officials.

The Ruling Family

The characteristics of the bureaucracy discussed so far find their concrete representation in the highest leadership of the Vietnamese government. President Ngo Dinh Diem is a non-Southerner; he is a Catholic; his public service began in the colonial period, although it terminated in 1933; and he has followed nepotistic practices in choosing the people who surround him.

It was inevitable that in post-Geneva Vietnam there should be a consolidation of administrative power at the highest level. The task of creating a strong central government, itself a necessity if Vietnam were to survive both sect and Communist challenges and to surmount its lack of economic development, required that this be done. It was likewise inevitable that President Diem should come to depend largely

[18] See John D. Montgomery, *The Politics of Foreign Aid* (New York: Praeger, 1962), p. 126.

upon a small group of trusted associates to help him carry the great burdens of his office. It was not necessary, however, that he should so concentrate decision-making in his own person, often even in the smallest matters, that government machinery could not function until he had given his assent, or that he should rely so heavily on his family for assistance in ruling his country.

The much-publicized reluctance of President Diem to delegate authority is not new to Vietnam. Writing of the governments immediately preceding his, one observer noted that "clearly routine matters all too often have to be referred to the President or the full Cabinet for decision," and that "throughout the administrative structure there seems to be an unwillingness or inability to delegate authority to subordinate officials to deal with minor matters."[19] What is new with Diem is the tremendous extent to which personal centralization has taken place. Until recently, his signature was required on every exit visa for Vietnamese wishing to travel abroad, and he still approves all "questionable" requests. At Cabinet meetings he is frequently preoccupied with the most minute questions, such as the location of trees or buildings in some public development. He once became concerned with the prospects of tourism in the resort city of Dalat in Central Vietnam and dispatched a trusted foreign adviser to make a special investigation. On another occasion, because he had doubts about the arrangement of booths and a parking lot at a new market in the same city, he sent a group consisting of another close foreign adviser and some foreign technicians to inspect the construction site. And he once vetoed a plan to install air conditioning in the documents library of the National Assembly on the ground that it was an unnecessary luxury. Important matters for decision pile up on the President's desk, or on those of his subordinates at the Presidency, and many more minor matters flow to him from the lowest administrative levels, glutting the channels of decision-making, because subordinate officials are incapable or fearful of resolving them. Several years ago, the academic council of the National Institute of Administration concluded that it lacked the power to grant a student permission to take an examination he had missed, and routed the matter to the Presidency, apparently to the President himself. The fear of making decisions, as has been noted, was part of the baggage inherited from the strongly hierarchical pre-1954 administration. It stems too from the unsureness of many government officials. But the President's ingrained distrust of other men's judgments has aggravated these conditions. The condescending attitude he displays toward his administrators — he

[19] Walter R. Sharp, "Some Observations on Public Administration in Indochina," *Public Administration Review,* 14 (Winter, 1954), 46.

once described a secretary of state as having the requisites of a good clerk — is a corollary of his conception of the Vietnamese people as a whole: they are immature, even childish, when they are not capricious, and must be guided along their development by the paternalistic hand of those who know what is best for them.

If Ngo Dinh Diem has played the part of the Emperor, it must be added that he has not been a stay-at-home one. Until the deteriorating security situation slowed him down, the President frequently made excursions from Saigon. Between July 7, 1957, and July 7, 1958, for example, his travels within Vietnam covered 14,000 miles in thirty-three separate trips out of the Presidential Palace. These trips, which totaled thirty-four days, took him to all parts of South Vietnam, though his special interest was the land development centers being created in the Central highlands, and he traveled by plane, small boat, car, and jeep. During this same period, President Diem spent twenty-three days abroad, in good-will trips to Thailand, Australia, Korea, and India.[20] Diem never acted as the reckless demagogue in the many speeches he delivered on his travels — he almost invariably lectured his audiences on the necessity for hard work and the virtue of good living; but neither could he, after the exhilarating days of 1955, arouse his carefully managed listeners to spontaneous displays of enthusiasm.

Closely related to his propensity for one-man rule is President Diem's reliance on his family to help him govern Vietnam. Although the evidence is rather sketchy, it does not appear that nepotism was traditionally a significant feature of Vietnamese administration, at least at the higher levels. But traditional administrative ways were greatly disrupted by eighty years of French rule. The traditional cohesiveness of the Vietnamese family was less affected, especially in Central Vietnam where the Western impact was much weaker than in the North and, especially, in the South. It may be that family solidarity was able to insert itself as a principle of administrative behavior in the chaotic situation after 1949, when Vietnamese began taking over government positions from the French in large numbers. Although some nepotism existed in pre-1954 high-level Vietnamese administration — General Nguyen Van Hinh, for example, was the son of Premier Nguyen Van Tam — it appears to have pervaded the administrative system only after Ngo Dinh Diem took power.

One of his brothers, Ngo Dinh Nhu, has the title of Advisor to the President. Another brother, Ngo Dinh Can, though he holds no government position, is in effect the governor of Central Vietnam. A third brother, Ngo Dinh Thuc, the Archbishop of Hue and Dean of

---

[20] These data have been calculated from the reports of presidential trips carried by the *Vietnam Press* during this period.

the Catholic episcopacy, also holds no government post but functions as an unofficial advisor and exerts his influence with the Catholic clergy and population on behalf of the regime. A fourth brother, Ngo Dinh Luyen, is ambassador to Great Britain and his country's diplomatic representative in Belgium and The Netherlands as well, but he spends occasional extended periods of time in Vietnam. One of the President's sisters-in-law, Mme Ngo Dinh Nhu, is the Official Hostess at the Presidential Palace, a deputy in the National Assembly, the founder-chairman of the Women's Solidarity Movement (the government's mass organization for women), and generally in charge of women's activities in the country. Mme Nhu's father is ambassador to Washington and diplomatic representative to Argentina and Brazil, and his wife is the permanent Vietnamese observer at the United Nations. Three family members, Tran Van Chuong, Tran Van Do, and Tran Van Bac, served in Diem's initial Cabinet, and two other in-laws, Nguyen Huu Chau and Tran Trung Dung, held the important portfolios of Secretary of State at the Presidency and Assistant Secretary of State for National Defense (the President has held the National Defense portfolio) for long tenures, until 1958 and 1961, respectively. Certain government officials in whom Diem has placed trust have been incorporated into the family by having the affective designation "nephew" applied to them. Other high officials have taken the less direct route of converting to Catholicism since Diem came to power.

In April, 1955, a group of Vietnamese nationalists headed by former Premier Nguyen Phan Long wrote to General J. Lawton Collins, the American ambassador to Vietnam, urging that the United States withdraw its support from Ngo Dinh Diem. Among the reasons given were that Diem was strongly influenced by his brothers who, it was claimed, formed a "camarilla" around him, and that he refused to give any authority to his ministers. This accusation has been borne out as the President's brothers, in particular Ngo Dinh Nhu and Ngo Dinh Can, have increasingly gathered power into their own hands and as the President has diminished the role of once influential non-family advisors like Vice-President Nguyen Ngoc Tho. In fact, members of the broader family — like Nguyen Huu Chau and Tran Trung Dung — fell by the wayside as the power of Nhu, Mme Nhu and Can increased. Nhu works and lives at the Presidential Palace, as does the President, sees the President daily, and participates in most of the important matters which come before the President. He is also the philosopher of the regime, the author of many of the lofty sentiments found in the speeches of the President; and at the same time he takes a special interest in intelligence matters and in the activities of government and other political groups, as well as in keeping opposition activity under control. The operations of Nhu's eyes and ears, euphemistically called the Social and Political Research Service, will be discussed in Chapter 7.

Nhu's extensive authority stops at the borders of the Central Vietnamese coastlands, for here, at Phan Thiet province, Ngo Dinh Can's domain begins. Can, who, in contrast to Nhu and the President, is rarely seen by foreigners, rules the Central lowlands from his home in the city of Hue. Government officials in the Center must take orders from Can, and officials appointed from Saigon have been unable to assume their posts when Can objected to them. Can has even, on at least several occasions, successfully defied the President's authority and has at other times given reluctant obedience to presidential directives. His rule is exercised not only through the regular government administration of Central Vietnam, in which he holds no official position, but also through an extensive private network of agents; and it extends to certain agencies of the central government through the placement of loyal Can men. This is particularly evident in the police and security services.

Of all the Ngo brothers, Can is the only one who did not receive a Westernized education — Nhu, Thuc, and Luyen studied in Europe, and the President attended French schools in Vietnam — and he is the only one who has never traveled abroad. Indeed, he very seldom leaves his native Hue where, as the next to youngest brother, he assumes the responsibility for looking after his mother. He is also considered the most severe, some would say primitive, member of the family, and he rules his domain with a strict and sometimes brutal hand. On his own part, Can considers himself, according to what he once told a Vietnamese official, the only true revolutionary in the family. It is ironic that administrative regionalism should have been suppressed by President Diem in 1954 only to reappear under the aegis of one of his brothers.

These in brief are the two most powerful men in the Vietnamese government after Ngo Dinh Diem. Some close observers would say that Nhu is more powerful than the President because he is the channel for nearly everything which passes to and from Diem and because he appears to have such a strong influence on his brother's thinking. Also, Nhu, who had shunned the public spotlight in the past, emerged more and more into view during 1962. He assumed the chairmanship of the interdepartmental committee coordinating the strategic hamlet program, officiated at several ceremonies, and, in October, 1962, had himself elected the supreme leader of the mass Republican Youth organization. Some people, including a former high official in the Vietnamese government, believe that Mme Nhu has in certain respects become the dominant member of the family. It has been observed that she occupies herself increasingly with matters outside her original feminist domain and that she seems to seek a position of equality with the President, to the point of suggesting that she be referred to officially as Madame Ngo.[21] Ngo Dinh Thuc, while perhaps the most respected member of the family, does not take the same consuming interest in government affairs as Can and the Nhus, but when he does speak his voice carries heavy authority. Ngo Dinh Luyen, the youngest of the brothers — Thuc is the oldest — and the person around whom a number of the foreign-trained technicians in the government have gathered, is the least influential of the family.

The President's family constitutes an extralegal elite which, with Diem, directs the destiny of Vietnam today. The family is in class, regional origin, religion, and temperament sharply set off from the population over which it rules. With the partial exception of the President, and probably of Thuc and Luyen as well, it appears to have incurred the strong enmity of the people, certainly of the vocal segments of the population. And yet the Ngos have a feeling for the Vietnamese people in the mass which is almost mystical. The Ngos are proud to the point of arrogance, self-sure to the point of sectarianism, and dubious of the abilities, if not the motives, of others to the point of contempt. They are also intelligent, capable, hardworking and devoted to what they believe to be their country's interest. The reports are prolific that Can and the Nhus have devoted themselves to their personal enrichment in office. Their lofty conception of their mission as the resurrectors of Vietnam and the absence of lavishness in their personal living would seem to argue against their having used their trusts for purposes of jobbery, though it is possible, of course, that they have secreted assets abroad. So intense were the stories about the Nhus a few years ago that they felt it necessary to issue a statement denying that they had ever transferred money out of the country, engaged in financial or commercial activities, or accepted bribes.[22]

If the Ngo family has not been guilty of personal corruption, it has made corruption serve political ends. There apparently was no hesitation in buying off sect leaders during the period of trouble with the sects. Leaders of the minor political parties are kept docile by regular payments, and certain people who work for Nhu, including key members of his Personalist Labor Party, have their loyalty assured by high

[21] Thai, "The Government of Men in the Republic of Vietnam," pp. 191–95.

[22] All Saigon newspapers, reprinted in USOM, *Saigon Daily News Round-Up,* August 24, 1957, p. 2.

salaries and the disposition of villas, cars, and other favors. Also, both Nhu and Can take in large sums of graft for their party and other private activities, through business and other contributions. Such activities are particularly noticeable in the Center, where Can maintains the National Revolutionary Movement, his network of agents, and certain philanthropic endeavors (including several schools) through graft in government contracts, in the cinnamon trade, which he treats as personal monopoly, in local shipping, and by various other methods. Further, there is a strong personal flavor in government administration under the Ngos. The security of high government officials depends upon their personal standing with members of the President's family, especially Nhu, Can, Mme Nhu, and sometimes Thuc; an official who loses favor with a certain faction of the family, as happened to Nguyen Huu Chau, the Secretary of State at the Presidency, or who gets caught between factions, as happened to Tran Chanh Thanh, the Secretary of State for Information, has his days numbered.

Chau's case illustrates the extreme personal element which may enter into government affairs. The husband of Mme Nhu's sister, Chau was a brilliant young administrator and high in the President's esteem. Marital difficulties led him to seek divorce in the Vietnamese courts, and the scandal his action threatened to bring on the family gained him the enmity of Mme Nhu. She eliminated the possibility that the President might select Chau as his Vice-President in 1956 by seeing to it that the Constituent Assembly defeated the presidential proposal to lower the qualifying age for the Presidency and Vice-Presidency from 40 to 35 years of age. She then prevented Chau's divorce case from being taken up by the judiciary until her family bill, which prohibits divorce, was enacted into law. Chau, his position at the Presidency gradually undermined, finally resigned from the government and then fled to France.

Many persons, both critics and friends of the present Vietnamese regime, have wished that the President might eliminate his family from the places of influence they occupy. The family, it is said, is dragging the President down to its level of unpopularity. But it is futile to hope that Diem might displace his family. His attitude towards any criticism of it is so strong that very few people have dared broach the subject, certainly not officials of his government nor even his two American advisors of the past who were known to disapprove of the behavior of Nhu, Can, and Mme Nhu. And one American ambassador who spoke his mind about Nhu to the President was listened to in cold silence. It seems impossible, moreover, that Diem could dispense with the services of his family, for, given the way in which he governs Vietnam, his family is indispensable to him. Together the Ngos constitute a balanced system, no important part of which may be removed without wrecking its operation. And thus is Vietnam governed, by paternalism and nepotism, and with a growing gulf between the very few rulers and the very many ruled.

The Limited Revolution

The word "revolution" is a constant part of the Vietnamese government's vocabulary. It appears in the names of the government mass party, Nhu's elite group, and the civil servant's league, and it finds frequent expression in the discourses of the President and other government officials. The revolutionary theme was set forth by Diem in 1949, when he publicly announced the conditions under which he would accept the leadership of his country. "The [present] struggle," he said, "is not only a struggle for national independence. It is also a social revolution for the economic independence of the Vietnamese farmer and laborer." He proceeded to "advocate the most advanced and bold social reforms," and to declare that "the best positions" in the Vietnamese government should be reserved to those "who have merited the country's gratitude" — that is, to persons serving in the Resistance.[23]

In a limited sense, Diem did effect a revolution after coming to power. He established the authority of a sovereign centralized government over all of South Vietnam. This achievement necessitated the elimination of sect and Binh Xuyen power, of pro-French and other disloyal elements in the army and the administration, of regional autonomy, of France's political influence over Vietnamese affairs, of the traditional monarchy itself. But these actions were essentially negative and, it is equally important to note, they were directed to securing Diem's rule against rivals for the control of Vietnam's fate. The test of the nationalist revolution began in early 1956, once the emergency phase of South Vietnam's rebirth had been safely passed. Political stability had been achieved, the refugee influx had been largely resettled, the dislocations of war were being rapidly remedied, and there was at least a temporary surcease from the menace of Communism.

Succeeding chapters will consider the character of the Diem regime's social, economic, and political efforts at revolutionary change. The present and preceding chapters strongly support the conclusion that

[23] "Statement of June 16, 1949," *Major Policy Speeches by President Ngo Dinh Diem,* 3rd ed. (Saigon: Republic of Vietnam, the Presidency, July, 1957), p. 3.

its efforts have been hardly revolutionary in the creation of a new governmental system and in infusing this system with a new spirit and with new leading personnel. Symbolic of its tie with the Bao Dai regime which it replaced are the flag and national anthem it has adopted. President Diem quite naturally wished to dissociate the new Republic of Vietnam from the Associate State of Vietnam, and he assigned the Constituent Assembly the task of producing a new flag and anthem. This body, after due deliberation, was unable to come up with replacements — indeed, the need for any change was questioned there[24] — and the task was passed along to the National Assembly, which did nothing. For want of innovation, the flag which flies over all public buildings and the anthem dedicated to an independent Vietnam are those of the puppet Bao Dai regime. Symbolic of the change wrought by the Diem regime is the hymn, which enjoys the same status as the anthem, that gives praise to the leadership of Ngo Dinh Diem. Again illustrating the connection between the two regimes, President Diem's first official action upon abolishing the monarchy was to preserve the validity of all pre-existing legislation "not inconsistent with the republican regime."[25] This vast inheritance of colonial law has since undergone only minor modification. Still effective as law in South Vietnam are decrees requiring official approval for any kind of meeting and for the formation of any type of private organization, including political parties. Nationalists still carry legal disabilities for having been convicted during the colonial period for political crimes, and as a result a special government commission had to be established in 1959 in order to pass upon applications of those who wished to run for the National Assembly.

The President of the Republic of Vietnam has assumed the powers formerly possessed by His Majesty Bao Dai and, before him, the French Governor-General, and has perpetuated an autocratic tradition which antedates the arrival of the French in Indochina. While he does not possess the awesome powers of the pre-colonial emperors, who operated under the mandate of heaven, his authority ranges over a broader array of subjects and has more efficient mechanisms at its disposal. He does possess much more power than the governors-general, who had to share theirs with a Parliament and Minister of Colonies in France and with a Governor of Cochinchina and superior residents of Tonkin and Annam. In fact, most of the legislation promulgated for Vietnam during the colonial period originated in

[24] *Vietnam Press* (English edition), October 15, 1956 (evening issue), pp. I–III.
[25] Republic of Vietnam, *Official Journal* [*Cong Bao Viet Nam Cong Hoa*], Provisional Constitutional Act No. 1 of October 26, 1955.

France and could only be amended there, while President Diem is free, with only minor participation by the National Assembly, to create, modify, and abolish the rules by which Vietnam is governed. Like the Governor-General, Diem governs his country largely by colonial law; like the pre-colonial emperors, he does not seek to lead his people by democratic, or demagogic, means but by providing in his own austere behavior and his public pronouncements the proper example for them to follow. The passion which animates him, in the summation of two competent French observers, "is born of a profound, of an immense nostalgia for the Vietnamese past, of a desperate filial respect for the society of ancient Annam. . . ."[26]

His 1949 declaration notwithstanding, Diem did not fill the best positions in his government with those who had fought in the Resistance, but then few persons qualified to hold such positions left the Viet Minh ranks after the 1954 cease-fire. The most notable convert to the nationalist side, Tran Chanh Thanh, who was Diem's propaganda chief until late 1960, had come over several years prior to Geneva. Below the highest levels, the old bureaucracy was hardly affected. The Secretary of State for Interior, in a talk he gave in 1962, frankly acknowledged the government's mistake in using colonial-trained personnel in local government. The Viet Minh, he pointed out, eliminated experienced civil servants when they took power in 1945, introducing in their place a new class of cadres. "These cadres worked and learned at the same time." He then observed that "on the contrary, for the last seven years, we continued to use an outmoded group of cadres because they have diplomas and experience," and further that the government's local administrators "fight against Communism [in order] to go backward. . . . Some of them have antagonized the people, driving them to the Communist side."[27]

Diem made little effort to rally persons active in nationalist politics, of whom he was very suspicious, but he did win over some *attentiste* intellectuals and he did attract home a number of people from the large Vietnamese colony in France. According to official figures released in mid-1961, 325 Vietnamese holding university degrees had returned from overseas to serve their country since the establishment of the Republic.[28] Perhaps many, if not most, of these persons had been sent abroad by the government itself under grants provided by the United States.

[26] Jean Lacouture and Philippe Devillers, *La fin d'une guerre: Indochine 1954* (Paris: Éditions du Seuil, 1960), p. 306.

[27] Bui Van Luong, "Strategic Hamlets to Keep the Roots in the Ground," *Times of Vietnam Magazine,* May 20, 1962, pp. 4, 20.

[28] *Vietnam Press* (English edition), June 1, 1961 (evening issue), p. C-8.

Indeed, the main external source of trained civil servants is the study programs financed by the American government. Those sent abroad under these programs are either civil servants or persons who have contracted to work for the government upon their return to Vietnam. Leaving aside brief trips and stop-overs in other countries, nearly all have gone to the United States. The Vietnamese government is unwilling to send its people to Europe for study and, because it fears defections, will not (with some exceptions) allows its American-trained people to return to Vietnam by way of Europe. It is difficult to say how many Vietnamese have participated in foreign-training programs, but the actual number is but a fraction of the number (1,037 persons) given by an American official source for the period 1954–1961.[29] These training programs offer the greatest hope for invigorating and transforming the present conservative mentality of the Vietnamese administrative system, but neither the Vietnamese nor American governments have taken full advantage of the opportunities they present. An American who had been involved in educational programs in Vietnam has recently pointed out two serious shortcomings in them. The Vietnamese government, he observed, has lacked a broad and imaginative program for sending its people abroad, and the American agencies in Saigon — he would exempt the Michigan State University government-contract group — have failed to develop a program for providing Vietnamese universities with American instructors as a means of filling the teacher gap until sufficient Vietnamese teaching personnel have been trained abroad.[30] The main domestic source for producing trained administrators, the National Institute of Administration, has been severely handicapped by the government's insistence upon furnishing it with weak leadership, using its faculty positions as a convenient dumping place for civil servants not wanted elsewhere, and otherwise assigning to it largely mediocre persons. (The Institute's vice-rector is a notable exception.) It does not enjoy a high reputation among high government officials and intellectuals generally.

The prospect of government employment is not — for the young,

[29] U.S. Operations Mission to Vietnam, *Annual Report for Fiscal Year 1961* (Saigon, November 20, 1961), p. 67. This source also reports 668 persons as having been sent to "third countries." Actually, the American aid mission has no exact record of the number of persons who have participated in its programs, and personal inquiry reveals that the statistics it does present are based on the number of trips, not the number of persons, and include goodwill trips, attendance at foreign conferences, and other short visits.

[30] Edgar N. Pike, "Problems of Education in Vietnam," in Fishel (editor), *Problems of Freedom,* pp. 95, 97.

the capable, and the ambitious — very attractive. It should be pointed out, however, that a survey of students enrolled at the National Institute of Administration revealed that four-fifths of them would seek a government career even if they were not obliged by the conditions of their educational scholarships to do so.[31] To what extent the students disguised their real attitudes and to what extent the figure simply reflects on the quality of the students, the writer is not sure. In any event, many talented persons did seek government employment in the early days of the regime. In 1954, Diem exhibited a strong interest in administrative reform, and to this end he created a study group consisting of his brother, Ngo Dinh Luyen, an engineer by training, and some other technically trained persons who had just returned from abroad. The proposals this group made were never acted upon, and Diem gradually lost his interest in reform.[32] Old-line civil servants were left in their positions rather than being retired or otherwise replaced, and younger civil servants found themselves frequently thwarted by their older rivals and unable to make themselves heard.

Government administration took on an increasingly conservative cast after 1956. It has been filled largely — to use the expression of a former American advisor to President Diem — with city jobholders. It has been led by a man who requires even the smallest details to be passed on to him for decision, and who by temperament inclines to the older, conservative officials around him. Government administrators came to find that it did not pay to take risks, for these led to official displeasure in cases of error or difference in judgment. Officials devote too much time to pleasing those above them, with the trail often leading to the Presidency, and too little to carrying out their substantive responsibilities. One result has been the neglect of rural rehabilitation. As one perceptive Vietnamese official has remarked, urban areas in Vietnam have "witnessed the realization of many beautification projects; while in the rural areas a great many villages are in need," because officials concern themselves only with projects which are visible to their superiors.[33] A more pervasive result has been a general orientation of government administration away from the people and toward Saigon, with a commensurate break between the

[31] Jason L. Finkle, *A Profile of NIA Students* (Saigon: Michigan State University Vietnam Advisory Group, July, 1961), pp. 36–37.

[32] Thai, "The Government of Men in the Republic of Vietnam," pp. 28–29.

[33] Do Van Ro, "Suggested Solutions to Help the Village Budget Attain Autonomy," translated and reprinted in Lloyd W. Woodruff, *Local Administration in Vietnam: Its Future Development* (Saigon: Michigan State University Vietnam Advisory Group; Republic of Vietnam, National Institute of Administration, June, 1961), p. 350.

government and the Vietnamese population. Only since the fall of 1962 has the Vietnamese government given serious and concerted attention to rural rehabilitation, when it undertook, with the help of American aid, to furnish villages under its control with sizeable amounts of social and economic assistance.

The attrition among capable administrators in the Diem government has been high, especially in the younger group. Perhaps the greatest loss to the government was the departure of Vũ Van Thai, the General Director of Budget and Foreign Aid, probably the most brilliant of the regime's high-level administrators. Thai found his reforms countered at the Presidency and in the old-line agencies, and his personal status sapped; he quit the government and Vietnam in mid-1961. A favorite device used by the President to get rid of top-level administrators, both competent and otherwise, who are feared as rivals or suspected of political duplicity, is to funnel them abroad into ambassadorships. The list of people so handled apparently begins with the President's family: Ngo Dinh Luyen was, according to reliable report, early despatched as ambassador to Great Britain at the instigation of his intrafamilial rival, Ngo Dinh Nhu. Tran Van Lam, a very popular Southerner who was, as Diem's first delegate to the Southern region of Vietnam, pronounced by one foreign source to be the second most powerful man in the government in 1956,[34] was sent to Australia in 1961 after he had descended by degrees to the posts of President of the National Assembly, leader of the majority bloc of that body, and ordinary deputy. Tran Chanh Thanh, who also enjoyed a period of power as Secretary of State for Information and chairman of the National Revolutionary Movement, found himself sent off to Tunisia in 1960 after his party leadership had already been taken from him and his administrative authority eclipsed. Bui Van Thinh, who, as Secretary of State for Interior, controlled the police and security agencies and the organization of civil servants and in addition was head of the then-strongest government party, was suspected of furthering his own political advancement. He was made ambassador to Japan right after the Bao Dai referendum, which he had directed. Lam Le Trinh, who also headed the Interior Department, was linked to a group hostile to certain key members at the Presidency and was sent to Turkey. It is not known what caused the fall of certain other Cabinet-members-become-ambassadors, including Tran Huu The, Nguyen Cong Vien, and Nguyen Duong Don, who traded the departments of Education, Agriculture and, again, Education, for posts in the Philippines, China, and Italy, respectively. Finally, Nguyen Huu

[34] J.A.C. Grant, "The Vietnam Constitution of 1956," *American Political Science Review,* 52 (June, 1958), 442.

Chau, whose story has already been told, was not sent but fled abroad.

If revolutionary change has occurred anywhere in the South Vietnamese government, it has occurred in the military organization. Precise figures are not available, but it appears that about one-half of the officers corps of the army and a considerable number of enlisted technicians have studied in the United States for periods of about one year. Military rank is not tied so closely to educational status, and able and dynamic men have been able to rise, under the test of the present emergency, to leading positions in the armed forces of Vietnam. Military personnel, moreover, are being increasingly assigned to civil posts in provincial and district administration, and some of the government's far-reaching programs, such as land development and the creation of strategic hamlets, have been under military direction or have involved strong military participation. Indeed, those areas in which the government has been most dynamic have directly concerned security. The present program of regrouping much of the rural population in order to cut off Communist guerrilla sources of supply and manpower certainly has revolutionary implications. It is ironic, but an irony not limited to Vietnam, that the potentiality of revolutionary change in modernizing an underdeveloped country should lie in those trained in the skills of destruction.

4

Politics in an Underdeveloped State

The Colonial Imprint

The emergence of political parties in the United States and Western Europe was intimately related to the growth of representative government. As the franchise broadened in various Western countries in the nineteenth and twentieth centuries, so did political parties develop as necessary agencies in the competition of candidates for office for support from enlarging electorates. The development of representative government itself appears to have been related to certain social and economic conditions, such as urbanism, industrialism, a fairly high standard of living, and literacy; and to liberal doctrines of the seventeenth century which paved the way not only for the Industrial Revolution but for popular rule as well.

In Vietnam, as we have seen, the representative tradition has been largely absent. There was little place for it in the traditional society of pre-colonial Vietnam with its predominantly agricultural population, its small, and according to Confucian ethics, little-esteemed business class, and its mandarin system of rule topped by an autocratic Emperor. Only in the villages was there a semblance of representative government, and here the selection of councils of notables, and probably of the nominally elected village chiefs as well was by co-optation and not by popular election. On their part, the French introduced capitalism to a limited sector of the Vietnamese economy and developed a working class which numbered, at the eve of the Second World War, about one million, but the native middle class constituted only a thin crust of Vietnamese society because of French control of most government and private economic enterprise. Inadvertently introduced to Vietnam through Vietnamese students and workers returned from France were the ideals of the French Revolution, some French political practices, and, after World War I, the teachings of Marx and Lenin. Hardly introduced at all were French democratic institutions; the experiment in elective village councils was abandoned in 1941 after the Pétainists took over in France, and the elective provincial and regional councils were French-dominated, chosen by extremely limited electorates, and had but meager powers of consultation. Not advanced at all under French colonialism was popular literacy; Vietnam, with 80 per cent of its people unable to read or write in 1944, had a lower standard of literacy under French rule than it had had in the early nineteenth century.

Thus, Vietnamese political parties developed under different circumstances and had different objectives from those in the West. They were essentially instruments for dealing with the foreign ruler. Some groups, like the Constitutionalist Party active in the 1920s and 1930s, sought accommodation, limiting their demands to greater economic opportunity and political freedom for Vietnamese and some participation in the running of the country; but for most the goal was independence, and as moderation failed to achieve concessions from the French, extremist parties steadily increased their strength. In the protectorates of Tonkin and Annam organized political activity was prohibited, and in consequence politics took an exclusively clandestine and revolutionary form. Only in the Colony of Cochinchina were political parties and opposition newspapers (although only if published in French) legally permitted, and both were there subjected to the hazards of colonial control and repression. This greater freedom in the South enabled indigenous political parties to participate in elections to the Saigon Municipal Council and the Colonial Council of Cochinchina and to gain some representation in these bodies. But since the councils were weak adjuncts to the colonial administration and since their Vietnamese membership was fixed below that of French membership, they were regarded by extremist groups as forums from which the struggle for independence could be supported and not as important institutions in themselves. For collaborators with the colonial administration elective office had honorific rather than political utility or was used merely for material gain. For the most part, Vietnamese parties in Cochinchina operated as in the other parts of the country: as underground conspiracies for disseminating propaganda, instigating strikes and demonstrations, and engaging in acts of terrorism ranging from sabotage and assassination to occasional armed attacks on French outposts. Colonialism in Vietnam provided a rich training ground in intrigue, negativism, and violence.

A significant feature of Vietnam's pre-independence politics was the heavy influence of foreign countries upon the ideology, organization, and methods of domestic political groups. The need to look abroad for inspiration was made apparent by the failure of a series of revolts led by mandarins and scholars against the French between 1862 and about 1910. Outmatched by French technology, dependent upon the qualities of individual leaders, seeking no more than to restore the traditional monarchy, these attempts were doomed to failure. The Japanese defeat of Russia in the Far East in 1905 spurred the first great interest in enlisting the ideas and, it was hoped, the help of other countries in the cause of Vietnamese independence. Many Vietnamese went to Japan to study and to establish contact with Japanese political circles. Among them was a member of the Vietnamese royal family, Prince Cuong De, who lived most of his life after 1906 in Japanese exile, nourished by the hope of returning to Vietnam as its monarch in a Japanese-patterned government. Cuong De's support came from the Association for the Restoration of Vietnam (*Viet Nam Quang Phuc Hoi*) created in 1912 by his associate in exile, Phan Boi Chau, but many other nationalist groups, including important segments of the Cao Dai sect, looked to Cuong De as well.

Sun Yat-sen and Republican China in their turn exerted a strong influence on internal political developments. Several groups sprang up during the 1920s, espousing republicanism and modeling themselves on the Chinese Kuomintang. The most significant of these was the Vietnamese National People's Party (*Viet Nam Quoc Dan Dang*) organized by Nguyen Thai Hoc in 1927. The People's Party, in fact, received more than inspiration from the Chinese. The Kuomintang paid financial subsidies to the Canton headquarters of the party and a number of the party's members were trained at the Yunnan Military Academy. France too had its reflections inside Vietnam, most notably in the Constitutionalist Party which, formed in Cochinchina in 1923 by Nguyen Phan Long, Bui Quang Chieu, and other intellectuals recently returned from study in French universities, shunned revolutionary action but asked only that France grant greater economic and political opportunities to its subjects while guiding them along the way to maturity. Most ominous of all international events in its Vietnamese repercussions was the Russian Revolution. By 1925 its influence had reached Vietnam through the creation in Canton of an Association of Revolutionary Vietnamese Youth (*Viet Nam Thanh Nien Cach Mang Dong Chi Hoi*) under a Comintern agent of great ability, Nguyen Ai Quoc, later to be better known as Ho Chi Minh. In 1930 competing factions of the youth organization were brought together under Ho's leadership to form the Indochinese Communist Party (*Dong Duong Cong San Dang*) which has had an unbroken existence since that date despite its apparent absorption by the Viet Minh in 1941. Since 1951, Vietnamese Communism has functioned under the name of the Vietnamese Workers Party (*Dang Lao Dong Viet Nam*).

Japan appeared once more as an internal political influence during its wartime occupation of Vietnam, encouraging the creation of a number of pro-Japanese groups, such as the Vietnamese National Restoration League (*Viet Nam Phuc Quoc Dong Minh Hoi*), the Great Vietnam People's Nationalist Party (*Dai Viet Dan Chinh Dang*), and stimulating a number of others, like the Cao Dai and Hoa Hao, to adjust their political lines in order to play the Japanese game. Meanwhile China, in October, 1942, collected a number of the groups nesting on its soil into the Vietnamese Revolutionary Allied League (*Viet Nam Cach Mang Dong Minh Hoi*) in order to develop anti-Japanese guerrilla and intelligence activities inside Vietnam.

In short, every major power operating in Southeast Asia, including, as we shall see, the United States, has produced political progeny in Vietnam. There have been advantages to this foreign parenthood. It has, for example, furnished native political groups with political direction, obscure as it often has been, and with organizational techniques. Sometimes it has brought strong political and material support. It did not guarantee well-organized, broadly based parties, however, and most of the groups which it fathered were limited by the colonial situation to conspiratorial networks and by the character of their leadership mostly to the urban areas. There were dangers in relying too heavily on foreign sponsors, for not only did this reliance tend to sap local initiative, but foreign friends too frequently displayed a willingness to sacrifice their protégés for more tangible interests. The Japanese, for all their talk about Asia for the Asians, never helped Cuong De against the French; indeed, they expelled a number of his followers in 1910 when they were found to be an embarrassment to amicable relations with France. Japan again disappointed Vietnamese nationalists during its wartime occupation of Vietnam, for it did not replace the French administration until March, 1945, and then only because of growing Gaullist sentiment among the Indochinese French. The Japanese showed no interest in bringing Cuong De back to the country in the spring of 1945, nor in giving the newly established Vietnamese government any substantial authority until just prior to the military collapse of Japan in August.

The French treated their friends no better. The chances that Vietnamese moderates might constitute a weighty force in domestic politics were killed when the French government, unwilling to make even small concessions to Vietnamese nationalism, brusquely rejected the mild demands of the Constitutionalist Party and refused to permit the Progressive Party of Pham Quynh, which also preached collaboration with France, to operate in Annam.

The Indochinese Communist Party was fortunate during the early 1930s in its strained relations with the Comintern, for it was enabled thereby to adapt its Communist principles to the Vietnamese situation and, in particular, to carry on a mutually profitable alliance with the Trotskyites in Cochinchina — an arrangement not tolerated elsewhere in the Communist camp. The Trotskyite group was organized in 1932 under the leadership of a remarkable young Paris-trained Vietnamese Communist, Ta Thu Thau. In 1935 the Vietnamese Communists affirmed their allegiance to the Comintern and accepted the new Soviet line of forming a united front against fascism. The Communist Party thus espoused collaboration with the French — its representatives in the Saigon Municipal Council approved new taxes for the national defense of France — while the Trotskyites, attacking their erstwhile allies as traitors, became the dominant revolutionary party in the southern part of the country. In the Cochinchinese Colonial Council elections of 1939, the Trotskyites captured 80 per cent of the votes cast by the Vietnamese electors, the paltry remainder being divided between Communist and other candidates.

Political groups which relied upon nationalist Chinese help did not fare very well either. Although Chinese authorities initially favored their Vietnamese friends when they established the Vietnamese Revolutionary Allied League in 1942, they and their American military partners came to lean more and more on the Viet Minh element within the League, for only the Viet Minh could supply them with reliable intelligence on Japanese military activities inside Vietnam. The Chinese army which occupied the northern half of Vietnam at war's end did give some assistance to the pro-Chinese Vietnamese groups, but this assistance was tempered by the realities of the local situation. The Viet Minh were in firm control of the Vietnamese administration in Hanoi and of most of the countryside, and the Revolutionary Allied League, its affiliates having split into competing groups, was just another political faction. Wishing to avoid chaos in their sphere of control, and perhaps induced by Viet Minh bribes to Lu Han, the commanding Chinese general, the Chinese pushed the Revolutionary Allied League and the People's Party into a deadly embrace with the Viet Minh by constituting a coalition government in February, 1946, in which the Viet Minh held the main levers of power. Actually, China was not interested in Vietnamese independence, either under its protégés or under the Viet Minh, but rather in extracting a price from France as a condition for the return of French troops to the

North. This price was met in the French renunciation of extraterritorial rights in China and in other concessions, and French troops moved in during the month of March. The immediate losers in the French take-over were the nationalists, for the French assisted the Viet Minh in clearing the People's Party and Revolutionary Allied League from the provinces they controlled, and permitted the nationalist forces in the North to be crushed and dispersed.

After World War II the Communist-led Viet Minh became the dominant native political force in Vietnam. The only significant group in North Vietnam which survived Viet Minh repression was the Great Vietnam Civil Servants Party, which became a factor in nationalist politics during the Bao Dai period because of its control of many high government positions under Nguyen Huu Tri, the governor of North Vietnam. Remnants of the People's Party and other groups broken up by the Viet Minh in 1946 drifted into the French zone in the South. The Trotskyites had suffered seriously from French repression in 1939–1940, and the Viet Minh finished them as a political force after the war by killing some of their leaders, including Ta Thu Thau, and terrorizing others.

In the South, the wartime dislocations enabled the Cao Dai and Hoa Hao sects to develop power in broad stretches of the countryside, and both groups created political appendages called, respectively, the National Restoration League (*Phuc Quoc Hoi*) and the Social Democratic Party (*Dan Chu Xa Hoi*). A number of other groups, including Catholic supporters of Ngo Dinh Diem, also sprang up during this period. Most of the groups, faced with the choice of the Communist-controlled Viet Minh or the French-controlled Bao Dai government, chose the latter, though some refused to make the choice, at least on the terms which were then available. The number of political parties operating in Vietnam prior to independence was large, their memberships, outside of the sects, were very small, and their relations with each other, with the Bao Dai regime, and with the French were volatile, intricate, and frequently devious.[1]

---

[1] Those interested in detailed examinations of political parties before the Republic are referred to Anh Van and Jacqueline Roussel, *Mouvements nationaux et lutte de classes au Viet-Nam* (Marxisme et Colonies, publications de la IVe Internationale; Paris: Imprimerie Réaumur, [n.d.]); Virginia Thompson and Richard Adloff, *The Left Wing in Southeast Asia* (New York: William Sloane Associates, 1950), chapter 2; Philippe Devillers, "Vietnamese Nationalism and French Policies," in William L. Holland (editor), *Asian Nationalism and the West* (New York: Macmillan, 1953); Bernard B. Fall, "The Political-Religious Sects of Vietnam," *Pacific Affairs*, 28 (September, 1955), 235–53; and Jean Lacouture, *Cinq hommes et la France* (Paris: Éditions du Seuil, 1961), chapter 1.

The Government and the Opposition

The conditions under which political parties function in Vietnam would seem to have changed with the gaining of independence. For one thing, Vietnam has been run by Vietnamese, and no longer by foreigners, since 1954. Thus anti-colonialism, which had been the rallying call of practically all political groups prior to Geneva, has lost its meaning, and new issues have had to be found. In the second place, political parties have been given, at least in theory, functions more nearly comparable to those they perform in the West. Legislative and presidential elections provide parties with the tasks of producing candidates and competing for the control of government through the organizing of the electorate.

As we shall see, Vietnamese Communism has not accepted the notion that the colonial period has been ended in the South. It claims that only the controlling foreign power and its domestic puppets have changed since France and the Bao Dai regime disappeared from the political stage. As we shall also see, political parties, outside of those controlled by the government, have not been given a part in the one presidential and two National Assembly elections which Vietnam has held since independence. In fact, it is in the growth of government parties that politics in the new Vietnam has mainly differed from the politics of pre-republican days. An examination of parties in Vietnam under the Republic must start with these new instruments created to support the regime of Ngo Dinh Diem.

The government political parties in Vietnam are organized to meet different needs. There is an elite organization, the Personalist Labor Revolutionary Party (*Can Lao Nhan Vi Cach Mang Dang*), which functions out of public view in the southern region of the Republic. There is a mass party, the National Revolutionary Movement (*Phong Trao Cach Mang Quoc Gia*), which operates throughout the country and commands a majority in the National Assembly. Finally, there are several minor parties which direct their appeals to special groups in the electorate and, like the Personalist Labor Party, confine their activities to the southern region.

The Personalist Labor Party is the party of Ngo Dinh Nhu. It originated in a small group of labor leaders and intellectuals which worked with Nhu in the pre-1954 period, but it was not formally organized until after Diem came to power and is not, despite its title, a party of labor except in the sense that Nhu also controls the trade union movement of the country. The Party has a philosophic base known as Personalism (*nhan vi*), which is, in fact, the official doctrine of all the pro-government political parties, studied (in diluted form) within the civil service, and proclaimed as the bedrock of the Constitution itself. Personalism lays its main emphasis on harmonizing the material and spiritual aspirations of the individual with the social needs of the community and the political needs of the state, and seeks a middle path between capitalist individualism and Marxist collectivism.[2] While it purports to derive its inspiration largely from Asian tradition, it reminds the Westerner strongly of the social encyclicals of Popes Leo XIII and Pius XI. It was noted in the preceding chapter that the special school for teaching Personalism is run by the Catholic clergy. The economic individualism which Nhu attacks is more a caricature of nineteenth-century capitalism, seen through a Marxist lens, than any system found in the Western democracies today.

In August, 1959, Nhu told the author his party had 20,000 members; in May, 1960, the *New York Times* reported him as claiming 70,000 members, most of them workers and peasants.[3] In actuality, the Personalist Labor Party consists of a small number of trusted persons, nearly all of whom are in the government. There they occupy key, though not necessarily the highest, positions in the Saigon bureaucracy, the army, and some provincial administrations. The Party has held no congresses, its governing committee of five section heads has never met as a group, it claims no positions on issues of the day, runs no candidates in elections, seeks no publicity in the press. Some Personalist Labor members, including Nhu, ran as independents in the National Assembly elections of 1956 and 1959; fifteen deputies declared themselves to be Personalist Labor members after the first election, and two deputies after the second election. The modest legislative representation of the party is entirely irrelevant to its political influence because of Nhu's leadership of the group and his general control over National Assembly deliberations. The usefulness of the Personalist Labor Party to Nhu apparently consists in the intelligence which its members provide him about suspect members of the government and about each other. Its usefulness to party members consists in the access they have to Nhu and the material benefits which flow to them through the party's financial graft and related sources of income. Despite the awesome reputation which the Personalist Labor Party has had in certain circles, especially among foreigners, it is not much more than a select though by no means harmonious group of officials held together by their personal relationships with Ngo Dinh Nhu.

The National Revolutionary Movement is of more substance. As the official party of the regime, it is closely identified with the person

[2] See the discussion in John C. Donnell, "National Renovation Campaigns in Vietnam," *Pacific Affairs,* 32 (March, 1959), 77–80.

[3] May 22, 1960, p. 4.

and policies of President Ngo Dinh Diem, its honorary leader. The Movement was founded in October, 1954, despite its claim to have originated in a "clandestine struggle for the revolution of national independence and human emancipation" at the time Ngo Dinh Diem withdrew from the Bao Dai Ministry in 1933.[4] The President does not concern himself with the general operations of the NRM. The first two party chairmen were members of his official family — the Secretary of State for Information (and personal physician to the President), Bui Kien Tin, and a subsequent Information Secretary, Tran Chanh Thanh; the third chairman of the organization, Pham Van Nhu, was also President of the National Assembly, and the present chairman, Truong Vinh Le, is now President of the Assembly. None of these persons has been able to develop strong personal power from his position of party leadership, with the partial exception of Tran Chanh Thanh, and his influence ended with his replacement as party head in 1958, if indeed it did not in part lead to his replacement. Real power within the organization is divided between Ngo Dinh Can, who runs the party in the Central delta area of the country, and Ngo Dinh Nhu, who directs it, less strictly, in the South, with the Central highlands area divided between them. Suggestive of the differences in the regional organizations of the party is that the National Revolutionary Movement is the only pro-government party in Can's domain, whereas several government parties function in the South. It should be added that Can's power in the Center has diminished since 1962.

The National Revolutionary Movement describes itself as a "vast political organization grouping in its midst revolutionary forces from all classes of the population."[5] This would be true if one accepted the Movement's own membership figures, which claim a leap from 10,000 persons in 1955 to about one and a half million in 1959,[6] a highly improbable figure unless it is based on paper members with little or no active identification with the party. Actually, the backbone of the Movement is the government administration. Its national leaders are deputies and administrative officials; province chiefs have presided over its public meetings; district information chiefs, at least in some areas, have acted as district NRM chairmen, and the village political commissioners usually act as local chapter chairmen. While membership in the Movement is voluntary, it is, in village Vietnam, strongly encouraged and provides the peasant and his family with a certain

[4] "Historique du Mouvement de Révolution Nationale," (Saigon, about January, 1956, typewritten).

[5] "Mouvement de Révolution Nationale: Appel à la Nation," (Saigon, about February, 1956, mimeographed).

[6] *Vietnam Press* (English edition), October 3, 1959 (morning issue), p. II.

security in dealings with the government. The recruiting efforts of the National Revolutionary Movement have been less successful in Saigon which, with about 13 per cent of the Nation's population, contains only about 3 per cent of the Movement's claimed membership.

Closely related to the National Revolutionary Movement is the organization for civil servants, the National Revolutionary Civil Servants League (*Lien Doan Cong Chuc Cach Mang Quoc Gia*), membership in which is practically a concomitant of government employment. If there is an important difference between the League and the National Revolutionary Movement, many civil servants are not aware of it, for they tend to equate their membership in one group with membership in the other. In fact, the NRM's propaganda states that the Movement created the League. The two groups differ mainly in that the Movement draws much of its membership from outside the government, puts up candidates for election, and engages to a limited extent in related political activities. Also, whereas the formal leadership of the Movement lies in the National Assembly, that of the League has been vested in high administrative officials, presently in Nguyen Luong, the Secretary of State for Finance. Both groups devote much of their time to anti-Communist indoctrination, and the materials they use in their study sessions are prepared by the General Directorate of Information.

Because of the nature of its membership, the League is better organized than the Movement. Its own hierarchy more closely parallels that of the government, and it has at its ready disposal thousands of civil servants for participating in government-sponsored parades, for lining the streets to welcome visiting dignitaries, and for contributing labor on special public works projects. The League's study program is probably its single most important activity and represents a major effort by the regime to gain the support of the bureaucracy. In the three regular elections thus far held, the National Revolutionary Civil Servants League has not run or officially supported any candidates, but has acted as a sort of good-government group, conducting get-out-the-vote campaigns and sending its members into the countryside to explain the purposes and procedures of voting to the people. At the same time, civil servants have been given the word about favored National Assembly candidates and government machinery has been made available to such candidates.

The pro-government stamp can be affixed to six other political groups which have functioned in South Vietnam since 1955. Three of them no longer exist; ironically, all were supporters of the government but were dissolved by it. The three still-functioning groups, on the other hand, were all in opposition to the government about the end of 1955, though none is today. One of the eliminated groups, the Popular Revolutionary Committee (*Hoi Dong Nhan Dan Cach Mang*), was not really a political party but a coalition containing representatives of all five of the other groups. The role of the Popular Revolutionary Committee in supporting Diem against the Binh Xuyen and Bao Dai in 1955, and its dissolution by the regime once it had served its purpose, were described earlier (see pp. 23–24). A second progovernment group also expired after the Bao Dai referendum, though its organizational skeleton rattled in Vietnamese politics for another three years. This was the Movement to Win and Preserve Freedom (*Phong Trao Tranh Thu Tu Do*), which, established about February 1955, carried the names of eminent intellectuals and high government officials on its roster, including five secretaries of state and several professors of the University of Saigon. The influence of the party did not derive so much from the quality of its membership or its leading role in the Popular Revolutionary Committee as from the circumstance that its leader, Bui Van Thinh, was Secretary of State for Interior and consequently in charge of the police and security forces of the country and the organization for civil servants as well. After Thinh was sent off as ambassador to Turkey in late 1955 by a suspicious superior, the Movement to Win and Preserve Freedom quietly faded from public view.

The third of the defunct parties, the Citizens Assembly (*Tap Doan Cong Dan*), was formed in 1955 under the leadership of Tran Van Lam, the government delegate for the southern region of Vietnam. Lam was gently eased from power, first by his replacement as party leader in 1957 and then by the liquidation of his party in mid-1958 through merger with the National Revolutionary Movement. There were no perceptible program differences between the two parties. The Citizens Assembly had a number of prominent Southerners among its claimed 600,000 members, and both members and National Assembly deputies were easily absorbed into the National Revolutionary Movement. Tran Van Lam was made an "adviser" to the merged party.

The minor pro-government parties which were first oppositionist are the National Restoration League and the Social Democratic Party, the political outlets of the Cao Dai and Hoa Hao sects, and the Socialist party (*Dang Xa Hoi*), a former affiliate of the French socialist movement. The National Restoration League was organized in 1943, the Social Democratic Party in 1945, and the Socialist Party, after some false starts, about 1952. Factions of all three groups participated in the Popular Revolutionary Committee, and Nguyen Bao Toan, the head of the Social Democratic Party, was chairman of the Committee. The Social Democratic Party was purged by the government in late 1955, as Toan fled the country, and emerged with new, pro-Diem leadership; and the other two groups, after fighting a weak rearguard action against the government's procedures for establishing a Constituent Assembly and a Constitution, followed suit after the March, 1956, elections. The Socialists had never been an important factor in Vietnamese politics, and the sect parties lost their sources of strength with the elimination of their military and administrative power; it was an easy matter to convert all three groups into weak and willing supporters of the government. Very little was thereafter heard of the three groups until mid-1959, when they participated in a minor way in the National Assembly elections, electing a total of nine deputies.

There is from a legal standpoint no opposition party in Vietnam. The approval of the Secretary of State for Interior is required for any political party to function, and his disapproval need not be explained and cannot be appealed. This power is based on regulations promulgated in 1950 and continued in force under the Republic. The only parties which have thus far received this approval have been the pro-government groups. All opposition activity in Vietnam is either suppressed, and its participants arrested, as in the case of the Communists and a number of too energetic nationalists, or watchfully tolerated so long as its scope is restricted to small group discussions and the issuance of mild criticisms against the government. There have been no opposition newspapers since the *Thoi Luan* was closed in March, 1958, and attempts by opposition spokesmen to speak to public gatherings or hold press conferences have been controlled by the requirement of government authorization.

By far the strongest opposition to the regime comes from the Communists. Their activities are carried on primarily through three organizations: the Vietnamese Workers Party, the official party of North Vietnam; the Vietnamese People's Revolutionary Party, an avowedly Marxist organization created at the end of 1961, perhaps to provide South Vietnam with an "indigenous" Communist organ in place of the Workers Party; and the National Liberation Front, which, like the Viet Minh of a decade ago, is designed to attract non-Communists to the Communist-directed guerrilla war against the Ngo Dinh Diem government. Since Communist political activities are so overwhelmingly directed to military ends, they will be reserved to a later chapter dealing with the renewal of armed conflict in Vietnam. Two observations, however, are relevant at this point. First, Communist adherents are much more numerous than those of all the nationalist opposition groups put together. Second, the Communists are well organized, and their organization is sustained and given direction by a coherent body of theory. In both these respects the nationalist opposition and the government parties alike are sadly deficient. It is difficult to say how clandestinely active Communist agents are in political affairs. Vietnamese government officials express strong concern about Communist and pro-Communist infiltration of political parties, the press, and government agencies; Communist agents have been arrested in the civil service and labor organizations; and the government has from time to time moved against newspapers or organizations suspected of being pro-Communist.[7] But what the government believes or claims to be Communist activity may sometimes be no more than plain opposition to the regime, and government authorities have used the excuse of Communist infiltration to justify strict controls of private activity ranging from the letting of government contracts to freedom of the press and of economic enterprise.

The non-Communist opposition to the government consists of a number of small groups gathered around leaders having little or no real organization and but few direct followers. For the most part these groups are made up of the remnants of the pre-independence political parties, of those politicians who are conditioned to functioning in a context of illegality and intrigue. The opposition also contains a number of former supporters of Ngo Dinh Diem who have broken with him since his coming to power, though most Diem defectors have not attached themselves to particular groups, as well as a smaller number of others from the intellectual class, mostly young people, who have been alienated by policies of the Diem regime.

The best known of the old political groups are the Vietnamese People's Party, the Great Vietnam Civil Servants Party, and some of their quondam affiliates and close allies.[8] A number of Great Vietnam members swung to the support of Ngo Dinh Diem before or just after he took power, finding positions within his regime, and some elements of both groups sided with the sects and Binh Xuyen in the armed conflict of 1955 or engaged in the uprising levied in the name of their organizations the following year in Central Vietnam; in both cases many of them ended up dead, in prison, or in exile. Today the two parties are little more than labels used to identify persons by their past associations. Practically all of the former People's and Great Vietnam Party members have either become inactive or have gone into or formed other groups.

[7] See Roy Jumper and the sources he cites in "The Communist Challenge to South Vietnam," *Far Eastern Survey,* 25 (November, 1956), 165–66.

[8] These include the Great Vietnam National Socialist [Fascist] Party (*Dang Dai Viet Quoc Xa*), the Great Vietnam People's Party (*Dang Dai Viet Duy Dan*), the Great Vietnam National People's Party (*Dai Viet Quoc Dan Dang*), and the People's Party (*Quoc Dan Dang*).

A word should be said about the opposition-in-exile. Most of it consists of pre-1954 politicians, including some persons who had been closely associated with French colonialism. Opposition ranks are being swelled, however, by military officers, high-level administrators, and former intimates of Ngo Dinh Diem who have broken with the regime in recent years. The foreign opposition is centered in Paris, though Cambodia and, to a lesser extent, the United States also provide homes for the regime's overseas critics. Opposition sentiment abroad runs the political gamut, from pro-Communism (among some of the Paris-based Vietnamese) to neutralism (mostly France and Cambodia) to strong anti-Communism (mostly the United States). There is a segment of the Great Vietnam People's Party in Paris which, under Nguyen Ton Hoan, issues an occasional magazine and claims to have an underground network in Vietnam. There is a segment of the Free Democratic Party, also in Paris, under Pham Huy Co, which in mid-1962 established a "National Revolutionary Executive Committee" consisting of opposition leaders in France, Cambodia, and Vietnam. It includes military officers who led the attempts against Vietnam's leadership in November, 1960, and February, 1962. There are Nguyen Ngoc Bich and Nguyen Bao Toan, perhaps the two most popular of the Paris oppositionists; and there is a growing list of others. None of the foreign groups appears to be much more active or any larger than the numerous small groups operating within Vietnam itself, and all of them appear to look to foreign help for achieving their purposes.

Much of the flavor of opposition politics can be shown by the activities of the most active and, until November, 1960, most successful of the opposition leaders, Dr. Phan Quang Dan. Like many other Vietnamese politicians, including Ho Chi Minh, Dan comes from the North Central province of Nghe An. A medical student in Hanoi in 1945, he was swept into nationalist politics by the end-of-the-war political ferment, associating briefly with the Vietnamese People's Party and the Great Vietnam Civil Servants Party and then forming his own group around the newspaper *Thiet Thuc*. Dan twice turned down Viet Minh offers of a Cabinet position in 1946, according to his own account,[9] and decided to follow Bao Dai to China and then to Hong Kong where, during 1947 and 1948, he was an adviser to the Emperor in his negotiations with the French for a return to Vietnam. When a Provisional Central Government was established in 1948, without Bao Dai but with his blessing, Dan joined it as Minister of Information, resigning after several months because, again by his

---

[9] Personal interview, June 6, 1959. A short [auto?]biographical statement on Dan was published in the *Thoi Luan* (Saigon), July 22, 1957.

account,[10] he saw that the French were unwilling to grant real autonomy to Vietnam. In 1949 Dan simultaneously established his own group, the Republican Party (*Cong Hoa Dang*) and went abroad, where he continued his political activities and also managed to study medicine at the Harvard Medical School. Dan's refusal to serve in any of Bao Dai's cabinets after 1948 extended to the early cabinets of Ngo Dinh Diem's rule, but it is not clear whether this was due, as Dan claimed, to Diem's having been appointed by Bao Dai or, as the Vietnamese government claimed, to his holding out for a more important ministry than those offered him.

At any rate, Phan Quang Dan returned to Vietnam in September, 1955, and from then until the end of 1960 was the center of much of the open opposition to the regime. First he headed a coalition of opposition groups which fought the government's arrangements for the election of a Constituent Assembly. This coalition had a legal basis in that its three main component groups — the National Restoration League, the Socialist Party, and the Social Democratic Party — had government approval, granted prior to 1954, to engage in politics. The coalition foundered three months after the Constituent Assembly elections, with the imprisonment of the leaders of the first two parties and the pressured withdrawal of the third party. Dan himself did not escape entirely untouched; he was arrested briefly on the eve of the 1956 elections and accused in the government press of Communist and colonialist activities, and shortly thereafter lost his position at the University of Saigon Medical School. Undaunted, he continued his political activities and, in May, 1957, formed another opposition coalition called the Democratic Bloc, which managed somehow to obtain its own newspaper, the *Thoi Luan*. After having submitted to one sacking by an organized mob in September, 1957, the *Thoi Luan* was closed down by court action the following March. In April, 1958, the Democratic Bloc collapsed when Dan withdrew from it to seek legal authorization for his own group, the Free Democratic Party, and permission to publish a newspaper. No action was ever taken on either application, and a number of members of Dan's party were subsequently arrested for varying durations for engaging in illegal political activity. In March, 1959, the newspaper *Tin Bac* printed an article by Dan; that edition was seized and the newspaper was closed down. In June, 1959, another newspaper, the *Nguoi Viet Tu Do,* met the same fate for the same indiscretion. In August, 1959,

[10] A Vietnamese newspaper, the *Tu Do,* in what may have been a government-inspired story, claimed that Dan had embezzled funds during his tenure as Minister of Information. See U.S. Operations Mission, *Saigon Daily News Round-Up,* May 6, 1957, p. 3.

Dan ran for the National Assembly from Saigon and was elected by a six-to-one margin over the government candidate, but he was disqualified by court action from taking his seat. Dan's political history ended with the November, 1960, attempted *coup d'état*. He appointed himself political advisor to the rebel organization after the *coup* had been launched, was subsequently arrested, and has not been heard from since, although a government source announced in February, 1961, that he would shortly be brought to trial before a military tribunal.[11]

Phan Quang Dan's opposition record is exceptional. No other opposition leader has sustained the same level of political activity nor, except for those who engaged in the 1960 *coup,* has any one else taken the same risks in crossing the regime. Dan had gained the admiration of other opposition leaders, but they also distrusted him and few answered his repeated call to join forces with him. In general, the nationalist opposition has been fragmented, largely inactive, and preoccupied with the past. In an unusual show of unity, most of the major anti-government politicians banded together in late April, 1960, to issue a manifesto of grievances against the Ngo Dinh Diem administration. The document, which was released to the press, called for Diem to liberalize his government, to reorganize his administration — which meant, among other things, to eliminate party and family influence from the civil service and army — and to encourage domestic and foreign economic enterprise.[12] This opposition action is interesting for three reasons. First, the signers of the manifesto were all old-time politicians, leaders of the Hoa Hao and Cao Dai sects, the Great Vietnam and Vietnamese People's Party, and dissident Catholic groups. Eleven of the eighteen signers were former Cabinet ministers and four more had held other high government posts. Second, the action marked a coalescence of opposition fragments and a willingness on their part to engage in public political activities, for the petition-signers (known as the Caravelle group, after the hotel in which their public announcement was made) organized themselves as the Bloc for Liberty and Progress (*Khoi Tu Do Tien Bo*). While the Bloc's membership was quite heterogeneous, it did agree upon certain policies,

[11] This statement was made by the Chairman of the National Revolutionary Movement and President of the National Assembly, Truong Vinh Le, and reported by the *Times of Vietnam,* February 21, 1961.

[12] *New York Times,* May 1, 1960, pp. 1, 21. Dated April 26, the manifesto was considered by some to have been motivated by the Korean students' revolt in Seoul some eight days earlier, but an American correspondent states that he had received a copy of the document on April 14. ("Where Danger Threatens Another U.S.-Backed Country," *U.S. News & World Report,* May 16, 1960, p. 120.)

including constitutional revision in the direction of a less authoritarian regime, new elections for the National Assembly, and a government responsible to the Assembly. And third, the appeal of opposition unity was not sufficiently strong to induce Phan Quang Dan and his group to enter the Bloc.

The story of the Bloc for Liberty and Progress ends where Dan's does, with the November, 1960, *coup*. Although only one Bloc member, Phan Khac Suu, was apparently involved in the attempted overthrow, the government made use of the occasion to arrest most of the Caravelle group. Some of these persons were quickly released and several are still being held without charge. Since that time, aboveboard opposition activity has subsided to coteries of frustrated individuals, endlessly discussing Vietnam's problems in the privacy of their homes or in the restaurants and bars of Saigon. There has been one attempt at *bona fide* activity, led by Dr. Dang Van Sung, one of the former Great Vietnam leaders, but his group, the Front for Democratization (*Mat Tran Dan Chu Hoa*), has not attracted much public attention since its formation in April, 1961.[13] Part of this group's problem may lie in its program, which seeks government cooperation in the development of a democratic climate and calls for the creation of an appointive national advisory council, elective village councils, and free political activity. This program is not sufficiently mild to wring concessions from the government, such as permission to publish a newspaper, but is too mild to enlist opponents of the government in its ranks.

Nature of the Party System

The outstanding characteristic of the legal Vietnamese parties is their artificiality. This is most evident in the case of the minor government groups, the Socialist Party, the Social Democratic Party, and the National Restoration League. All three were taken over by the regime and their continued existence depends upon its benevolence and subventions. These groups appear to serve largely as showcase parties, evidence that Vietnam is a democracy, and as gestures designed to satisfy the political interests of their old clienteles, though their appeal is extremely limited. They might possibly be viewed as hothouse parties, passing through a stage of very slow incubation before being permitted an independent and meaningful part in Vietnam's political life. The National Revolutionary Movement, with its civil

[13] A published American account of Sung's group is contained in the *Christian Science Monitor*, April 19, 1961. A Vietnamese report can be found in the *Ngon Luan* (Saigon), April 28, 1961.

servants' wing, has the appearance of a large company union employed to control, mobilize, and indoctrinate large sections of the population and to give it tutelary experience in the business of running election campaigns and electing public officials. By virtue of its close governmental ties, the Movement is better organized and has more important functions than its minor allies, but affiliation with it and adhesion to its principles assume a highly formal character. Indeed, as the security situation has worsened, the political anti-Communist activities performed by the NRM have given way to the quasi-military activities of an organization established early in 1960, the Republican Youth (*Thanh Nien Cong Hoa*). The Personalist Labor Party, even more than the National Revolutionary Movement, has its functions intimately related to those of the government, and its atmosphere of secrecy, restricted membership, and special role as watchdog of the regime against its enemies and defectors — not to mention the eminence of its leader, Ngo Dinh Nhu — endow it with a special position.

The artificiality of the government parties can be seen in their role in the National Assembly. In the first place, legislative elections, as we shall see later, have been carefully manipulated by the government to produce mostly safe deputies, and there has not yet developed any close relationship between the deputies as a whole and their constituencies. Secondly, the bulk of government policy-making is carried out through the executive branch, and whatever comes before the National Assembly is under heavy executive guidance. In general, party labels have no significance in the National Assembly, for there are no real differences among parties. The same thing is true of the two blocs into which the deputies have been organized.

The most obvious characteristics of the nationalist opposition are its weakness and fragmentation. The political elite in Vietnam has always been small in relation to the population, and only a few of those who were active in pre-1954 politics can be counted among the opposition today. The rest have either gone with the Communists, the French, or the government, have been killed or imprisoned, or have turned away from politics. Those still active are hampered by government constraints, by their association in many people's minds with Bao Dai and the French, or at least with times gone by, and by their difficulty in adjusting to the post-1954 state of affairs. The nationalist opposition does not appear to have much appeal for the new generation of urban-educated and still less for the urban masses or the rural peasantry, though it is difficult to estimate the influence which some of the anti-government Hoa Hao and Cao Dai leaders have in areas where these sects have strong followings. The government has confiscated many of the buildings belonging to the sects, particularly in the Hoa

Hao zone, and there is considerable resentment towards the national authorities within both groups, some of which has spilled over into cooperation with the Communist guerrilla forces. Those who have grown to political maturity in the urban areas since 1954 have tended to avoid political involvement; the opposition's lack of appeal, the existence of a nationalist (even if disliked) government, and the sanctions which that government may exert against those who associate with the opposition probably account in fair part for this behavior. Also contributing is the feeling of a number of people that the Communist threat compels them either to go with the government or, at least, not to oppose it. The political apathy of the new generation, on the other hand, has been wearing somewhat thin in the past two years. Some of its members have been enticed by the clear-cut alternative offered by the Communists, and still more have been groping for their own forms of political expression.

The weak nationalist opposition has not been able to develop sufficient internal cohesion to present a united front to the government. It is not differences of program which keep the opposition fragmented, but personality clashes and status considerations, which frequently have long histories, coupled with the difficulty of opposing a nationalist government entrenched in power which is willing to employ force against its competitors to keep itself there. The opposition has found it difficult to translate talking, of which it has done a great deal, into concerted action, except of a negative and violent kind. There is, moreover, a strong tendency for oppositionists to rely on the United States, sometimes with a fantastic optimism, to do for them what they cannot achieve themselves. If CIA agents, or even politically impotent American professors, establish contact with opposition leaders, it is sometimes concluded that the United States is shifting its support from Diem or, at the least, providing "American protection" for its chosen allies. When Kennedy was elected President, it was concluded by some that a change of regime in the United States meant support for a change of regime in Vietnam. When Averell Harriman stopped briefly in Saigon in the fall of 1961, reputable opposition leaders believed the rumor that he had presented the Vietnamese President with a list, which included their names, of required Cabinet changes. Many people in Saigon believed, and even the government suspected, that Phan Quang Dan was being supported by the American Democratic Party, a supposition apparently deduced from the circumstance that the Vietnamese government was receiving *its* aid from a Republican administration in Washington. Dan, incidentally, may well have encouraged this belief, and it is interesting that he should in 1958 change the name of his party from the Republican to the Free Democratic.

Two aspects of the relationship between the government and the nationalist opposition deserve discussion. First is the inequality of power between the two sides. South Vietnam is for practical purposes a one-party state, if one does not take into account the outlawed Communist movement. On the government side there exist several legal parties controlled from a common center. Two of them, the National Revolutionary Movement and the Personalist Labor Party, have special roles in the functioning of the administrative system and receive material and other benefits from this association. There is a party press, subsidized, as are all newspapers, by the government, and a government news agency to publicize the government's policies. Finally, there is the National Assembly, practically all of whose members belong to the government parties while the rest follow the government's line.

The opposition, on the other hand, exists in a penumbra between legality and illegality. It cannot run candidates under party labels, cannot hold meetings, and faces the continuous risk of suppression. Those newspapers which supported it have been closed down, and all requests in recent years to start new ones have been ignored. With very rare exceptions there is no public outlet for the expression of opposition views. The statement of the Caravelle group was published only in the foreign press — no Vietnamese newspaper dared handle it — and the same is true of most other opposition pronouncements.

A second aspect of the relationship between the government and the opposition is the mutual distrust and antagonism. The leaders of the government regard the opposition as conspiratorial, inclined to violence, and unwilling or unable to adapt itself to the conditions of the republican regime. It is, in their eyes, imbued with a "feudal mentality" and interested mainly in clandestine activity and in enriching itself. While some distinction is made by the President and his supporters among the different opposition leaders, they profess the view that the existing opposition groups are not yet ready to be accorded a place in the nation's political life; indeed, there is a strong tendency to speak of *creating* an opposition. In one of his rare public statements concerning his nationalist rivals, which can be considered conciliatory in comparison to his private comments, President Diem referred to them as "persons of good faith," but, he added, "who, in the same name of liberty, are trying to crush the social revolution."[14] On its part, the opposition regards the regime as a family dictatorship run by a man incapable of sharing power who will go to almost any length to preserve it. It maintains that government under Ngo Dinh Diem is a compound of favoritism, inefficiency, and corruption, and

[14] *Times of Vietnam,* July 7, 1960, p. 1.

that this has resulted in the squandering of both the nation's resources and of foreign aid and in the alienation of the Vietnamese people. In public statements and open conversation, opposition members generally take the position that Diem is all right but must institute reforms; in private conversation, they increasingly take the position that political change must begin at the top.

There is a basis in the past for the attitudes of both sides. The opposition, it is true, largely refused to support the government during its uncertain first year in office or else imposed demands which could not have been met without drastically weakening the regime. Furthermore, the Binh Xuyen and some elements of the Cao Dai, the Hoa Hao, the Great Vietnam Party, and the Vietnamese People's Party did resort to armed action during 1955 and 1956 when their private armies and special privileges were threatened, and well-known civilian politicians were connected with the military group which launched the November, 1960, attempt against the regime. And domestic oppositionists have been linked with sworn enemies of the regime residing in Cambodia and France. On the other hand, the government has on many occasions employed police-state coercion against the opposition. When, for example, security agents moved against the National Restoration League before it was "purified," they searched and closed down local party headquarters, physically injured party members, arrested other members, and compelled still others to repudiate the organization.[15] The government has prohibited opposition newspapers by court action, and wreaked its wrath against the press on other occasions through well-organized mob action; and it has since 1957 withheld its consent from all opposition requests to start new papers. It has prevented oppositionists from using public forums and has constrained their activities in numerous other ways, including surveillance of their movements and on occasion the sacking of their places of business and arrest on trumped-up charges. Persons arrested following the abortive 1960 *coup,* the innocent as well as the culpable, were rather severely beaten — apparently by special agents under the control of Ngo Dinh Can and not by the regular security police.

It has been mentioned that Vietnamese government leaders speak of creating an opposition. In late 1960 they did just that. Through the covert activities of two officials, Lieutenant Colonel Nguyen Van Chau, then head of the army psychological warfare branch, and Le Van Thai, a lieutenant of Ngo Dinh Nhu attached to the presidential

---

[15] The then secretary-general of the party, Nguyen Thanh Danh, issued detailed charges of the government's behavior in a mimeographed statement, "Liste des actes de terrorisme par le Gouvernement contre le Viet Nam Phuc Quoc Hoi" (Saigon, March 22, 1956).

secret police service, a number of opposition and other personalities agreed to form a Popular Anti-Communist Front (*Mat Tran Nhan Dan Chong Cong*), generally referred to as the National Union Front. The government's motivations were clear: it had been shaken by the attempted *coup d'état* and wanted to propitiate both Vietnamese and foreign opinion by providing an outlet for popular dissatisfaction. Some of the persons who participated in the experiment, including pro-government people, thought the regime was prepared to make concessions to a semi-autonomous political movement, and others hoped they could play the government's game to their own advantage; but most critics of the regime were wary. In fact, the chairman of the Front, Dr. Phan Huy Quat, a respected former Great Vietnam member and minister in the early Bao Dai governments, accepted the position only after repeated government urging, fearful as he was of being charged with selling out to the regime.

The Front called four public meetings between January and July, 1961, when its public activities came to an end. The meetings were rather heavily attended — the last two drew about 1,200 and 700 persons, mostly middle-class politicians, professional persons, intellectuals, and religious group representatives. A good portion of each audience was made up of government people. Two resolutions adopted at the final meeting, held July 2, called for the creation of a national advisory council, to be appointed by the President, and of public tribunals where free opinions could be expressed; they were approved nearly unanimously. Two other resolutions, urging the government to authorize nationalist political activity and to release nationalist political prisoners, were carried by solid majorities. The Front's directing committee was ordered at this meeting to follow through on these resolutions and to carry on other necessary activities until the next open meeting, set for six months later. This was the end of the Front. The Vietnamese government leadership was evidently disturbed by the actions of its creation, particularly the resolutions concerning legalization of opposition parties and release of political prisoners which had been pushed at the July meeting by Dang Van Sung, the leader of the Front for Democratization. In late August one of the government representatives on the National Union Front's directing committee informed the other committee members that the government could not, in that difficult period, afford an opposition group. Privately, he said that the President and Ngo Dinh Nhu, among other things, distrusted the direction which the Front appeared to be taking. Its existence was based on government permission, and when permission was withdrawn, the National Union Front quietly collapsed, and with it the Vietnamese government's sole venture in creating its own opposition.

The strength of the Communists constitutes a final attribute of the Vietnamese party system. In fact, the Communists are the only political force within Vietnam which presents a serious alternative to the present government. Thus, Vietnamese politics are marked by a sharp polarization. For those who oppose the regime, the room for maneuver, even within the narrow gambit permitted by the government, is extremely limited. For those middle-class persons who dislike the regime, the absence of a practicable alternative between Communism and Diemism often leads to grudging acceptance of the Diem government or to withdrawal from political involvement. Choice is most difficult for the peasantry, for both the government and the Communists demand their allegiance and to support one side is to invite retaliation from the other. Probably more than any other group, the Communists have influenced government policy in Vietnam. Nearly every major policy — whether it has concerned road construction, the location of new industry, development of the highlands, agrarian reform, or the allocation of foreign aid — has been shaped by the government's political and military rivalry with the Communists. In this pervasive competition, the Diem government has adopted many of its rival's methods. It has its political re-education camps, its Communist denunciation rallies, its ubiquitous propaganda extolling the leader and damning the enemy, its mass organizations. In short, the government has transformed itself into a light image of its rival.

Elections in a One-Party State

Even if elections were completely free in Vietnam, they would be ineffective channels of democratic expression. The control by the government of all political party life, of the press, of the trade union movement, and of most other organized activities make serious electoral competition a most difficult task. In the three general elections held in Vietnam so far, the government has taken advantage of its initial assets to impede the efforts of those who would challenge its authority. These were the Constituent Assembly election of March 4, 1956, the National Assembly election of August 30, 1959, and the presidential election of April 9, 1961. The National Assembly deputies were elected from single-member districts by plurality vote, and the President was elected on the basis of a national plurality vote. With minor exceptions, all Vietnamese citizens over eighteen years of age were eligible to participate in the elections.

The Assembly elections of 1956 and 1959 and the presidential election of 1961 all followed a fairly similar pattern. Complete responsibility for conducting the electoral campaigns was given to special committees composed of representatives of the different candidates. These committees were established on a national basis and in each election district — in each province, in the case of the presidential election. They decided upon the number, color, size, and kind of paper to be used for handbills and posters, and the dates and places for their posting or distribution. They approved the texts of these various campaign materials. They set up public meetings for the candidates, arranged for radio time and newspaper space, and assigned loudspeaker trucks. Behind these committees stood the government, which defrayed the committees' expenses, provided the manpower for various campaign tasks and, in addition, conducted its own get-out-the-vote campaign. The candidates and their supporters were not permitted to spend their own money nor to engage in activities, such as public meetings, outside of this planned framework. The campaign periods were about two weeks for the National Assembly elections and 25 days for the presidential election.

Numerically, all three elections demonstrated satisfactory competition. The mean number of candidates per district in both National Assembly elections was about 3.5, and there were three contesting tickets in the 1961 presidential election. There was not, however, much genuine conflict in the Assembly elections. The Communists, of course, stood outside the legal pale, though the government claimed they tried to introduce pro-Communist candidates in the 1959 election.[16] The nationalist opposition boycotted the 1956 election when their complaints against the electoral arrangements went unheeded. In 1959 a number of oppositionists indicated a willingness to participate in the election if the government would substitute proportional representation for election by plurality vote in single-member districts, accord them certain procedural safeguards, and permit opposition parties to operate and offer candidates. None of these conditions was met, and most of the opposition sat out this election as well. Perhaps six clearly opposition candidates ran as independents in 1959, five of them in Saigon or its suburbs. Two opposition slates were entered in the presidential election, but their candidates were relatively unknown to the electorate. One slate (called List II in the absence of political labels) consisted of Nguyen Dinh Quat, a businessman, and Nguyen Thanh Phuong, who had commanded the Cao Dai military forces but who had led a quiet life since the 1955 turbulence. List III featured

[16] *Journal d'extrême-orient* (Saigon), 3 septembre 1959, p. 4.

Ho Nhut Tan, a 75-year old practitioner of Oriental medicine, a person with a long political record which had ended with his retirement from politics in the late 1940s, and Nguyen The Truyen, a chemical engineer in his early 60s who had withdrawn from public activities about the same time.

The most noticeable evidence of the campaigns was the great number of posters, banners, and similar pieces of electoral propaganda. Hardly a tree in the beautifully shaded city of Saigon, hardly a house or business place, hardly an unused wall did not bear witness to the electoral campaign in progress. Outside the capital, the amount of electoral propaganda was somewhat less, though still substantial. It is interesting that, including the slogans placed on homes and shops, exhortations to vote greatly outnumbered those on behalf of the candidates. Also, beneath the veneer of campaign bustle, there was not very much purposeful activity. In the cities and countryside, meetings were held and candidates set forth their programs, but it was difficult to discern much spontaneous voter activity or excitement. The greatest relief in this electoral calm was occasioned by some disturbances at opposition candidate meetings in Saigon in 1959 and 1961; but then the opposition provided the only stir in otherwise dull campaigns, and their public motions were severely confined by the election procedures and were, in any case, almost entirely concentrated in the capital. In the presidential election, none of the candidates campaigned much outside of Saigon. Vice-President Nguyen Ngoc Tho made brief trips to several provinces, but it appears that the other candidates hardly, if ever, left the outskirts of the city. Any campaigning on their behalf was left to provincial representatives and the officially created campaign committees.

There was no danger that the government might lose control of the Presidency or the National Assembly in any of these elections. Its control over political, social, and economic activity was sufficient to give it an advantage over any hastily improvised attempts to defeat it. But this was insufficient assurance for a regime which was unfamiliar with democratic methods and fearful even of their most unlikely consequences. In Saigon, the elections were relatively fair. Some advantages were, to be sure, given to government candidates: certain among them sent out special mailings in 1959, an illegal action under the "equality" rules, to lists drawn from records furnished them by the police; civil servants were carefully informed about favored legislative candidates; although all candidates seemed to receive roughly equal treatment in the placement of posters, posters favoring government candidates appeared around a number of polling places on the eve of the 1959 election; and there is strong evidence that the government was responsible for disorders created at opposition meetings and the small bombs set off in 1959 outside certain printing houses. Nor was the press exactly neutral in the campaigns. President Diem, according to reports of the Vietnam Press, the official news agency, "answered questions from the audience with gracefulness and simplicity," but Nguyen Dinh Quat "confused and frustrated his audience with his answers to their questions," and Nguyen The Truyen "did not suggest any positive and constructive plan."[17] Finally, the government made free use of the army in certain competitive districts in Saigon to give support to its candidates. Soldiers were given the names of government candidates, transported to polling places, sometimes in uniform and sometimes in civilian clothes, and sent into the polls in groups. The actual voting, however, was secret, and apparently the counting of ballots was fair.

Outside of Saigon, particularly in rural Vietnam, things were run quite differently. There legislative candidates were screened and undesirable ones pressured to withdraw from the campaigns. The election campaigns were firmly under government control and were used to help the government candidates. The National Revolutionary Movement leaders, who were often government cadres, were told in no uncertain language that the government's candidates were to be elected, and in many places NRM members, civil servants, and military personnel had to submit for inspection their unused ballots in order to prove how they had voted. (At the polling station each voter is given as many ballots as there are candidates, each ballot containing the name and symbol of a single candidate; he is required to place one ballot in an envelope for deposit in the election box and he discards the unused ballots in a trash basket.) The government did not hesitate to tamper with the ballots in rural Vietnam, and in at least one district in 1959 it distributed spurious campaign literature intended to discredit a candidate among Catholic refugees by purporting to give her Communist backing.[18]

The flavor of provincial campaigning can be gleaned from the following eyewitness account related of a meeting held in a rural village in 1959. Each family in the village was instructed to have at least one adult representative at the affair; the audience was passive except when

---

[17] *Vietnam Press* (English edition), April 7, 1961 (morning issue), p. H-1; *ibid.*, (morning issue), March 29, 1961, p. H-3; *ibid.*, (evening issue), March 30, 1961, p. H-1.

[18] For one candidate's experience in the 1959 election, see Nguyen Tuyet Mai, "Electioneering: Vietnamese Style," *Asian Survey*, 2 (November, 1962), 11–18; for a detailed examination, see this writer, "The Electoral Process in South Vietnam," *Midwest Journal of Political Science*, 4 (May, 1960), 138–61.

prompted to applause by non-village "strangers" in its midst; and all questions, which did not exceed two to a candidate, were posed by the hamlet chiefs. In place of questioning the government candidate, one hamlet chief simply shouted, "Long live the National Revolutionary Movement," which the audience dutifully applauded. The presidential election appeared to accord greater freedom to President Diem's rivals for office, and they made use of it to express sharp and sometimes acid criticism of the government's policies and the President's family. The representatives of all three lists joined in a statement at the end of the campaign in which they said that the election had taken place in "an atmosphere of complete liberty and true democracy,"[19] although the opposition candidates themselves charged, without citing specific instances, that the election had been rigged.

Given the degree of government solicitude for the outcome, it is not surprising that its candidates fared so well. In the two legislative elections, the government parties won 83 seats in 1956 and 89 seats in 1959, but these figures do not adequately measure the government's success. For example, in 1959 government party candidates lost only 22 of the 105 contests they entered, and nearly all of them lost to other government party candidates or to independents who were really government-favored. Indeed, a number of government candidates, including Ngo Dinh Nhu and his Personalist Labor group, ran as independents in both 1956 and 1959. Thus, very few government candidates, avowed or disguised, were beaten in either election, and the only significant upsets took place in Saigon. The most famous of the two opposition winners who won through the maze of government precautions in 1959 was Phan Quang Dan, and he and another unintended winner lost their seats by court action on charges of having violated the election law.[20]

The real issue in the elections was not victory or defeat for the government, but how many people could be led to the polls and how big a victory the government could extract from them in the face of Communist and other opposition. In other words, the elections were more a test of the government's strength than of its popularity. The Communists carried out harassments during the two legislative contests and launched a major effort to disrupt the presidential election. Although one may doubt the government's claim that the Com-

[19] *Vietnam Press* (English edition), April 11, 1961 (evening issue) p. H-1.

[20] In answering the charge of having promised free medical care in exchange for votes, Dan pointed out that, if this were true, he would have sought election where his medical practice was conducted and not in a district located on the other side of the city. (*Times of Vietnam,* September 9, 1959, pp. 1–2.)

munists hoped in the 1961 election to unleash a general insurrection that would lead to a seizure of power, Communist guerrillas did carry out extensive attacks, destroying election and identification cards, ransacking polling places, organizing protest meetings, sabotaging bridges and roads, and propagandizing against participation in the election. The government claimed it killed 350 guerrillas and captured as many more in the last ten days of the campaign alone, not including the 2,000 persons who were seized as they arrived in Saigon from the provinces on election day, supposedly to stir up riots.[21]

The vote totals testify to the greater loyalty, or strength, which the government was able to muster. About 85 per cent of the eligible voters turned out for each of the legislative elections and about 93 per cent for the presidential election. There was, of course, strong pressure to vote, especially in rural areas, and the government tended to equate voting with loyalty to the regime against its enemies. "Every ballot," one 1959 poster read, "is a shell through the Vietnamese Communist flag." "The whole people," another announced, "have a duty to participate in the National Assembly election of 1959"; and so on nearly ad infinitum. Before the 1961 campaign even got under way, information cadres had put up over 300,000 posters and banners and had distributed almost seven million leaflets, all urging a large turn-out. Waves of civil servants were sent out in each election to propagandize in the countryside, when it was not too unsafe, and parades and demonstrations were organized to publicize the event. As for the voters, voting was probably considered another government-imposed obligation, and it was widely believed in Saigon, and probably even more widely held in the provinces, that failure to have a voter's card duly stamped by the election officials could lead to difficulties with the authorities. That there was some resentment is not surprising when official pressure to vote was accompanied by directed voting or, particularly in the National Assembly campaigns, a choice of often meaningless alternatives; and where, in addition, the citizens were called upon to attach slogans to their houses and, in the countryside, to participate in campaign meetings. At least some of the government employees sent out to evangelize in the countryside encountered critical citizens; there was some defacement of election posters, and the more independent and sophisticated Saigon inhabitants stayed away from the polls in fairly large numbers. It is not known how many Saigon residents were eligible to vote in 1961, but of those who registered only 75 per cent actually turned out on election day, in contrast to 95 per cent in the rest of the country — much of which, it

21 *Vietnam Press,* week ending April 16, 1961, pp. 4–6.

should be observed, was under Communist influence. In 1959, when the regime's prestige was less at stake, 82 per cent of the registered Saigon voters went to the polls.[22]

The overall margin of government victory was high in all three elections. Adequate data are not available for the 1956 election, but in 1959 the winning candidates, of whom all but about three were government-supported, received 79 per cent of the vote in the country as a whole.[23] President Diem obtained 89 per cent of the votes cast in 1961, as against 4 per cent for List II and 7 per cent for List III.[24] As in the case of voter turnout, opposition to the government did not come primarily from the Communist-infested areas. In fact, government candidates generally did best where the Communists were strongest. In the province of An Xuyen in the Camau Peninsula, which serves as a Communist base-area, the government-favored candidates garnered 95 per cent of the vote in 1959 and 98 per cent in 1961. President Diem got over 99 per cent of the votes cast in Kien Tuong, another Communist base-area in the Plain of Reeds, and in the highland province of Pleiku the opposition presidential candidates together got 7 votes to his 102,031. The principal opposition to the government was in the secure — and freer — cities. The winning legislative candidates in 1959 averaged 57 per cent of the vote in the 22 urban districts of Vietnam, in contrast to 84 per cent of the vote in the rural districts. In Saigon itself, the government's winners averaged only 42 per cent of the vote, and Phan Quang Dan obtained 63 per cent of the ballots cast in a field of 15 candidates. President Diem also found Saigon least tractable to his persuasion, obtaining only 64 per cent of the votes there compared to the 95 per cent he got in the rest of the country. Fewer than half of the registered voters of Saigon gave their support to the President.

To sum up, assuming that rural votes were counted accurately, the Diem regime has achieved impressive results in getting its people to vote and to vote for government candidates. Given the various and potent political weapons at its disposal, the government's accomplish-

[22] These percentages have been derived from data given in the *Vietnam Press* (English edition), August 31, 1959, (evening issue), p. I; *ibid.,* April 3, 1961 (evening issue), p. H-9; and Republic of Vietnam, Presidential Press Office, *President Ngo Dinh Diem and the Election of April 9, 1961* (Saigon, 1961), Appendix.

[23] This and subsequent legislative percentages were derived from the voting results reported in the *Vietnam Press* (French edition) during the period August 31-September 3, 1959. The votes received by minor candidates were not published.

[24] Republic of Vietnam, *President Ngo Dinh Diem and the Election of April 9, 1961,* Appendix.

ments are more notably expressions of its power than of its popular backing. Ironically, its power was weaker in the urban areas, particularly the capital city of Saigon, where it has the greatest military security, than in the rural areas where the Communist-directed guerrilla movement challenges the regime's control of its population. The victory of Phan Quang Dan is especially illuminating, for Dan had fashioned for himself the role of leading critic of the Ngo Dinh Diem regime. Dan's case is interesting because his record does not contain any substantial accomplishments for his country. Except for a brief period in the Provisional Government of 1948 he has been a politician out of power. But the same was true of Diem's career from 1933 to 1954. Both Dan and Diem gained their strength not for what they were but for what they symbolized: in the one case, unyielding opposition to French colonialism; in the other, dissatisfaction with the policies of the present regime.

The Vietnamese government sought to make a good showing before the outside world in its elections. Its audience was not only the West and the underdeveloped countries, but also the Communist bloc — in particular, North Vietnam. The Diem government made the most of the South's ability even under difficult conditions to allow popular selection of its leaders, in contrast with the North where national elections had not been held since 1946. The North finally held legislative elections in early 1960, evidently in order to keep up with *its* rival. To be successful, the elections in the Republic of Vietnam had, on the one hand, to be or appear to be fair enough to impress the outside world and, on the other hand, had to be sufficiently controlled to produce satisfactory results. If the extent to which the government manipulated its elections was out of proportion to the threat from the opposition, this can be explained by its lack of experience with the democratic process and its extreme sensitivity to divisions within the electorate and to any challenges to its authority

Conclusion

The winning of independence and the establishment of a Republic have introduced the forms but not much of the substance of representative government to Vietnam. It is likely that there is less political freedom in Vietnam today than there was under the French. Three reasons why even a limited political democracy has not flourished in Vietnam since 1954 may be noted. First is the problem of security. In a newly partitioned country which is confronted with an imminent Communist threat to its survival, political liberty must necessarily be circumscribed. In the second place, Vietnam is an underdeveloped country, and its underdevelopment is displayed in its political institutions no less than in its economic and social institutions. Underdevelopment means that parties tend to lack organization and defined programs, to be largely city-based, and to depend heavily on the personalities of their leaders, who come from a small intellectual elite. In such a society power falls to those groups which, like the Communists, can form tightly knit organizations around an ideology of religious intensity or which can use the public bureaucracy or the armed forces for political purposes. Indeed, in the brief history of the Republic of Vietnam, the only effective challenges to the government have come from military organizations. The Ngo Dinh Diem government has found it necessary to crush those of the sects, and is currently engaged against the military forces of the Communists. It must rely upon the military organization which it has itself developed, and in this, its own army, lies the greatest non-Communist threat to the regime. Underdevelopment also means for the nation which wishes to improve its condition the centralized direction of human and material resources, which in turn requires that it limit political liberty, particularly those political activities which create disputes over goals or the broad means of reaching them or which in other ways threaten to divide the society.

Internal security problems and underdevelopment account for much of the restraint placed upon political life in Vietnam. Indeed, the problems posed by underdevelopment would place sharp restraints upon democratic political development even if there were no Communist problem. President Diem's observations on this subject are worth quoting: "If you want to emerge rapidly from this humiliating condition, and not in a few centuries, you are led to adopt some sort of forced march. The democratic problem consists precisely in our ability to determine the limits of this forced march, which is in itself indispensable even without the added pressure of Communist neighbors and even in conditions of pure neutralism and peaceful coexistence."[25] It is unfortunate that full-scale elections and other democratic trappings should have been introduced into Vietnam during a period of great transition when its rulers' lack of self-confidence, the ideological tensions within the society, and the importance of the issues at stake have all militated against the growth of fragile democratic institutions. Both of the dominating forces in present-day Vietnam, the Communist Democratic Republic of Vietnam and the Ngo Dinh Diem regime, have permitted elections only to the extent that they could control the results; both have used elections to mobilize mass approval of the regime; and in each, minor parties exist only as

[25] *Vietnam Press,* week ending February 21, 1960, p. 18.

fronts for the ruling group. The two regimes differ politically, of course. The dictatorship of the North is more secure, more far-reaching in its control of the population, and less tolerant of opposition and more willing to employ drastic methods to eliminate it. Further, the nature of the political doctrines of the two regimes encourages more optimism toward future developments in South Vietnam.

The restrictive policies of the Ngo Dinh Diem government have been a third reason why even limited democratic development has not taken place in post-Geneva Vietnam. These policies have exceeded the requirements of internal security and the impulsion from underdeveloped status. Except in the most superficial and thus, in the eyes of many Vietnamese, hypocritical way, Diem and his brothers have not been interested in building republican institutions. Furthermore, they have been unnecessarily cautious and largely concerned with narrow advantage in dealing with political freedom for their critics. As a result, the Diem regime has alienated important sections of the population and has deprived itself of healthy checks on the excesses of administrative officials. If Vietnamese parties have lacked maturity, the government's treatment of them has frozen them in their immaturity. A less rigid control of the press, a more meaningful role for the National Assembly, and greater tolerance for the expression of opposition and those who express it would not undermine the foundations of the Vietnamese Republic. They might well, on the contrary, serve to reinforce them.

5

Economic and Social Development

The Vietnamese economy in 1954 bore deep scars from the drawn-out war between the French and the Viet Minh. Roads, bridges, and public buildings had been destroyed or damaged. Much of the irrigation system had fallen into disrepair. Arable land had been abandoned as many thousands of peasants sought the security of the cities. Very little investment had been made in productive enterprise, since businessmen were hesitant to risk capital and since wartime conditions provided quicker avenues for making money, not all of which were legal. Heavy French military expenditures prevented economic collapse and even provided an artificially high standard of living for Saigon and other main cities, but this prop would be removed with the coming of peace.

The partitioning of the country in 1954 worsened the economic situation in the South. The North contained most of Vietnam's natural resources and hence most of its industry; it had provided the South with paper, cement, textiles, glass, coal, and chemical products for rubber processing, receiving in return part of the South's rice surplus. The South's traders and banks lost the control which they had over most of the foreign trade of Cambodia and Laos, for independence also meant the break-up of the Indochinese Union, with a concomitant loss of Saigon's commercial prominence in the Union as a port.[1] The withdrawal of the French increased these other economic dislocations. The French Expeditionary Corps alone had been a major source of foreign exchange and the most important income-generating

[1] See Buu Hoan, "Vietnam: Economic Consequences of the Geneva Peace," *Far Eastern Economic Review,* December 11, 1958, pp. 753–57.

factor in the domestic market. The departure of French troops, completed in 1956, directly cost 85,000 people their jobs.[2] And private French capital was shifted from Vietnam in considerable amounts during the uncertain period following independence. As if all this were not enough, the new Vietnamese government had to devote much of its energy to meeting the threats posed by its own army and the sects in its first year in power. The mountainous task of feeding, clothing, and resettling the refugees from the North was to occupy the government for an even longer period.

Thus, the obstacles to economic and social development were formidable. But there were, nevertheless, favorable factors as well. Unlike most of Asia, including the Communist-controlled North, South Vietnam has a relatively small population for its large amount of arable land, and partition placed within its borders 65 per cent of the total rice acreage of the country and practically all of the rubber plantations. Besides, the South Vietnamese and their government could expect substantial and quick returns from relatively modest efforts. There was idle land to be tilled, a well-constructed canal and irrigation network needing only to be restored, a fairly modern road system to be repaired, excellent though aging rubber plantations to be rejuvenated, a nation to be put once more to productive work. What Vietnam needed were energetic people (which it had), relative peace and stability (which ensued in late 1955), and a government with the means and competence to assist the people in the task of economic reconstruction. The means were not lacking, for the United States moved quickly to underwrite most of the costs of the Ngo Dinh Diem regime.

The Pattern of Development

The sequence of social and economic development in Vietnam may be conveniently described as passing from relief to rehabilitation to economic growth. The three phases in the sequence occurred more or less in the order stated, though there was considerable overlap between them. The problem of providing relief to a people unsettled by war dominated all else during 1954 and 1955. During the second year the Vietnamese government began giving attention to restoring and expanding the material preconditions of economic growth and to developing the human resources of the country as well. This second phase has by no means been completed, but it merged with the third, the achievement of agricultural and industrial growth, sometime in

[2] Buu Hoan, "Impact of Military Expenditures on the South Vietnamese Economy," *ibid.,* December 25, 1958, p. 839.

1957. Both rehabilitation and economic growth have been seriously impeded since late 1960, when the tolls of guerrilla warfare began mounting. The phase of economic growth was thus a brief one, and most gains remained at a standstill or were reversed during 1961 and 1962. A fair assessment of Vietnam's economic achievements since independence must be based, for the most part, on 1960 production levels.

During the first year after independence the Vietnamese government's major economic role was that of a relief agency. Its main problem was the refugees from the North. Most of them were peasants, and most of them crowded into the Saigon area. Practically all arrived with very few possessions. The government resettled most of the refugees in new villages, provided them with tools and materials, and fed them until they could fend for themselves. The United States supported the refugee resettlement program through generous aid grants totaling 93 million dollars, and Catholic and other private organizations also gave a helping hand. By 1956 the program had been substantially and very successfully completed.[3]

Aside from aid to the refugees, government relief was provided on a large scale by pumping consumer goods into private channels of commerce. With the end of heavy French spending the Vietnamese lost their main source of foreign exchange. A drop in imports would have meant a sharp drop in living standards and in government customs revenues, if American aid had not filled the breach. With this aid importers were able to purchase a wide variety of foreign products, ranging from food to automobiles to air conditioners, the great bulk of which were consumer or quasi-consumer goods. With a government-fixed overvaluation of the piaster, Vietnamese businessmen were able to sell and Vietnamese consumers could buy this flood of goods at prices below their real value, and the government was enabled at the same time to gain the bulk of its public revenues through various import taxes. The piasters importers paid for the aid-dollars went into a special counterpart fund which was used to support government programs and services. The American government, moving rather slowly and against strong official Vietnamese resistance, took the first steps during 1957 to shift its commercial aid program from one subsidizing a high level of consumption to one stimulating economic development. Its program continued, however, to bear many of the marks of an international relief project.

Rehabilitation was the second phase in the pattern of economic and

[3] The study of the refugee program has been told in Richard W. Lindholm (editor), *Vietnam: The First Five Years* (East Lansing: Michigan State University Press, 1959), pp. 45–103.

social development. The most important and necessary job for economic rehabilitation was rice production. Rice is Vietnam's main domestic crop, and had been its chief export before World War II. The rehabilitation of rice cultivation required more than a simple restoration of prewar conditions in the countryside, for the Indochina War had irrevocably severed the old relations between peasants and landowners. Although the Viet Minh's greatest strength was in the North, they were also strong in parts of the South; in areas they controlled they carried out land reform, and in areas under their influence they assisted the peasants in their efforts to avoid paying rents to landowners. In many parts of the rich Mekong delta the landlords made no attempt to collect rents, but retired to the safety of the cities; about 400,000 acres of riceland were simply abandoned by both owners and cultivators during this troubled period.

In response to awakened peasant aspirations for land, the government in 1955 initiated a three-pronged land reform program. Its aims were to settle peasants on abandoned land, to safeguard tenants' rights by means of land contracts, and to transfer land from large holders to tenants and others with the aim of reducing the size of land holdings.[4] The land transfer program was begun in early 1958. Landlords were required to give up all individual holdings that exceeded 247 acres (rubber, tea, and coffee plantations were exempt), though another 37 acres might be kept if used for maintaining the ancestral tombs. The government purchased the excess land directly, paying the owners 10 per cent in cash and the rest in government bonds maturing over twelve years at 3 per cent annual interest. The peasants had to pay the government for the land they obtained in six annual installments, without interest, and they gained ownership when the full payment was made. For most of Vietnam's 1.2 million tenant households, land-tenure contracts were of greater direct impact than land transfers.[5] These contracts limited rents to no more than 25 per cent of the gross yield, and assured tenants a secure holding for three to five years; they were renewable at the tenant's option unless the owner himself wished to resume cultivation for his family. Three-fourths of all tenant farmers had entered into these contracts by the middle of 1959.

In its resettlement program, the Vietnamese government has undertaken to place people on abandoned land in the Mekong delta and,

[4] A detailed study of agrarian reform in South Vietnam by an American technician who worked on this program can be found in J. P. Gittinger, *Studies on Land Tenure in Vietnam, Terminal Report* (Saigon: U.S. Operations Mission to Vietnam, December, 1959).

[5] The limited effect of land transfers in a single Vietnamese village is examined in James B. Hendry, "Land Tenure in South Vietnam," *Economic Development and Cultural Change,* 9 (October, 1960), 27–44.

more ambitiously, to open up the 3.7 million acres of public domain in the Central Vietnamese highlands where very few Vietnamese had penetrated in the past. The economy of the highlands, aside from a number of large French rubber, tea, and coffee plantations, had been based on the shifting agriculture of the scattered tribes which inhabited the region. The government's land development program has concentrated on the highlands, and most of the Vietnamese now occupying its newly-established centers came from the overpopulated and land-scarce coastal strip of Central Vietnam. The government chose the settlement sites, cleared the land, transported the settlers, allocated plots, and provided food, livestock, seed, and other supplies until the centers could maintain themselves. Since the program was inaugurated in April, 1957, over 210,000 persons have been resettled in 147 centers carved from 220,000 acres of wilderness. By the end of 1961, nearly one-half of the centers had become sufficiently self-sustaining to be integrated into the regular local administration.

The second most important area of reconstruction was the transport system. In the nation almost 700 miles of main roads, over a third of the railroad trackage, hundreds of bridges, and a large part of the canal system had suffered from destruction or deterioration during the war. On the 860 miles of railway alone, 68 reinforced concrete bridges had been damaged beyond repair by Viet Minh action, and travel along even main highways was slow and in places nearly impossible. Rehabilitation of the communication arteries was an essential condition to economic development, and a major effort went into the task after 1956. By late 1962 the railroad system between Hue (near the seventeenth parallel) and Saigon was in its fourth year of operation and much of the road and canal system had been rehabilitated. Adequate roads linked the highlands with the delta area and with Central coastal cities, a most important accomplishment from both the economic and military viewpoints.

A third area of government action in laying the basis for economic development was education. Under the French, the quality of secondary and university education was high but extremely limited in extent; there were in 1939 only 5,000 high school students in all of Indochina, and a mere 700 students attending the University of Hanoi, the sole university serving the three-country Indochinese Union. The total number of students in lower education came to about half a million.[6] In 1955 there were, in South Vietnam alone, 2,500 university students and over 400,000 students in public and private schools

[6] Claude A. Buss, *The Far East* (New York: Macmillan, 1955), p. 640, and Nguyen Dinh Hoa, "Higher Education in the Republic of Vietnam," *The Burman,* January 10, 1960.

below the university level. While the government has not achieved its objective of providing a school for every village, it has tripled the number of classrooms and students in primary and secondary education. Perhaps 70 per cent of all young people between the ages of five and fifteen now get some schooling. Higher education has also expanded with the creation of three universities at Saigon, Dalat, and Hue, and the number of students at the university level, most of whom attend the University of Saigon, totals around 12,000.[7]

In the field of health, the most notable activity of the government has been its malaria-control program, which has sought to eliminate the principal cause of illness and death in Vietnam. Since 1959, over 2,500 workers have been engaged in the nationwide spraying of houses, and over six million people have thus far benefited from the program. Rural health in general has been improved through rudimentary medical stations established in about 3,300 villages and hamlets, and through district and provincial health centers. Health activities have, however, lagged behind other government efforts, in part because of lack of trained personnel — there are, for example, only 600 doctors in Vietnam, and over half of them are in the military services and most of the rest in Saigon — and in part because the government itself has given inadequate attention to health needs, especially in the countryside. The security situation has now forced a change, and since 1962 medical supplies have been flowing in large amounts to the villages. Indeed, the government hopes to expand the number of its rural health stations to 10,000 during 1963.

The third phase in the development sequence is the promotion of economic growth. This became an increasingly pressing need after 1956. Its objective has been to make Vietnam self-sufficient; this has required both the development of domestic production to meet many needs which had been filled by imports, and a heavy increase in exports to close the gaping trade deficit. The United States, since it has been meeting this deficit through its aid program, has had an interest in seeing Vietnam achieve self-sufficiency. In the relief and rehabilitation phases of post-independence development, the Vietnamese government necessarily played a primary role. It could continue to play a primary role in economic development if it chose the path of a socialist economy; it could play a very minor role if it chose to allow private enterprise an open field. In fact, the government took an intermediate position. Agriculture and trade were left in private hands, with the government exercising important but indirect controls,

---

[7] University enrollment figures are high, since a student is counted for each university faculty in which he takes course work.

while industrial activity was frequently made a joint private-government matter.

Agriculture constitutes the dominant sector of the Vietnamese economy. It supports about 80 per cent of the population, and provides Vietnam with its two main exports, rubber and rice. Rice production rose quickly with the coming of peace, moving from 2.6 million tons of paddy in 1954 to a peak of 5 million tons in 1959; the national insecurity has reduced this since that date to 4.5 million tons in 1961.[8] Rubber production likewise rose steadily, from 51 thousand tons in 1954 to 79 thousand tons in 1961; guerrilla activities have not seriously interfered with the maintenance and tapping of rubber trees. Other agricultural commodities — sweet potatoes, sugar cane, peanuts, coconuts, tobacco, and corn — also increased steadily in production, though, as in the case of rice, production drops were registered for all of them after 1960. The production of livestock and poultry rose more spectacularly than almost anything else. There were 149 thousand cattle, 222 thousand buffaloes, and 961 thousand pigs in South Vietnam in 1954, and over 1 million cattle, 754 thousand buffaloes, and 3.6 million pigs in 1960; and there were nearly 10 million chickens and ducks in 1955 and 26.6 million in 1960. Livestock and poultry showed a decline similar to that of the plant crops in 1961. An interesting if minor success in the development of new crops has been the kenaf and ramie introduced in the highlands resettlement villages only a few years ago; combined with the older production of jute, they now supply most of Vietnam's fiber-bag and twine needs. Finally, the Vietnamese fishing industry, which engages 10 per cent of the population on a full- or part-time basis, increased its catch between 1955 and 1961 from 52 thousand tons to 212 thousand tons.[9]

There was little industry in Vietnam before independence, for under French colonial policy Vietnam was a market for manufactured goods. What industry did exist was mostly located in the North, close to the sources of energy and raw materials. Industries in the South were small and mainly engaged in producing such consumer goods as beer, soft drinks, cigarettes, and matches. There were also large rice-milling plants in the Cholon area to process the paddy coming from

[8] These and some of the succeeding statistics on agricultural and industrial production have been taken from U.S. Operations Mission to Vietnam, *Annual Statistical Bulletin, Data through 1961* (Saigon, July, 1962). The economic and social data reproduced in this and other USOM documents depend almost entirely on Vietnamese official sources and are frequently based on rough estimates, if not sheer guesses.

[9] U.S. Operations Mission to Vietnam, *Annual Report for Fiscal Year 1961* (Saigon, [1962], p. 21.

the Mekong delta, and a number of sugar mills and handicraft industries producing textiles, pottery, and the like. Since independence, these existing industries have been modernized, though, with the important exceptions of sugar refining and textiles, their output has not substantially increased, and in some cases was actually lower in 1960 and 1961 than it was in 1954. Modern equipment has helped to increase sugar production from 3,526 tons in 1954 to 90,000 tons in 1961, eliminating the need of importing refined sugar, and Vietnam's modern textile plants now meet much of the country's consumer needs. It should be added that Vietnam is presently producing goods never before manufactured in the South, including paper, aluminum ware, plastics, pharmaceuticals, and glassware.

Vietnam's old and new industrial development has been for the most part in the Saigon area, but the government plans to divert a good share of the country's future development to Central Vietnam. The only known coal deposits are located there, as is the large hydroelectric plant being readied for operation through Japanese reparations aid. The Nong Son coal mine, not far from the important port of Da Nang, yielded no coal in 1954 and had a production of 100 thousand tons in 1962. When it reaches full capacity in 1965, it should produce 250 thousand tons annually. The Da Nhim hydroelectric plant, near Dalat, will be producing 160,000 kwh of power by 1965, enough to take care of all of Vietnam's industrial needs for the foreseeable future. By contrast, the total electrical production in Vietnam was 181,000 kwh in 1954 and 315,354 kwh in 1961. To take advantage of the power made available by the Da Nhim and Nong Son projects, the government is planning the development of an industrial complex in the Nong Son area which will include thermal, chemical, and calcium carbide plants, as well as an oil refinery.

Vietnam's economic progress since independence should be reflected in a rising level of exports and in an improved import-export ratio. Of course, not all of the country's economic expansion has gone into the export market: there were about three million more people to sustain in 1962 and the population as a whole was better off economically than in 1954. Exports did in fact increase substantially between 1954 and 1960, the peak year, by about two-thirds, from a dollar value of $50.6 million to $85.6 million. It is important to note that the increase was due almost entirely to two commodities, rubber and rice. Rubber exports rose from 62 thousand tons to 70 thousand tons in the period, and rice exports increased even more strikingly, from 70 thousand tons to 340 thousand tons. Indeed, rubber and rice are the dominant factors in Vietnam's whole export trade; they accounted for 70 per cent of all exports in 1955 and nearly 90 per cent of all exports in 1960. The third major export commodity, hogs, constituted little more than 2 per cent of the total export trade of the latter year. The export picture turned bleak in 1961 with the suspension of rice exports in mid-year — in fact, rice had to be imported in large quantities later on — and with a drop in rubber prices, despite a volume increase in rubber exports to over 83 thousand tons. Exports were down to $70.8 million in 1961 and $22.1 million during the first half of 1962; 14 thousand tons of rice were exported in this latter period.[10]

While exports rose between 1954 and 1960, imports declined. The decline was not, however, either great or regular. In 1954 the dollar value of imports was $267 million; in 1956 it fell to $217.7 million, but it rose the next year to $288.7 million; and in 1960 it was $240.3 million. The decline between the two base years was thus only $26.7 million. The imbalance of imports over exports during this same period narrowed from $216.4 million to $154.8 million, yet the excess of imports to exports stood at three-to-one in 1960; economic chaos was averted in this perilous circumstance only because American aid was filling the gap. The imbalance was intensified in 1961, and by a considerable margin in 1962, as exports fell further and American-aid financed imports increased sharply. The total import figure for 1961 was 255.1 million, and while the 1962 figure is not yet available, it will probably be substantially higher. Even before the recent reversal in the export-import trend Vietnam was clearly a long way from economic self-sufficiency, and that goal is now receding further and further from attainment.

An important development in Vietnam's post-independence trade has been the shift from France to the United States as the main source of imports. In 1954 Vietnam got about two-thirds of its imports from France to only 8 per cent from the United States; by contrast, in 1961 France supplied only 15 per cent to the United States' 27 per cent. This puts the United States in first place in Vietnam's import trade, with Japan running a fairly close second and France a rather poor third. The emergence of the United States as Vietnam's biggest supplier is easy to explain. Until November, 1960, Vietnamese importers could buy anywhere in the non-Communist world market under the American-financed commercial aid program. The only exceptions were certain foods and fibers, in surplus in the United States, which had to be purchased from that country. Since the end of

[10] See Vu Quoc Thuc, "Economic Outlook in 1962," *Vietnam Review* (Washington: Embassy of Vietnam), June 6, 1962, pp. 12–14; François Nivolon, "Decline in Exports," *Far Eastern Economic Review,* October 25, 1962, p. 232.

1960, about eighteen countries, including France, Japan, Germany, and the United Kingdom, have been excluded as suppliers under the program, except under special circumstances. It appears that the final figures for 1962, the year in which American preferential trade regulations took full effect, will show the United States supplying two-fifths of Vietnam's foreign needs. On the other hand, France continues to be Vietnam's best customer, buying 36 per cent of what Vietnam had to sell in 1961, three times as much as any other country. Neither the United States nor Japan has been a heavy purchaser of Vietnamese goods.

Dominant Characteristics of Development

An understanding of economic and social development efforts in Vietnam would be grossly incomplete if it did not include some perception of three of its dominant characteristics. These are the strong role played by the government, the crucial contribution of foreign aid, and the pervasive effect of military and general security considerations on the activities of both the Vietnamese and American governments.

The Vietnamese government necessarily assumed an active role in the rehabilitation of the economy. Road construction, canal dredging, educational expansion, agrarian reform, and numerous other activities could be undertaken only by the state. But the Diem government has sought to direct other aspects of economic development as well. Much of its attention has been given to developing agriculture, through peasant cooperatives, farmers' associations, an agricultural loan agency, and fixed prices on agricultural products. The government operates or has majority control of industrial enterprises that range from sugar milling, the manufacture of paper, textiles, cement, and glass, coal mining and lumbering, through railway and airlines systems, to the bottling of mineral water. The planned industrial complex in the area of the Nong Son coal mine will be a state undertaking. The Diem government has demonstrated a lack of interest, apparent in its administrative requirements and its participation in a joint Vietnamese-American industrial loan agency, in the establishment of economic enterprises in which it does not participate.

This attitude of the Vietnamese government is expressed in its official philosophy of Personalism, which seeks to find a middle course between capitalist individualism and Marxist collectivism. This view sees economic growth as inseparable from social and political development; it does not admit narrow economic criteria of efficiency and profit as controlling considerations, and it wishes to achieve growth without concentrating capital and income in a few hands.[11] It should be observed that official suspicion of private enterprise accords with Confucian principles, which place tradesmen at the bottom of the hierarchy of social groups, beneath intellectuals, farmers, and artisans.

The second important characteristic of economic development has been the role played by foreign aid. Vietnam has received assistance from a number of Western nations. France has helped in the rehabilitation of the railway system, in the development of the Nong Son coal mine, in agrarian reform (through subsidizing the purchase of lands owned by French nationals), and has provided aid for a number of other programs as well. The Japanese, through reparations arrangements with Vietnam, have undertaken several projects, the most important of which is the construction of the Da Nhim hydroelectric plant; and British Commonwealth members, Nationalist China, and still other countries have contributed technical assistance and equipment to Vietnam. The overwhelming flow of foreign aid, however, has come from the United States. American aid has paid for most of Vietnam's imports since 1954. It has provided most of the revenues for the Vietnamese budget — about 60 per cent of all government revenues since 1954 have come directly or indirectly from American aid.[12] Without American aid, economic development would have been impossible. Indeed, Vietnam could not have preserved its independence.

The bulk of American aid to Vietnam was administered through the French prior to independence. Between 1950, when the United States began to absorb the costs of the Indochina War, and 1954, it contributed $2.5 billion for this purpose, most of which the French expended for Vietnam and the great part of which was used for direct military purposes.[13] Since 1954, the United States has poured another $2 billion of economic aid alone into Vietnam.[14] The size of this

[11] A succinct statement of the government's position can be found in Vu Van Thai, "Our Concept of Development," published in *Vital Speeches of the Day,* December 1, 1959, pp. 101–102.

[12] The director of the U.S. economic aid mission in Vietnam told a Congressional committee in 1959 that the total effective American contribution to the Vietnamese budget was about 75 per cent, but this is too high. See Senate Committee on Foreign Relations, Subcommittee on State Department Organization and Public Affairs, *Situation in Vietnam, Hearings, July 30 and 31, 1959* (Washington, 1959), p. 206; and *ibid., United States Aid Program in Vietnam, Report, February 26, 1960* (1960), p. 45.

[13] Agency for International Development, Statistics and Reports Division, *U.S. Foreign Assistance and Assistance from International Organizations, July 1, 1945–June 30, 1951* (revised; Washington, March 21, 1962), p. 32.

[14] USOM, *Annual Statistical Bulletin, 1961,* p. 120, places total economic

outlay can be seen more clearly in relation to that given some of Vietnam's neighbors. In 1960 Vietnam received from the United States the equivalent of $13.70 for each inhabitant. Taiwan received $12.50 per capita, Korea $8.60, India $1.90, and Thailand $1.20. Only Laos, with a per capita assistance of $17, surpassed Vietnam among the countries of South and Southeast Asia.[15]

The United States has injected over 80 per cent of its economic aid to Vietnam into an import-subsidization program, which works as follows: the United States government pays for foreign commodities for Vietnamese importers, using either dollars or other foreign currencies. The importers pay for these goods in Vietnamese piasters which are deposited in a "counterpart fund." When the imports arrive, they are assessed for customs duties and other taxes, some of which also go into the counterpart fund and, like other imports, they enter the general stream of commerce. The counterpart fund is drawn upon to pay for programs, services, and other expenses of the Vietnamese government which are agreed upon by the Vietnamese and American governments. The United States can control the level of the counterpart fund pretty well by determining how much money it will allocate annually to the commercial import program, and it also determines the commodities which are eligible for importation under the program. The remaining 20 per cent of American aid is provided in several ways: to import equipment used in development projects, to train Vietnamese civil servants and military personnel in the United States and other countries, to support American personnel in Vietnam, and so forth.

Whether it has been injected through the commercial import program or otherwise, American economic and technical assistance has ranged across the whole of Vietnamese society. It has supported school construction, the development of agricultural credit and cooperatives, police training, loans to industrial enterprises, and the education of future government employees. The financial emphasis of this aid has, however, been in three areas: transportation, agriculture and natural resources, and public administration. The lion's share of American project aid, 40 per cent of the total, has been spent on transportation,

---

assistance at $1.701 billion for the period July, 1954 through June, 1962. It appears certain, however, that its preliminary estimate of $156.8 million for the last twelve months of this period has been substantially exceeded as a result of the intensification in the American aid program during 1962. Indeed, by mid-1962, newspaper stories were referring to an American expenditure of $1 million per day.

[15] Milton C. Taylor, "South Vietnam: Lavish Aid, Limited Progress," *Pacific Affairs,* 34 (Fall, 1961), 244.

most of it in rebuilding and extending Vietnam's highway system. Aid to agriculture trailed far behind, with only 17 per cent of the total, and public administration received 11 per cent. The share expended on transportation completely overshadowed the meager amounts of counterpart and other funds used for health and sanitation (7 per cent), education (7 per cent), and industrial development and mining (6 per cent). Community development, social welfare, and housing received a puny 3 per cent of these funds, and the amount devoted to labor was only a minute fraction of 1 per cent.[16] Since American-supported aid projects are mutually agreed upon by the United States and Vietnamese governments, the allocations of economic and technical assistance reflect quite accurately the importance which both governments attach to different areas of development. The allocations also give a good indication of the areas where development has been strong and where it has been neglected.

The third influence on development has been security. Security considerations have, since the very beginning of Vietnam's post-Geneva history, directed and limited the course of economic and social development. The impact of security can be seen in both American-aid support of Vietnamese military expenditures and in the portion of Vietnamese total expenditures devoted to military purposes. Between 1956 and 1960, 43 per cent of all Vietnamese public expenditures were allocated directly to the military for the support of the army and Self-Defense Corps. The United States provided practically all of the money through the counterpart generated by the commercial import program. As a matter of fact, 78 per cent of all American aid given to Vietnam between these two years went into the military budget.[17] In short, from 1956 to 1960 the Vietnamese government spent two-fifths of its total revenues, including over three-quarters of the money it obtained from the United States, in order to maintain its military establishment. The aid projects for economic and social development discussed in the preceding paragraph made up only about 22 per cent of the total aid given to Vietnam. Thus, the 7 per cent of project funds which were devoted to health and sanitation constituted only 1½ per cent of total American aid, and the 3 per cent devoted to community development, social welfare, and housing constituted only about six-tenths of 1 per cent of total aid.

[16] These percentages were obtained through combining obligated dollar project aid and counterpart withdrawals for project aid through December 31, 1961. See Tables H-1B and H-1C in USOM, *Annual Statistical Bulletin, 1961,* pp. 120–21.

[17] These percentages were derived from the figures given in Senate Committee on Foreign Relations, *United States Aid Program in Vietnam, Report, February 26, 1960,* p. 45.

As impressive as they are, these figures do not reveal the full weight of the military emphasis on the development effort in post-independence Vietnam. They do not, for example, include the value of the military equipment the United States has given directly to the Vietnamese government. Direct military assistance averaged about $85 million a year before the massive build-up that began in early 1962. Between the middle of 1954 and the middle of 1962, it totaled $724 million.[18] Nor do the figures include Vietnamese expenditures for the paramilitary Civil Guard or the large police and security services, which, technically civilian, are headed and heavily staffed by military personnel and deeply involved in anti-guerrilla activities. Nor do the figures on military and civilian expenditures indicate the extent to which provincial and other local authorities are likewise preoccupied with security matters. Over the years — not just since 1960 — local officials have expended more time and money on the maintenance of security than on any other governmental business.

The effects of the pressure of security do not stop here. Security considerations have also shaped many of the Vietnamese government's economic and social programs. The land development centers created in the sparsely populated highlands may serve economic and social ends, but the prime motive in their creation was President Diem's desire to build a "human wall" against the Communist threat from the North. The army had the responsibility for carrying out the program, and strategic reasons usually dictated the location of the centers. Security was the dominant impulse behind the government's plan to build rural "cities" in 1959 and, subsequently, the strategic hamlets. It has influenced the location of new industry, agrarian reform, almost every important development which Vietnam has undertaken since 1954.

The importance of military factors in economic and social development can be seen by further examination of American aid. As we have noted, the great bulk of American economic aid has supported the Vietnamese military budget largely through funds generated by the commercial import program, while only about 22 per cent of all aid, whether from imports or provided in other ways, has been used in economic and technical assistance projects. Even these figures are somewhat misleading. The third most important use of economic project funds since 1954 has been for public administration, but in actuality most of the public administration expenditures went to support the Vietnamese police and security services, and most of this support was in the form of equipment. The primary use of project funds

[18] AID, *U.S. Foreign Assistance and Assistance from International Organizations,* July 1, 1945–June 30, 1962 (revised; Washington, April 23, 1963), pp. 61, 69.

since 1954 has been for transportation — 40 per cent of the total, it will be recalled, went for this purpose. Nearly all of the transportation projects entailed road construction, and while road-building served economic ends it was carried out in accordance with military strategy. To give but one illustration, we may take the Vietnamese government's plan to give first priority to rebuilding the coastal highway from Saigon to Hue. The chief American military officer in Vietnam opposed this plan, except for the 20-mile stretch extending from Saigon northeast to Bien Hoa. He found the Bien Hoa link necessary because, in his words, "there is no road out of Saigon now that could take care of heavy military traffic," but he considered the long coastal route unsuitable for military traffic and too easy for an enemy to destroy.[19] This 20-mile stretch of highway cost more money than the United States provided for all labor, community development, social welfare, housing, health, and education projects in Vietnam combined during the entire period 1954–1961.

Development in Perspective

How successful has Vietnam been in developing its material and human resources? The head of the American economic mission to Saigon proclaimed in 1960 that Vietnam was then "well on the road to a balanced economy."[20] This view, which has been echoed by both American and Vietnamese sources, does not square with the facts. It is true that Vietnam rebounded with vigor from the effects of war, partition, and withdrawal from the French colonial system. It is also true that the economic infrastructure of the country was developed at a fast rate, that production, particularly in agriculture, rather quickly regained prewar levels and in some cases surpassed them, and that the standard of living, at least in the cities, was raised by a comfortable margin. Certainly Saigon has shown many signs of prosperity. Visitors to the capital city have frequently noted how well-dressed and well-nourished the people are, how many cars, motor scooters, and bicycles crowd the city's streets, how plentiful consumer goods are in the stores and markets, and how much new commercial and residential construction has taken place since the coming of peace in 1954.

But certain unpleasant economic facts intrude themselves into this picture of apparent economic and social health. First of all, much of

[19] This revealing information is found in Senate Committee on Foreign Relations, *Situation in Vietnam, Hearings, December 7 and 8, 1959* (Washington, 1960), pp. 287–88.

[20] U.S. Operations Mission to Vietnam, *Annual Report for Fiscal Year 1960* (Saigon, October 1, 1960), p. 1.

it was achieved through foreign aid. The Vietnamese government has been unable — to an extent, unwilling — to obtain most of its necessary revenues from internal sources. Most of the revenues the government has produced, moreover, have come from taxes imposed on imports supplied by American aid. In the second place, Vietnam has had a heavy and, since 1960, increasing trade deficit. Despite all efforts, imports were three times as high as exports in 1959, the year in which the imbalance was smallest. In the third place, capital investment in Vietnam has been low, much below the 10 per cent of net national product which is considered to be the annual minimum investment rate for assuring adequate economic growth in underdeveloped countries. In 1955, 1956, and 1960, for example, private and public investment combined amounted to only 3.4, 1.8, and 4.8 per cent of net national product. Even so, Vietnam has been able to achieve a fair rate of economic growth with this low level of investment — gross national product increased nearly 24 per cent in the five years between 1956 and 1960, and living standards increased also[21] — this is because of the depressed state of the Vietnamese economy in 1954. An upward economic movement was bound to occur as people returned to uncultivated land and took up neglected pursuits, and as moderate efforts were expended in reconstruction.[22] Once basic reconstruction had been completed, however, larger increments of investment were required which have not been forthcoming from the government or from domestic or foreign entrepreneurs. Finally, there has been the problem of chronic unemployment. Despite its affluent appearance, according to a survey Saigon had in 1961 one-fourth of its working class unemployed and many others underemployed.[23] It is difficult to estimate the amount of unemployment in rural Vietnam, though it is known to be high; in one Mekong delta village researchers found fewer than half the farm laborers working more than four months of the year.[24] And a 1958 industrial study showed half of Vietnam's industrial capacity to be unutilized.[25]

[21] These figures are taken from Frank C. Child, *Essays on Economic Growth, Capital Formation, and Public Policy in Vietnam* (Saigon: Michigan State University Vietnam Advisory Group, May, 1961), pp. 6–9. More than most, figures on gross national product are tentative guesses.

[22] *Ibid.*, pp. 9–10.

[23] See, for example, the sample survey conducted by the Center for Vietnamese Studies, *Profile of the Vietnamese Population, the Saigon Pilot Study, Preliminary Report* (Saigon, April, 1961).

[24] James B. Hendry, assisted by Nguyen Van Thuan, *The Study of a Vietnamese Rural Community — Economic Activity* (Saigon: Michigan State University Vietnam Advisory Group, December, 1959), p. 75.

[25] Cited by Child, *Essays on Economic Growth*, p. 120.

One reason for Vietnam's recent economic troubles is clearly evident. The Communist guerrilla campaign against the Ngo Dinh Diem government has imposed a heavy charge on economic and social development since late 1960. While the campaign has not yet caused serious damage to basic economic installations, it has sabotaged road and railway communications and interfered sharply with internal trade and personal movement. In the reversal of economic trends after 1960 described earlier in this chapter, the most significant economic retreat was in rice production, when Vietnam in 1961 lost its position as a rice-surplus country. In addition to progressive decreases in rice acreage, recent shortages have resulted from the Communists' diversion of rice from the Saigon market as a means of applying economic pressure and maintaining their growing guerrilla forces. Conditions in the countryside have been responsible for the building-up of commodity inventories in Saigon and other cities, for, having little to sell to the cities, the peasants have less money for the purchase of manufactured products. The government has had great difficulty in collecting taxes from its rural citizens, and collections have fallen sharply, perhaps by over 50 per cent. Payments for land given to tenants under the agrarian reform program have also fallen sharply, and agricultural credit loans dropped in 1961 by 60 per cent from the 1960 level, and probably even more in 1962. On the industrial side, capital equipment outlays began their fall also in 1961, and a number of important industrial projects, including the Ha Tien cement factory in southwestern Vietnam and the Thu Duc power plant only a few miles outside Saigon, have been delayed or suspended. Unemployment has, since 1961, become even more acute.

Communist insurgency has affected the government's social and technical programs as well as its economic programs. Hundreds of village health stations have been sacked — medical supplies are an important guerrilla need. The malaria eradication program has been severely impeded, with many of its personnel killed, kidnapped, or intimidated. By the fall of 1961, between 400 and 600 classrooms had been closed because of guerrilla activities; indeed, the entire mechanism of government services has ceased to function in many areas of rural Vietnam.

So far we have talked about the effects of guerrilla warfare on economic and social development. But insecurity has had effects on this development which antedate the outbreak of extensive fighting in 1960. For example, over the years private businessmen have been reluctant to invest in long-range projects; the tendency has been to hoard wealth, to use it for the conspicuous consumption so common in Saigon, and to invest it in real estate, consumer loans, and other areas which promise quick returns but add little to the productive capacity of the nation. The overhanging Communist threat has also impelled the Vietnamese government since 1954 to apply the bulk of its own and foreign aid resources toward security objectives. A good part of Vietnam's manpower has been kept under arms; in 1955 the army, Civil Guard, and Self-Defense Corps totaled about 250,000 men; by 1962 these organizations had added another 120,000 men. Military defense has also withdrawn much skilled manpower from civilian pursuits, with most of Vietnam's trained doctors and many engineers and other specialists under arms.

It would be difficult to criticize the Republic of Vietnam for the size of its armed forces in the immediate post-Geneva period, in view of North Vietnam's even larger military establishment and the uncertain terms of the South's independence. It is true that many foreigners felt that the government was putting too much emphasis on military security and too little on helping the people. One foreign correspondent, for example, giving an unofficial but frequently expressed view, stated in 1957 that "far from giving security, there is every reason to suppose that the army, buttressed by the Civil Guard . . . is regarded by the Southern peasant as a symbol of insecurity and repression."[26] And one high American official in Saigon remarked in 1958, on the basis of intimate knowledge of President Diem, that the Vietnamese leader would, if he had the choice, sacrifice all American economic aid projects to add 20,000 men to his army.[27] It may be that the Vietnamese government could more easily have coped with the Communist rebellion if it had in the early years spent less money on its armed forces and more on social and economic objectives; but it is understandable that the Vietnamese should not have been willing to risk military insufficiency. Two questions may properly be raised concerning the use which the Diem government and its American ally have made of available resources. One is: how effectively have the Vietnamese military forces been developed? This question will be dealt with in Chapter 7. The other question is: how well have the nonmilitary resources of the country been used? To this question we now turn.

In the industrial sector, government policies have hindered development, partly because of the composition of the nation's entrepreneurial class. In 1954 there were few experienced Vietnamese businessmen. Economic activity was concentrated in French and Chinese hands, including most of the existing manufacturing, the rice trade, trans-

[26] David Hotham, "South Vietnam — Shaky Bastion," *New Republic,* November 25, 1957, p. 15.
[27] Personal interview dated January 27, 1958.

portation, and the export-import business. Government policies since 1954 have favored native businessmen and sought to solve the Chinese problem by requiring its resident Chinese to assume Vietnamese citizenship as a prerequisite for engaging in a number of key occupations and professions. To ensure native control of new industries, the government has insisted upon participation and control in most businesses established since 1954. Vietnamese businessmen have been given preference in the granting of government contracts, in the granting of business and export-import licenses, and in other ways. These various practices have not contributed to business growth in Vietnam, but neither, it should be added, have Vietnamese and Chinese businessmen shown much inclination to invest in productive economic activity. Much of their wealth has been hoarded or consumed or invested for high returns. Even though industrial investments have offered good profits, local entrepreneurs have been reluctant to engage their capital.[28]

But government policies have not strongly encouraged even Vietnamese businessmen. For example, the Industrial Development Center was created in 1957 and supported by American aid; among other purposes, it was to be a lending agency to new or existing enterprises. At the end of 1959, the government had approved only 27 of the 125 projects submitted to it,[29] of which a number appear to have been loans to pay off previous loans. The government displayed indifference, if not hostility, to the Center's operations, and the agency never achieved its stated function. Normal requests for business permits and licenses must wind their way through a labyrinth of government offices, and businessmen may wait months or even years before they get final decisions on seemingly routine requests. One government official told the author in 1958 that delays and special screenings were necessary to keep Communists out of the business life of the country. Much more likely, they reflect a distrust of entrepreneurs in general and a desire to give advantage to those who stand well with the government. The National Revolutionary Movement and Personalist Labor Party obtain much of their revenue from their influence or control over economic activities, and persons close to the Vietnamese leadership (including members of President Diem's family) have not been hindered from indulging their entrepreneurial proclivities.

The government has not offered much inducement to foreign capital. A presidential declaration of March, 1957, purported to encourage foreign investment and promised a number of exemptions and protections to foreign businessmen. These advantages turned out to

[28] Child, *Essays on Economic Growth,* pp. 133–34.
[29] M. N. Trued, "South Vietnam's Industrial Development Center," *Pacific Affairs,* 33 (September, 1960), 257.

be illusory, for foreign investors have in fact had to depend on whatever advantages the departments of Finance and National Economy have been willing to accord them in specific cases. Little foreign capital has been attracted to Vietnam, and foreigners doing business in the country frequently complain, justifiably or not, that their operations are heavily burdened with taxes and official red tape. Local business itself is not as a rule heavily taxed, but taxes are often arbitrarily set and collected. In addition, local businessmen, like their counterparts in other new nations (not to mention some more established nations) are sometimes subject to the shakedown.

Perhaps it is not realistic to expect local and foreign businessmen to contribute importantly to Vietnam's industrial development, even if the government had given them a fair chance. But the government has not used its own resources adequately in the promotion of industrial growth. It has, for example, been unwilling to limit consumption in favor of capital formation, largely because it fears the political effects of enforced austerity. Thus, it has resisted American efforts to shift the commercial import program to capital goods. In the words of one high American official, the Vietnamese government has preferred Chevrolets to dredges.[30] It has been unwilling to use its large accumulation of foreign exchange funds and gold to assist economic development, preferring money in the bank to investment in capital formation. These foreign reserves, which had risen from $138 million to $222 million between 1956 and 1960, finally began to fall in 1961 as a result of American pressures. The Vietnamese government is not to blame for all of the slowness of the country's industrial growth but, as the preceding paragraphs have indicated, it is responsible for much of it. The basic weakness of the Vietnamese government has been its refusal to allow private entrepreneurs to do the job and its reluctance or inability to do the job itself. As one American economist has put it, "the economic solution to the problem of economic growth in Vietnam is relatively simple; the real problems, the serious problems, lie in the areas of administration and politics."[31]

Inasmuch as the government's development policy has emphasized agriculture, its very limited record in furthering industrialization should be compared with its activities on behalf of Vietnam's rural population. Here its accomplishments have been more substantial, as the quick increases in farm crops and the implementation of agrarian reforms and land development programs demonstrate. However, it should not escape notice that, outside of agrarian reform and land development, the government has until recently given little attention

[30] This comment was made in an informal talk before a group of Michigan State University technical advisors, Saigon, September 4, 1958.

[31] Child, *Essays on Economic Growth*, p. 138.

to rural development. Most government expenditures at the local level have been for security, and most of the American-aid projects have not directly benefited the Vietnam's rural inhabitants. The commercial import program, through which most of the project funds came, has poured only about 20 per cent of its goods into rural Vietnam. Such major imports as automobiles, construction and raw materials, pharmaceutical supplies, and Western foods have been purchased in minor amounts, if at all, by the rural population. Nor have ordinary farmers bought heavily of the fertilizer and agricultural implements made available by the commercial import program; the main purchasers have been the plantations and large farms.

Agrarian reform is generally considered one of the great successes of the Ngo Dinh Diem government. When it is viewed in the context of the revolutionary situation in the Vietnamese countryside, one may question whether the Vietnamese government's moderate approach to reform has had a really substantial impact on its intended beneficiaries. In 1954, about 40 per cent of the land planted to rice was owned by about 2,500 persons — by a quarter of one per cent of the rural population. Rent alone commonly took 50 per cent of the tenant's crop and sometimes more; he either provided his own fertilizer, seeds, man- and draft-power, and equipment, or rented them at extra cost; he could be ejected from his leasehold at the landlord's whim.[32] The Indochina War relieved many peasants of these onerous conditions, though it added new burdens in the form of taxes paid the Viet Minh.

Previous Vietnamese governments had recognized the need for agrarian reform and had even promulgated programs, but none had translated program into action. Initially the Diem government gave indications of continuing this tradition. Its original agarian plan projected nothing more than certain changes in tenure rights and the sponsorship of some small pilot projects to be developed by cooperative groups on land purchased by the government; the government resisted American pressures for land transfer and effective rent control programs, "not wishing to disturb the strong landowning classes."[33] Action was produced only after General J. Lawton Collins, President Eisenhower's special ambassador, was dispatched to Saigon in November, 1954, with instructions that reportedly stipulated effective agrarian reform as a condition of the increased American aid which President Diem was seeking.[34] The first phase of the government program — the settlement of refugees and others on uncultivated land — finally

[32] Gittinger, *Studies on Land Tenure in Vietnam,* pp. 1, 50.

[33] John D. Montgomery, *The Politics of Foreign Aid* (New York: Praeger, 1962), p. 124.

[34] Gittinger, "United States Policy toward Agrarian Reform in Underdeveloped Nations," *Land Economics,* 37 (August, 1961), 203.

got under way in 1955, but the government still delayed on the implementing of land transfer and land tenure decrees. The problem, according to the report of American advisors, was "the lack of serious, interested administrators and topside command. Government officials, beginning with the Minister for Agrarian Reform, have divided loyalties, being themselves landholders."[35] In fact, land transfers, the heart of the reform program, did not get moving until the beginning of 1958 with the appointment of a new head of agrarian reform.

If land redistribution was an urgent issue in Vietnam, the government's response to it was not equal to the task. It should be noted at the outset that the land transfer program was limited to certain types of land. Against the advice of American technicians, the government decided to exempt non-rice land from the program,[36] thus excluding perhaps 235 million acres of land planted to other crops. In the case of rubber, at least, the exclusion seems to have been economically wise, given the efficiency of the large French-run rubber plantations. A serious weakness in the government's program was the exemptions it applied to rice holdings. For instance, the 284-acre maximum retainable by individual owners left only about 20 per cent of the total cultivated rice area, or about 1.2 million acres, eligible for transfer.[37] Setting the owner's maximum at 124 acres would have increased transferable land by about 625 thousand acres, bringing the affected portion to about one-third of total cultivated area.[38] The smaller maximum would have been economically feasible since large farms are not needed for efficient rice production in an underdeveloped country with a labor surplus like Vietnam, and since landowning Vietnamese have contributed precious little to the efficient operation of the lands they rented to tenants. The lower maximum certainly offered political advantages, given the land hunger of the Vietnamese peasantry.

The land transfer program was inadequate, too, in requiring the peasants to pay in full for the land they were to receive. Fair payment would have been a reasonable expectation under reasonable conditions, but conditions in war-torn Vietnam had not been reasonable. Landlords in much of South Vietnam had virtually ceased to exercise their proprietary rights against squatters and tenants during the Indochina War, and Communist agitation fed the peasants' belief

[35] Cited by Montgomery, *The Politics of Foreign Aid,* p. 126.

[36] David Wurfel, "Agrarian Reform in the Republic of Vietnam," *Far Eastern Survey,* 26 (June, 1957), 89.

[37] Gittinger, *Studies on Land Tenure in Vietnam,* pp. 5, 7. My evaluation of Vietnamese land reform is much less favorable than that of the author of this valuable study.

[38] See the table on rice land holdings, *ibid.,* p. 59.

that the land they occupied was theirs by right. The government did not follow a foreign adviser's recommendation that absentee owners not be permitted to keep any land,[39] and it made restitution for the 546 thousand acres of abandoned land which it took for redistribution. Finally, the number of people who lost and gained land under the program was not large. The amount of cultivated and abandoned land to be transferred was supposed to be 1.725 million acres, but President Diem reported in late 1962 that 1.062 million acres had actually changed hands. There were 1,584 landowners expropriated and 111 thousand benefiting peasant households, most of them tenants. In short, of an estimated 1 to 1.2 million tenant households existing in 1955, about 10 per cent obtained land under the government's land transfer program. Over 647 thousand acres of land marked for redistribution had been taken from French owners, for the expropriation of which the French government provided the money.[40]

For the great majority of Vietnam's farming population, the main benefits received through agrarian reform have been the government-supervised contracts which guarantee tenure for renewable three- to five-year periods and which limit rents to no more than 25 per cent of gross yield. Although some landlords have violated the tenure provisions, and although rents have run nearer one-third than the stipulated 25 per cent maximum, tenants have enjoyed greater protection against their landlords than in the peacetime past under these contracts. But the meaningful past for many tenants, as for the recipients of land, is the pre-1954 wartime period, during which they enjoyed great freedom from landowner influence, though not, of course, from that of the Viet Minh tax collectors. Also, peasants have not been able to understand why they have to sign tenancy contracts for unoccupied land which they assumed the Diem government was giving them. At the large Cai San development in southwestern Vietnam, for example, there was so much resistance to tenancy contracts by the 43,000 resettled refugees that the government cut off daily subsistence payments in order to bring the refugees around.

That peasant dissatisfaction with land reform has been a breeding ground for the growth of Communist power in independent Vietnam would seem indisputable. The Communists began in 1959 to interfere seriously with the government's agrarian reform programs and have, in the broad areas under their influence, replaced them with pro-

[39] Wurfel, *Far Eastern Survey*, p. 89.
[40] Compare Gittinger, *Studies on Land Tenure in Vietnam*, pp. 2, 5–7, with Republic of Vietnam, Directorate General of Information, *Message of the President of the Republic to the National Assembly, October 1, 1962* (Saigon, n.d.), p. 22.

grams of their own. As a Communist document, which analyzes the situation in one delta village, correctly observes: "The main interest of the farmer in 'XB' village is in land." It is, of course, the policy of the Communist guerrilla movement in Vietnam to satisfy that interest. But the guerrillas themselves appear to have taken a cautious approach to land reform, from a desire not to alienate the better-off peasants. So long as the latter do not side with the Vietnamese government the landowners among them are permitted to collect their rents, though at reduced rates; local cadres are enjoined from taking land from middle-level peasants for redistribution; and even the redistribution of uncultivated and communal land requires the approval of provincial committees of the guerrilla movement.[41]

As we have noted, American economic aid has been indispensable to the survival of Vietnam. We turn now to examine the impact of this aid on economic growth. The most important and controversial part of American aid has been the 80 per cent which entered Vietnam through the commercial import program. This program serves to increase the country's available resources beyond what domestic production and regular imports can provide. About two-thirds of the commercial imports under American aid in 1955 consisted of consumer goods, a reflection of the strong relief function which the program served. Some obvious luxury items, like water skis and hi-fi sets, were eliminated early from the list of goods eligible for importation, and many other consumer goods were dropped between 1957 and 1961. In 1960 consumer goods constituted only a third of the total American-aided imports, the rest consisting of industrial equipment and machinery (one-half) and raw materials, fuels, and what the American aid mission calls "other essentials."[42]

These figures are to some extent misleading. For one thing, the non-consumer categories appear to contain some quasi-consumer items; the largest import item in value in the industrial category in 1960, for example, was transportation vehicles (apparently not for personal use). More important, the decline in American-supported imports has meant neither a commensurate belt-tightening nor domestic satisfaction of consumer wants. The Vietnamese government has financed many consumer goods dropped from the American program, and the overall composition of the country's imports does not ap-

[41] This information is taken from what appears to be a high-level Communist document issued about August 1962.

[42] Compare the raw figures, from which these computations have been made, in U.S. Operations Mission to Vietnam, *Annual Report for the 1958 Fiscal Year* (Saigon, n.d.), pp. 54–55, and *ibid., Annual Report for Fiscal Year 1961,* p. 69.

pear to have changed significantly since 1957. The government's ability to finance the importation of these consumer items has, of course, been made possible only by American aid which provided the foreign exchange for the great bulk of imports. Finally, the decrease in United States-financed consumer imports has not been accompanied by an increase in imports related to capital growth, for these likewise declined between 1957 and 1960. The import of industrial machinery fell off by 38 per cent and that of raw materials by 20 per cent within this period.

Thus, the commercial import program has not served to induce substantial economic development in Vietnam. The reason in part is that there simply has not been enough industrial demand to absorb most of the money allocated to the program, and in part it is because the availability since 1954 of a large variety of Western-made products at low cost has tended to dampen the enthusiasm of potential local competition. Further, wealth which could have been put to productive use has been drained off in conspicuous consumption. And neither the Vietnamese nor the American government has made effective use of the program. Both governments — especially the Vietnamese — have looked upon it as a relief program, and the Vietnamese government has impeded the industrial opportunities the program offered by its treatment of private enterprise. The American government also has hampered industrial development. Not only was special permission from Washington necessary for several years for capital imports costing more than $500,000, but capital equipment could be imported only for enterprises entirely in private hands. Throughout the Eisenhower administration it was American policy to remonstrate against, if not block, industrial development in which the Vietnamese government was a participant.

If Vietnam's needs for economic growth were far less than what the commercial aid program could furnish, why was the program not reduced accordingly? The use of commercial aid as relief (or, to put it more broadly, a deterrent for political discontent) is one reason. A second is that the United States has, through several programs, made Vietnam a willing receptacle for surplus American agricultural products. An estimated $111.7 million dollars in agricultural goods was provided Vietnam *outside* of the regular commercial import program to mid-1962.[43] Nearly 7 per cent of all American economic assistance has been channeled to Vietnam through these separate but generally related programs.

It makes economic sense to include some consumer goods in Viet-

---

[43] USOM, *Annual Statistical Bulletin, 1961,* p. 120, Table H-1A.

namese imports, if domestic resources are thereby released to engage in basic economic development. The American aid program has, however, far exceeded an appropriate level of consumer goods. The pouring of consumables into Vietnam has had unfortunate political consequences, in addition to those of an economic kind. Although most Vietnamese have benefited from American consumer imports, the greatest beneficiaries have been the urban dwellers, especially the small middle and upper classes. Thus, American aid has functioned to accentuate the distinction between the well-off and the masses. It has also led the Vietnamese government to depend on a foreign power instead of its people for its own support. With less aid, the government would probably have been more responsive to the demands of its people, and quite likely would have engaged in badly needed administrative reforms in its assessment and collection of taxes.

The basic reason for heavy commercial aid imports was not the desire to provide relief or to dump American surpluses, let alone to promote economic growth. The commercial import program is a device for enabling the Vietnamese government to support a high level of public expenditure without causing disastrous inflation. Since Vietnam's resources are too limited to support these expenditures, American aid has filled the breach by pumping additional resources into the country. The United States maintains some control over the outlay of these resources by requiring that piasters paid by importers for commercial aid transactions be spent only for purposes agreed upon by both governments. Thus, in general terms, the level of the American commitment to Vietnamese public expenditures determines the level of economic aid which the United States provides Vietnam through the commercial import and related programs. And the heart of the American commitment is support of Vietnam's armed forces: about 80 per cent of all import-generated piasters have been used to pay and otherwise maintain the army and other military personnel. In short, American and Vietnamese military objectives have controlled the commercial import program, taking precedence over economic considerations.[44] The upward limit of commercial aid is determined by the capacity of the Vietnamese to absorb its bounty. They seem to have reached this limit about mid-1962, due to the decreased movement of goods out of the cities and to the higher price of goods caused by new

[44] Given the mixed consequences of the commercial import program, it is hard to understand how a responsible American official, in this case the director of the economic aid mission in Saigon, could call it "the greatest invention since the wheel." See the testimony of Arthur Z. Gardiner, Senate Committee on Foreign Relations, *Situation in Vietnam, Hearings, July 30 and 31, 1959*, p. 203.

taxes and the "Buy American" policy instituted in full force earlier that year. As a result, the Republic of Vietnam was for the first time in its short history faced with a budget deficit.[45]

American aid to Vietnam in the past has, to use Senator J. W. Fulbright's words, "been too heavily weighted on the military side."[46] Not only has the lion's share been used to support Vietnam's military budget, but most of the rest has gone for projects closely related to military security, like highway construction. The present crisis offers both hope and discouragement for economic and social development. The hope lies in the Vietnamese government's belated realization that effective counter-insurgency must include concrete social and economic benefits to village Vietnam, and a program is now in progress to do this in areas being cleared of Communist control. The discouragement is connected to the hope, for in order to devote economic project aid to activities which will help win the war, the United States economic aid mission in Vietnam has had to curtail or space out long-term projects for economic growth.

If it is to function more effectively in the future, the United States Operations Mission to Vietnam (USOM), which dispenses this country's economic aid, must surmount some of its serious weaknesses of the past. One of these has been an aimlessness of purpose. As a Congressional committee noted a few years ago, the economic aid mission "lacks a clear-cut plan with specific integrated goals, whereas," it added, "such goals do exist in the military program."[47] Like the Vietnamese government, USOM has lacked any real economic plan, and at the same time it has not encouraged planless capital formation on a scale large enough to achieve substantial results. Indeed, the mission did not have a professional economist on its staff from 1954 through 1961, though it has in the past intermittently drawn upon the services of trained economists attached to the Michigan State University government-contract group in Saigon. Many aid projects have been developed in a hit-or-miss fashion, with little thought given to their coordination with other projects or to their relation to overall goals. The mission has also lacked initiative in much of its activity, though there have been instances of bold and creative action, most notably in American support of the program of refugee resettlement. Many projects have dragged along slowly, and in certain ones there has been what the Congressional committee just quoted has termed

[45] See the *New York Times,* June 20, 1962, p. 6.

[46] *Congressional Record,* Senate, 87th Cong., 1st Sess., June 29, 1961, p. 11704.

[47] Senate Committee on Foreign Relations, *United States Aid Program in Vietnam, Report,* p. 8.

"extraordinary administrative delays and hesitancies."[48] The aid mission has been staffed with some very capable persons, including its director between 1954 and 1958; many more have been mediocre or worse.

Many of USOM's problems can be traced to Washington. The main foreign aid agency of the federal government, of which USOM is a field service, is the Agency for International Development (AID), known prior to 1961 as the International Cooperation Administration and before that by still different names. The Washington agency has since 1954 been much more concerned with bookkeeping than with program goals. It has insisted that the smallest details be cleared with it, and clearances, in which controllers have had an immoderate influence, have taken eight months and sometimes much longer. It has burdened Saigon technicians with a plethora of report-writing, record-keeping, filling in of forms, and other written communications, to the extent that much of their time has had to be spent in their offices. It has been very slow in its recruitment of personnel needed in the field, and it has, because of its reputation and its red tape, found it difficult to attract good people to overseas service.

The Kennedy Administration has, not unlike its predecessors, attempted to streamline its Washington aid operations and give more authority to those concerned with programs and less to the accountants. The results thus far appear encouraging, but one may wonder how well the Administration will succeed. For behind the foreign aid administration stands Congress, and within Congress a great suspicion of foreign aid. The caution, the slowness, the rigidity, and the ponderous red tape connected with foreign aid operations are due in great part to administrative fear of Congress and the absence of important domestic support for foreign aid; from this there is a resultant compulsion among foreign aid officials to protect themselves against the recurring attacks mounted from the Capitol. Until foreign aid becomes an accepted part of the American government's activities, many of the inadequacies found in American aid programs in Vietnam and elsewhere are bound to continue.

Summary

Generous infusions of American aid enabled the South Vietnamese government to cushion the economic effects which attended the ending of the Indochina War and the partition of Vietnam. Economic aid served well as a relief to economic stress and urban discontent. It

[48] *Ibid.,* p. 30.

also offered the means whereby the Vietnamese could rehabilitate their war-damaged infrastructure and engage their resources in economic growth. A fair measure of success was had in putting the country back in shape, though greater energy was applied to programs related to military security than to programs of more direct economic and social benefit to Vietnam's rural inhabitants. The Vietnamese government's economic and social achievements in some areas, like refugee resettlement, land development, road construction, and rice production, tended to obscure the general inadequacy of development achieved before 1961. The conspicuously good living enjoyed by many of Saigon's residents, thanks to American aid, further obscured Vietnam's serious economic problems.

Economic and social development has been carried on in the context of strong government involvement, indispensable American financial support, and a pervasive concern with security. The Vietnamese government has been more of a drag than a stimulus to economic development, and where its involvement has been necessary as, for example, in land reform, it has acted cautiously and, matched against Vietnam's needs, inadequately. American aid has both assisted development and placed difficulties in its way. The uncontrolled effects of the American commercial import program and the lack of imaginative thinking or systematic planning in its economic aid agencies are two illustrations. But much of the problem of economic development has been imposed on both American and Vietnamese authorities by the Communist threat. Even before the renewal of hostilities, about 1959, the concern for security impelled both governments to direct much of their resources to non-economic purposes. Since 1960, practically all economic and social advances have come to a standstill or have regressed. The Vietnamese government is today concerned above all else with political and military survival, and it is more than ever dependent on foreign aid as a substitute for domestic economic resources.

6

North Versus South

Geneva: The Unstable Peace

In 1946, the Democratic Republic of Vietnam, dominated by the Viet Minh and recognized by France, was in control of all territory north of the sixteenth parallel. The French occupied the southern half of the country and, with the agreement of the Viet Minh authorities, were permitted to maintain troops for a limited period in the North. The two parties had reached a *modus vivendi:* the Democratic Republic of Vietnam would associate itself with France through the French Union, in a manner which was left vague and which was to be the cause of sharp dispute, and a referendum would be held in the French-controlled areas to determine whether the people living there wished to accept the extension of Viet Minh authority over the entire country. There was no doubt that the rest of Vietnam would choose unification under a national government. The sudden outbreak of hostilities in Hanoi in December, 1946, which followed upon increasing tension between the two parties to the agreement, shattered hopes for a peaceful settlement in Vietnam, and it was not until eight years later that prospects for a settlement appeared again. On July 21, 1954, at Geneva, Switzerland, peace was once more restored after 400,000 people had been killed in a fruitless effort on the part of the French to "pacify" Vietnam. The conditions of peace, oddly, were similar to those which obtained in 1946: Vietnam was again partitioned, this time approximately at the seventeenth parallel, with French and Viet Minh forces withdrawing to their respective zones, and it was agreed that the country would be unified under a single authority in nationwide elections to be held in July, 1956.[1]

Thus, the two zones created by the Geneva Agreements were intended to be temporary. The opposing forces were given 300 days in

[1] For documents and discussion relating to the Geneva Agreements, see United States, Department of State, *American Foreign Policy, 1950–1955;*

which to regroup, and free movement between zones was promised to all inhabitants of the country; both sides agreed to refrain from reprisals against persons because of their activities during the fighting. In order to maintain the existing balance, no foreign or additional bases were to be established in either zone, nor would either zone associate itself with a military alliance or reinforce its military position, though the replacement of materiel was permitted. Supervision of the armistice was entrusted to an International Control Commission made up of representatives from India, Canada, and Poland, with the Indian member of the Commission acting as chairman. The Commission was also to supervise the reunification elections. Finally, it was specified that consultations for the elections would begin about July 20, 1955. The Agreements also required Viet Minh evacuation of Cambodia, which had not been the scene of much activity, and of Laos, which had been subjected to fairly heavy Viet Minh infiltration, but the pro-Communist Pathet Lao forces in Laos were permitted to assemble in the northeastern provinces of Sam Neua and Phong Saly pending integration with the central government.

Neither the United States nor the Bao Dai government (under the premiership of Ngo Dinh Diem) would join in the final declaration that gave approval to the various agreements reached at Geneva.[2] The United States did not wish to be associated with any settlement which consigned territory to Communist rule, and its ambassador at Geneva, Walter Bedell Smith, was authorized only to declare that his country took note of the agreements and would not use force to disturb them. The foreign minister for the Diem regime, Tran Van Do, had been no more than an observer at the Conference — the Vietnam settlement had been signed by the French and Viet Minh representatives only, and he protested against the decision to partition Vietnam; the non-Communist government had wanted a simple cease-fire with the opposing forces maintaining their existing positions. Other participants — France, Great Britain, Russia, Communist China, Cambodia, and Laos — were clearly satisfied with the results. Cambodia and Laos had achieved peace with the Viet Minh and independence from France. France had achieved surcease from a war which, even with the United States paying most of the military bill, had strained her

---

Basic Documents, vol. I (Washington, July, 1957); Jean Lacouture and Philippe Devillers, *La fin d'une guerre: Indochine 1954* (Paris: Éditions du Seuil, 1960), pp. 275–96; and Donald Lancaster, *The Emancipation of French Indochina* (London: Oxford University Press, 1961), pp. 332–37.

[2] There were three separate agreements providing for the cessation of hostilities in Vietnam, Cambodia, and Laos, and a final Conference declaration on the restoration of peace in all three countries.

resources and, more importantly, her military manpower; it was a war which had little meaning for the French people and little prospect of success. Great Britain, Russia, and China apparently feared that the United States would enter the conflict directly, wished to avoid this, and consequently bent their efforts to obtain a workable compromise between the immediate contestants. Anthony Eden, the British representative at Geneva, has reported that his Soviet counterpart, Molotov, "often came forward with some helpful suggestion or concession which enabled the work of the Conference to move forward," and that even Chou En-lai lent his persuasion to get the Viet Minh to agree to withdraw from Cambodia and Laos.[3] As for the Viet Minh, although they had obtained only half of what they had sought through the test of arms, they evidently believed the rest of the country would be theirs in the election which the Conference stipulated.

France has been criticized for its concessions at Geneva, particularly by the South Vietnamese government. What is surprising after an examination of the relative strength of the French and Viet Minh forces is that the French came off so well. The French position in North and Central Vietnam was extremely precarious. Not only had France suffered a crushing military and psychological defeat at Dien Bien Phu in May, 1954, while the negotiations were in progress, but the Viet Minh had followed this victory with another major success in late June at An Khe in Central Vietnam which opened that whole region to their control. There were, in fact, doubts that France would be able to maintain the Hanoi-Haiphong perimeter in the Red River delta, and Viet Minh guerrilla activity in the Mekong delta, which had not been the scene of major fighting, was sharply on the increase. Continuation of the war depended upon intervention by France's allies, particularly the United States, but American authorities in the spring of 1954 were unwilling to enter the war without at least British support, and the British in turn were unwilling to take any action while the Geneva negotiations were still pending. The most important gain won by the French was the line of demarcation. The Viet Minh had originally demanded that it be drawn at the thirteenth parallel while the French insisted on the eighteenth parallel; the French not only gained 80 per cent of their objective, but did so with a considerably weaker claim to having control of the intervening area. Also, the Viet Minh negotiators had wanted the reunification elections held within a maximum of six months and the evacuation of forces within three months. It should be noted too that the Southern government benefited from the provi-

[3] Anthony Eden, *Memoirs; Full Circle* (Boston: Houghton Mifflin, 1960), pp. 136, 145.

sion which permitted the replacement of war materiel, while prohibiting any reinforcements, for there was a great abundance of armaments on the French side but a scarcity on the Viet Minh side.[4]

Without notable incident, French and Viet Minh forces disengaged, transferred political prisoners, and moved to the provisional assembly areas assigned them as the first step toward total withdrawal from the zones allotted to the other side. The French assembly area embraced the Hanoi-Haiduong-Haiphong region, and most of the Northerners who chose to go south did so by passing into this small French-controlled zone. Hanoi was handed over to Viet Minh in early October, 1954, to become once again the seat of the Viet Minh Democratic Republic of Vietnam, and the last French forces departed from Haiphong in mid-May, 1955. The Viet Minh, who were assigned four assembly areas in the South — in Quang Ngai and Binh Dinh provinces in Central Vietnam, the Camau Peninsula, the Plain of Reeds, and the Xuyen Moc area east of Saigon — likewise withdrew their forces within the prescribed 300 days. With the completion of the regrouping operation, the movement of refugees between the two zones also, for all practical purposes, came to an end. It is not known with any precision how many people chose to live in the Communist zone, but their number was counter-balanced by the huge flood of about 900,000 refugees who went South during the period of free movement between zones.[5] This flood was more remarkable in view of the many obstacles the Northern authorities placed in the way of those who wished to leave the Communist zone. It was a great human and propaganda victory for the South, even if one accepts the charge that religious and other influences were employed and acknowledges that about 85 per cent of the refugees were Catholics, many of whom moved en masse under the leadership of village priests.[6]

A much more serious conflict in North-South relations emerged when the time came for opening consultations on elections to reunify the country. The Viet Minh had set heavy store by these elections and, on June 6, 1955, warned the South, "Whoever tries to partition

[4] See Lacouture and Devillers, *La fin d'une guerre,* pp. 283–86.

[5] Bui Van Luong, who was responsible for the Southern government's refugee program, has put the number of North-bound refugees at 4,358, while Bernard B. Fall says "it is generally estimated that about 120,000 Viet Minh troops and dependents chose to go North. . . . " (Richard W. Lindholm [ed.], *Vietnam: The First Five Years* [East Lansing: Michigan State University Press, 1959], pp. 50, 57.) The discrepancy between the two figures may be due in part to Fall's inclusion of military forces.

[6] The broad claim by a French observer in Hanoi that the refugee evacuation was "more or less forced" would seem to lack substantiation. See Gérard Tongas, *J'ai vécu dans l'enfer communiste au Nord Viet-Nam* (Paris: Nouvelles Éditions Debresse, 1960), pp. 15–29.

Vietnam is the enemy of the Vietnamese people and will surely be defeated."[7] The Ngo Dinh Diem government, with American support, refused to discuss reunification with the Northern authorities. In a statement rejecting a formal Communist request for a pre-election consultative conference, the Southern authorities observed that they had not signed and therefore were not bound by the Geneva Agreements and, further, that the conditions for free elections must first be evidenced in the North.[8] Inasmuch as the conditions which the Southern government sought were tantamount to a dismantling of the Communist regime, it was clear that the elections would not take place. It seemed equally clear that the South feared the outcome of any elections. Even if the International Control Commission were able to maintain strict supervision over the voting, the North possessed certain decisive advantages. Its population outnumbered the South's by nearly two million; its leaders were much better known in both the North and the South than Ngo Dinh Diem and his entourage, with Ho Chi Minh and Vo Nguyen Giap enjoying the status of national heroes for their leadership of the fight against the French; and its efficient dictatorship in the North and underground apparatus throughout the South was better able to influence the election results than the new, inexperienced administration of Ngo Dinh Diem.

The first and second anniversaries of the Geneva Agreements passed without any stronger reactions from the North than demonstrations against the Ngo Dinh Diem government for having reneged on reunification. But the North was not prepared to give up the goal of eight years of war so easily. The only alternative to peaceful reunification was reunification by force, and the Ho Chi Minh government possessed the means of employing it effectively. In the first place, its influence in the South was great. According to French reports, the Viet Minh at the end of February, 1955, prior to their withdrawal to the North, were masters of 60 to 90 per cent of the villages in the South, except for those areas under the control of the sects.[9] Joseph Alsop was surprised to find, in a trip to a Viet Minh-controlled region in the Mekong delta about this same time, that the people were happy, the country prosperous, and support for the Viet Minh strong. "I could hardly imagine," he reported, "a Communist government that was also a popular government and almost a democratic government."[10]

[7] Allan B. Cole and others (eds.), *Conflict in Indochina and International Repercussions, 1945–1955* (Ithaca: Cornell University Press, 1956), p. 209.

[8] *Ibid.*, pp. 227–28.

[9] Cited by Ellen J. Hammer, *The Struggle for Indochina Continues* (Stanford: Stanford University Press, 1955), p. 36.

[10] "A Reporter at Large," *New Yorker*, June 25, 1955, p. 48.

In the second place, the Viet Minh withdrawal from the South left behind a network of agents which extended into the army and government administration, and many hundreds of arms caches — Republic of Vietnam forces uncovered 307 of them between 1955 and early 1960.[11] Finally, practically all of the Viet Minh guerrilla troops who were evacuated to North Vietnam in the spring of 1955 were natives of the South who could easily infiltrate back to their local areas where they would have the protection of their families and friends.

The Renewal of Hostilities

It is difficult to pinpoint the time when the campaign to overthrow the Republic of Vietnam was launched, for Communist revolutionary warfare blends an accumulating number of small actions, political as well as military, into a heightened tempo of military combat. The writings on this subject by Vo Nguyen Giap, the military leader of the fight against the French and at present Minister of Defense in the Communist government, show a heavy dependence on Mao Tse-tung's teachings of the 1930s.[12] Writing about the war in Indochina, Giap saw an unresolvable difficulty besetting the French forces: if the French army concentrated its manpower in a limited number of locations, it was compelled to sacrifice unprotected areas to the Viet Minh; if it scattered its troops in order to prevent the loss of territory, it could mount no major attacks and opened itself to piecemeal annihilation by locally superior Viet Minh forces. Revolutionary war to Giap, echoing Mao, is a people's war; it is the duty of the party to educate, mobilize, organize, and arm the population, which, considering the social composition of Vietnam, means the rural masses. The organized peasantry will be directed by the party organization, and Giap makes the interesting revelation that between 35 and 40 per cent of the post-1954 army, including over 90 per cent of the officers, have been members of the ruling Workers Party.[13]

[11] *Times of Vietnam,* February 10, 1960, p. 1.

[12] Mao Tse-tung's principal writings on guerrilla warfare can be found in his *Selected Works* (New York: International Publishers, 1954). See especially Vol. II, 1937–1938, "Six Specific Strategic Problems of the Anti-Japanese Guerrilla War," pp. 119–56, and "On the Protracted War," pp. 157–243. The textual discussion of Giap's ideas is based on the collection of his materials which appeared as *People's War, People's Army* (Hanoi: Foreign Languages Publishing House, 1961). See also the analysis of Viet Minh doctrine, organization, and tactics by George K. Tanham, *Communist Revolutionary Warfare; the Viet Minh in Indochina* (New York: Praeger, 1961).

[13] *People's War, People's Army,* p. 56.

Revolutionary warfare is governed by an orderly "law" of development, the revolutionary forces passing from a defensive phase to an equilibrium and finally to an offensive phase. In the first phase, political action takes precedence over military; in the second, the two forms of action hold equal rank; and, in the third, the armed struggle occupies the chief position.[14] Giap appears to be saying that while revolutionary warfare must start with popular support, military might is the controlling factor in achieving victory. The same pattern can be seen in the progress of military activities. The first phase is characterized by guerrilla warfare, small-scale actions by local, often ill-equipped part-time fighters, the object of which is not to defend or gain territory but to cut down the enemy's strength. In Giap's words, "The enemy is avoided when he is the stronger and he is attacked when he is the weaker, now scattering, now regrouping one's forces, now wearing out, now exterminating the enemy, determined to fight him everywhere, so that wherever the enemy goes he will be submerged in a sea of armed people. . . ."[15] But in order to annihilate large enemy forces and to control territory, indeed, in order to maintain itself, guerrilla warfare must lead to mobile warfare. Mobile warfare emerges with the disposal of relatively large forces on a large field of action. It has gained most of its manpower from the rudimentarily trained guerrilla-peasant units and the intermediate regional troops; these, with better training and equipment, now become regular soldiers. Conventional principles of war increasingly characterize military operations, though emphasis continues to be placed rather on annihilating the enemy than on holding territory. During the equilibrium phase between revolutionary and enemy armies, mobile warfare shares an approximately equal importance with guerrilla warfare. Guerrilla troops lend support to large-scale military attacks by providing intelligence on enemy movements and by harassing communications and movements, and regional troops are frequently called upon to participate with the regular troops. As combat moves into its final phase, mobile warfare assumes precedence over guerrilla activity and, while retaining its rapidity of movement against exposed enemy positions, begins to present a new face: entrenched camp or positional warfare. The one example which Giap gives of entrenched camp warfare is the battle of Dien Bien Phu, in which Viet Minh troops laid siege to the French fortress for two months before finally subduing its defenders.

Although Giap speaks of "laws" of revolutionary warfare, he clearly does not regard them as rigid prescriptions. For instance, after he

[14] Vo Nguyen Giap, *Nhan Dan* (Hanoi), September 21, 1961.
[15] *People's War, People's Army,* p. 103.

states the "general law" of three stages through which such a war must go, he adds, referring to the Indochina War, "Of course, the reality on the battlefields unfolded in a more lively and more complicated manner."[16] What is essential does not appear to be the division of revolutionary war into three stages, but the general principles of combat and the rising tempo of activity. Revolutionary action must have a popular base, but be directed by the party; the enemy must be attacked relentlessly and everywhere, but not recklessly; political objectives must guide the struggle and be used to rally the population, but political activities will be superseded by military activities as the struggle progresses; the movement from small-scale harassment to continually greater attacks must occur if guerrilla activity itself is to survive, though no quick conclusion will be expected; and, influencing all else, final victory is certain, for the cause is both historically determined and morally just.

The Communist decision to overthrow the Ngo Dinh Diem regime probably was implemented in the spring of 1956, about the time of the March elections of the Constituent Assembly. There had been more or less of a lull in Communist activities during the preceding year, after the departure of the main body of Communist forces from Southern territory under the provisions of the Geneva cease-fire. Also, a number of persons who had worked with the Viet Minh rallied to the nationalist side in 1954 and 1955. The refusal of the Ngo Dinh Diem government to consent to reunification elections was a setback to Northern hopes of gaining the South by peaceful means, and the calling of a Constituent Assembly made it unmistakably clear that the Southern authorities intended to perpetuate the division of Vietnam indefinitely. The Communist response was to reactivate and strengthen its underground apparatus in the South, which included military units left behind in several remote areas, to increase the infiltration of its agents across and around the seventeenth parallel, and to embark upon a program to detach the rural population from the government administration. Propaganda activities constituted the thrust of this program until early 1959, and the main focus of Communist efforts was in the Mekong delta, particularly in areas such as Kien Hoa province, the Camau Peninsula, and the southwest coastal strip extending to the Cambodian border, where their influence had been strong during the Indochina War, though their agents were also active in the Tay Ninh area northwest of Saigon.

The theme of their propaganda during this period, and since, has been the American-supported republican regime of South Vietnam

[16] *Ibid.,* p. 101.

and the question of reunification. An illustrative appeal is the one contained in a circular distributed to government personnel in Ba Xuyen province, probably in early December, 1958: "Support the just struggle of the people to overthrow the government of the Americans and Diem, to establish a democratic regime in the South, and to work for general elections which will reunify the country by peaceful means." Around this theme Communist agents embroidered a variety of specific issues to appeal to real or fancied grievances of the people. The most emphasized and effective issue was that of land: preventing landowners who had fled to the cities during the Indochina fighting from recovering their rural property or collecting rents. Other issues have been political arrests, corruption on the part of officials, military conscription, and unfair taxation. As their network became more solidly established in the hamlets and villages of the South, propaganda spilled over more and more into action. Anti-government meetings, threats, kidnappings, tax collections, interference with government programs, and other activities increased in a steady rhythm. The main government forces assigned to deal with this growing threat were the Self-Defense Corps, organized on a village basis with locally recruited personnel, and the Civil Guard, a paramilitary force under the control of the province chiefs. The army was but rarely employed against the small Communist units, and the latter were careful to avoid contact with regular military units. Skirmishes with Self-Defense and Civil Guard patrols were, however, fairly frequent, and by 1958 the government was losing about 40 military personnel a month, in addition to an equal number of civilian officials.

In February, 1959, the newspaper of the main government political party acknowledged that "the situation in the rural areas is rotten."[17] The Communists, it said, had set up cells in every village which were entrusted with collecting regular "taxes," as well as rice, and with conducting espionage. In isolated villages, according to this source, the guerrilla forces possessed administrative and military committees which ruled the populations through instructions received from regional and provincial organizations. A sharp turn for the worse was noticed in the security situation during the early months of 1959, as Communist control over villages increased, and the government found itself increasingly opposed in its efforts to carry out administrative and economic programs in rural areas. Landowners were reported to be abandoning rents due them on rice lands, sabotage of roads was increasing as part of the plan to isolate the villages from military and provincial control, and minute but accumulating engagements with

[17] *Cach Mang Quoc Gia*, February 23, 1959; see also *ibid.*, February 24, 1959.

Civil Guard and Self-Defense units were beginning to cause concern. During May alone, 21 tractors and a $245,000 canal dredge, all gifts of American aid to Vietnamese reconstruction programs, were sabotaged by explosives. While the Communists sometimes used their army units in attacks upon the government, they still relied mainly on individual terrorists and small groups, usually operating under the cover of night, and travel on most of the roads of Vietnam was considered safe, at least during daylight hours.

The political struggle continued to hold primary focus in Communist activities during 1959 and 1960, though military action gained steadily in importance as progressively larger armed units were formed and put into action. And while the Mekong delta still constituted the main arena of the struggle, subversive activities began to stir up the previously calm Central region of the country. The dominant political objective was still the control of rural areas, and the fight to isolate the government from the villages of the southern provinces grew in intensity. From their control of villages the Communists sought to isolate the district towns, which usually range between four and seven to a province. Methods included indoctrinating peasant inhabitants of the villages and involving them, wherever possible, in actions against the legal authorities, and assassinating or intimidating into silence those who remained loyal to the government. Village and hamlet officials, police and security officials, information officers, and other government agents were main targets of Communist terrorism. It was also necessary to cripple the operations of Civil Guard and Self-Defense forces, either by driving them from strongly infested areas or by keeping them holed up in district towns or fortified posts.

The control of the peasant population was essential to protect the increasingly extensive operations of the Communist guerrilla forces, and to furnish a fresh supply of recruits. It was also essential if food and funds were to be provided for these forces. So long as Communist activities depended upon guerrilla troops, supply was not a serious problem, for these were peasants-turned-soldiers at night or for special operations who could provide for their own needs. But the growth of regional and regular army forces, and a host of political cadres, administrative personnel, couriers, special agents, and so on, required regular and sizeable logistical support. To an extent, food could be supplied from abandoned land or land seized from landowners and cultivated by the Communists themselves, but for the most part food, money, and other supplies could come only from the peasantry. An additional purpose in controlling the countryside was to strangle the cities economically. Communist control of the rural areas was not sufficiently decisive to make its economic effects strongly felt until the beginning of 1961, though tax collections, agricultural loans, and other government activities began to suffer in late 1959.

Communist military operations during 1959 and 1960 were directed largely to compelling the government to thin out its military forces, to decimating these forces in piecemeal attacks, and to obtaining much-needed weapons in the process. Often small military posts, almost always manned by Civil Guard or Self-Defense units, were offered the alternative of peacefully surrendering their arms, which occasionally they did. Communist military objectives did not include the defense of territory, and their forces always dispersed before superior government firepower, only to return to "pacified" villages or bases after government troops withdrew. The Communists particularly avoided engagements with army troops unless conditions were extremely favorable, but concentrated instead on poorly equipped and trained Civil Guard and Self-Defense forces. In carrying out their campaign to separate the government from its peasant population, Communist military units and individual terrorists, by government count, killed about 1,400 local officials and civilians during 1960.[18] The highest official was the chief of Vinh Long province, who was ambushed along a lonely road in May, 1960.

There was a steady increase in 1960 in the size of Communist military forces operating in South Vietnam. To an extent, this was due to the deterioration of the situation in Laos after July, 1959, and to the control established by the Pathet Lao over the eastern corridor of Laos that extends from North Vienam to the highlands region of the South. The first important attack on the Vietnamese army itself took place on the evening of January 25, 1960, when Communist forces overran army regimental headquarters at Tay Ninh, carrying off large quantities of arms and leaving destruction in their wake. This was followed by a heightening of attacks in other parts of the delta, especially in the province of Kien Hoa, where six of the eight districts were cut off for several months from any ground communication with the chief provincial town, in the Camau area, and in the provinces adjacent to the Cambodian border. At the same time, increased activities were noted in the Center. In the highlands of Thua Thien province, the Communists had established during 1958 an organization extending down to the village level, and it appears that similar actions were being followed in other parts of the highlands. Also, the infiltration of agents and troops into the highlands, and into safety bases on the Laotian side of the frontier, increased in late 1959 and during 1960. One major mili-

---

[18] United States, Department of State, *A Threat to the Peace; North Vietnam's Effort to Conquer South Vietnam,* Far Eastern Series 110 (Washington, December, 1961), Part I, p. 13.

tary action took place, a two-pronged attack of nearly 1,000 Communist troops in the Kontum-Pleiku-An Khe area, which began on October 21, 1960, and in which the attackers overran several government posts before they had to withdraw under counterattack by regular army units. The government stated that the attack was part of an attempt to create a Communist base in the highlands, and it claimed that North Vietnamese army units were involved in the action.[19]

It appears that Communist leaders believed in early 1961 that their revolutionary movement had entered a new phase. "At present," a captured Communist document dated June 16, 1961, read, "we must consider the armed struggle on the same footing with the political struggle." Previously, this document noted, armed struggle had been used to support the political struggle, but the changed relationship between the Communist position and that of the government made this policy no longer appropriate. "Numerous areas have been liberated, the coercive mechanism in rural areas is disintegrating. We must develop our armed struggle in order to create conditions to destroy the enemy and to annihilate the last support of the U.S.-Diem regime." This Communist estimate of the changed situation was supported by authoritative reports in Saigon that the guerrillas were no longer waging war in small groups only and that attacks of company strength, and greater, were increasing rapidly.[20] The Communists had reason to be proud of the success they had achieved. As of the end of 1960, they either controlled or were contesting for control of at least one-half the territory of the country, including most of the southern area, and they had prepared the way for strong military efforts in the highlands and Central coastal strip. Their armed forces numbered about 10,000 despite heavy losses during the year (which a government source placed at 6,800), and they had killed, by government count, which is probably low, about 1,600 government military and security personnel.[21] An American source estimated that over 3,000 local government officials had been killed or kidnapped during 1960.[22]

There was a further large build-up in Communist military power in 1961. Estimates vary widely, due in part to the difficulty of determining the number of part-time guerrillas, village guards, and other irregulars, which was certainly in the thousands, but reliable information placed regular and regional troop strength at about 16,000 in October,

[19] *Vietnam Press,* week ending November 13, 1960, pp. 1–3.

[20] Reuter despatch from Saigon, May 31, 1961.

[21] Government figures for nationalist and Communist losses are given in Wesley R. Fishel, "Political Realities in Vietnam," *Asian Survey,* 1 (April, 1961), 17.

[22] *New York Times,* May 5, 1961, p. 10.

1961. Government and Communist losses were running between 700 and 1,200 a month each, and the Communists engaged more and more frequently in large-scale mobile operations, using as many as 1,000 men in a single combat. The most striking Communist military success was the seizure on September 18, of the capital of Phuoc Thanh province, located about 55 miles northeast of Saigon. Guerrilla forces quickly overran the defending forces in a surprise early morning attack, killed many of the government troops and officials, including the chief of the province, released a large number of military and political prisoners, and withdrew before relieving forces could be despatched, taking with them a large quantity of arms and ammunition. More ominous than this attack, however, was the development of Communist units of battalion size and greater in the highland regions of Central Vietnam. Savage attacks were made on government posts near the Laotian frontier in the Kontum area at the beginning of September and in Quang Nam province about the middle of that month. The highlands, once considered secure nationalist territory, now began to totter. The mountain tribesmen, according to a Vietnamese government document, had been won over to the insurgents by a combination of terror, political indoctrination, and promises of autonomy. Thus, in addition to the assistance which North Vietnam could send through the eastern corridor of Laos, Communist forces in Central Vietnam were now able to make use of mountain tribesmen for augmenting their forces, supplying porters, and raising food.

At the end of 1961 the Vietnamese government was clearly on the defensive. The Hanoi claim that the guerrillas had "liberated" 1,100 of 1,290 villages in the southern region and 4,000 of 4,400 hamlets in the highlands does not seem to be too much inflated.[23] From other sources, it appears that about 80 per cent of the Vietnamese countryside had come under Communist influence. In areas where influence was strong, the population in effect lived under Communist rule; government officials, where they continued to exist, confined their movements mainly to district and village centers, and Civil Guard and Self-Defense forces made little effort to patrol away from their posts. Where control was partial, officials either lived in fear of their lives or followed government orders by day and Communist orders by night. Unless confronted by sizeable army incursions, Communist military units were free to move as they wished within the areas under strong control. Even large government forces ran the risk of annihilation. Also well established was a group of large "base areas" where military units could be grouped, troops trained, weapons manufac-

[23] United States Foreign Broadcast Information Service (Saigon), *Press and Radio Highlights,* Supplement for September 25, 1961.

tured, administrative and military headquarters located, and food grown. Most of the bases were in areas adjacent to the Laotian or Cambodian borders, like those located in Quang Tri and Pleiku provinces and in the Plain of Reeds, embracing Kien Phong and Kien Tuong provinces, or else bordered on the sea, like the U Minh base in the western part of An Xuyen province in the far south. There were also reliable reports of Communist bases in eastern Laos and claims, hotly disputed by the Cambodian government, of extensive bases on Cambodian soil.[24]

The military erosion was halted about the beginning of 1962, and the situation has since then remained in tenuous balance. Communist capability has not weakened; indeed, Communist forces now number about 30,000 and are better trained, better armed, and better led than ever. There has also been a further increase in the size of Communist combat units. The change in the war was brought about by the rapid build-up of American military aid to the Republic of Vietnam and the rapid augmentation of the Republic's armed forces. Nationalist troops have taken the offensive against Communist-dominated areas throughout the country, with the major moves in the Mekong delta and the provinces running northwest and north of Saigon. The size of many government operations has been impressive. In broad sweeps carried out in the Camau and Tay Ninh areas in August and October, 1962, for example, between 4,000 and 5,000 troops, many of them transported by helicopters, participated against Communist strongholds, and in one air attack on a Communist headquarters and base area north of Kontum in March, 50 aircraft unleashed 100 tons of bombs against their targets. As a result of the stepped-up fighting, casualties on both sides averaged about 1,000 a week during most of the year.

The results of the Republic's operations have likewise been impressive. Large quantities of stores have been captured, and Communist guerrilla units have been thrown off balance, thereby decreasing their ability to conduct large-scale operations of their own. Also, the government made the claim in mid-1962 that it had reversed the ratio of losses of men and weapons in its favor, that more Communists were defecting to the government side, and that more intelligence was coming out of the villages.[25]

[24] A four-day inspection by a newspaper correspondent, at the invitation of Cambodian authorities, failed to uncover any evidence of Communist installations where the Vietnamese government claimed they existed. See the *New York Times,* November 22, 1961, pp. 1, 5.

[25] The *Washington Post,* July 12, 1962, p. 1, reported the casualty ratio as running 5 to 3 in the government's favor, and the *New York Times,*

The success of the government, however, has been limited. For one thing, the main body of Communist troops has been able to slip through the nets cast in the large-scale military sweeps. The October sweep through Tay Ninh province, for example, resulted in only 40 or 50 enemy killed and was described as "futile" by American advisers.[26] Moreover, the Communists have thus far had no trouble in making up their losses through local recruitment and infiltration from North Vietnam. Most important, these military activities have not been translated into political gains, and as government troops withdraw the Communists move back into the areas which have been swept. Thus, the countryside remains under Communist control, and, in fact, the spread of guerrilla influence has rendered the immediate environs of Saigon and other large cities unsafe for government authority. The seriousness of the government situation is starkly illustrated in an ambush in mid-June, 1962, in which guerrillas smashed a military convoy just south of the town of Ben Cat, about 40 miles north of Saigon. The shocking aspect of the episode is that two companies of Communist troops were able to lie in wait for three hours, deployed over a half-mile stretch of a well-traveled highway in broad daylight, without any inhabitants of the area warning the government of their presence.[27]

Only in the Central highlands has Communist control over the population been noticeably weakened. Starting in the summer of 1962, mass movements of highlands people, swelling to over 100,000 by the end of the year, abandoned their mountain and forest habitations for government-controlled areas. It is not certain how much coercion the government might have employed in this exodus, but it appears that many highlanders have become discontented with the heavy exactions that growing guerrilla forces have been imposing on them. In any event, the exodus constitutes an important break in the government's efforts to win back control of those who have fallen under Communist influence, and it has considerably strengthened the government's military position in the Central highlands.

A potentially greater success for the government lies in the clear-and-hold strategy which is replacing the large-scale sweep in military operations. The plan is to secure areas cleared of Communist forces

August 12, 1962, p. 28, raised this figure to 2 to 1. Radio Hanoi, on the other hand, reported that 15,000 government troops had been killed or captured, and an additional 8,000 had defected to the guerrilla side, during the first half of 1962. (United States, Foreign Broadcast Information Service, Daily Report, *Foreign Radio Broadcasts,* September 26, 1962.)

[26] *New York Times,* October 20, 1962, pp. 1, 3.

[27] *Ibid.,* June 18, 1962, p. 5.

by maintaining government troops in them and by fortifying the rural localities. The strategic hamlet program, as the building of rural forts is called, is discussed in the next chapter. Clear-and-hold operations were, at the time of this writing, in progress in Binh Duong province, about 50 miles north of Saigon, in the coastal area of Phu Yen province in Central Vietnam, and in Binh Dinh province, just north of Phu Yen. Much hangs on the success of these operations.

To sum up, the Communist pattern in South Vietnam has proceeded from small to ever-increasing political penetration of the countryside, and from isolated terrorism to ever-increasing guerrilla activities, developing into mobile warfare during 1961 and 1962. As political efforts achieved sufficient success and large areas of rural Vietnam fell under their influence, Communist forces were able to expand the scale of their military operations. Vietnam as a whole appears to be early in the second phase of Communist revolutionary warfare, though the government's build-up and offensives since 1962 have slowed down, if they have not reversed, the rhythmic movement of guerrilla war. An uncertain equilibrium exists between government and insurgent forces. The National Liberation Front has not yet succeeded in gaining such secure control over territory that it could establish "liberated zones." Moreover, the safety bases in the Central highlands are in largely uninhabited country, and those located in the Camau Peninsula and north of Saigon (the famous Maquis D base of the Viet Minh period) do not enclose much population. Mountains and forests provide natural protection for the highlands bases, thick forests do the same for the Maquis D base, and extensive swamps for the base in the Camau Peninsula. It should be observed that the guerrillas are contesting for much of the Vietnamese countryside, which they have already infected politically. Outside of the cities and district towns, over two-thirds of the Vietnamese people are under Communist influence. To put the matter somewhat differently and using the estimate of American officials in Saigon at the end of 1962, about one-half of the South Vietnamese support the National Liberation Front for different reasons, of whom perhaps 300,000 are active in their support.

This is the situation in which the Republic of Vietnam finds itself today.

International Dimensions of the Struggle

Not long ago, a high-level North Vietnamese official angrily remarked that the Northern regime had driven the French into the sea and that it would drive the Americans into the sea as well. This remark is at variance with the standard line of the Democratic Republic of Vietnam that the struggle in the South is an uprising of the people against their oppressive rulers, but it agrees with compelling evidence of Hanoi's involvement in the movement to overturn the Ngo Dinh Diem government.[28] The ruling Workers [*Lao Dong*] Party of North Vietnam controls the movement through a Special Committee for Supervision of the South. The South itself is organized into two interzones, one for South-Central Vietnam, sometimes called Interzone V, which includes the highlands and Central coastal region, and the other for the Nam Bo, or Southern, Interzone, which embraces the southern and southwestern provinces. The Special Committee for Supervision of the South directs the operations of the executive committees of these two interzones. Within each interzone are four interprovincial regions, each with its own executive committee and containing between three and nine provinces. Below this level the Workers Party organization parallels the administrative structure of the Republic of Vietnam, progressing from the provincial to the district, village, and hamlet levels. Military and intelligence operations are similarly directed from Hanoi, by the Armed Forces high command and the Central Research Agency. It is the Workers Party Central Committee, however, which supervises military, intelligence, and related activities, and also the vast political apparatus created within the South, down to the village or neighborhood cell. In fact, political cadres are assigned to all military units down to the platoon level.

The Workers Party organization in the South bases its policy on Marx, Engels, Lenin, Stalin, and Mao Tse-tung, and "Vietnam's revolutionary realities"; its objective is "a people's democratic regime, gradually moving to a socialist regime"; and it is organized on the Leninist principle of democratic centralism.[29] For the same reason that the Viet Minh movement was created during World War II, the Communists have now created a National Front for the Liberation of South Vietnam to attract broader support to their cause. The creation of the National Liberation Front was approved by the Third National Congress of the Workers Party, held at Hanoi in September, 1960, in a call for "a broad national united front directed against the U.S.-Diem

[28] The publication of the Department of State, *A Threat to the Peace,* contains impressive proof, based on documents provided by the South Vietnamese government, of Northern responsibility for guerrilla operations within the South. Unless otherwise indicated, the textual discussion of the organization of these operations is taken from this source.

[29] *Regulations of the Labor Party of Vietnam,* 1961. (Translated, Mimeographed.)

clique and based on the worker-peasant alliance."[30]   The Front made its appearance three months later.   Its program, while designed to appeal to all segments of the population, appears to be aimed especially at intellectual and other middle-class groups.   It calls for the overthrow of the Ngo Dinh Diem regime and its replacement by a national democratic coalition government which would include all political, religious, and nationality groups; the interests of all classes, "except for a few very reactionary elements," would be respected; and it would pursue a neutral foreign policy and establish normal relations with the North as a first step to peaceful reunification of the country.[31] There are separate organs within the Front for peasants, workers, students, intellectuals, women, and so forth, and the Workers Party constitutes but one element in it.   Despite its pretensions of broad representation, and although its secretary-general, Nguyen Van Hieu, calls himself a Radical Socialist,[32] it is clear that the National Liberation Front is controlled by the Workers Party.   Indeed, captured instructions intended for Party members make it clear that the Front is a temporary tactic and that the Workers Party will overtly lead the revolution once the Ngo Dinh Diem government has been overthrown. In December, 1961, a new group calling itself the Vietnamese People's Revolutionary Party made its appearance.   Based frankly on Marxist-Leninist principles and appealing specifically to the peasantry and urban workers, this party may be nothing more than the Workers Party behind a Southern disguise.   It is affiliated with the National Liberation Front, and its pronouncements do not differ from the line followed by the Front.

There were persistent rumors during 1961 and early 1962 that the immediate objective of the National Liberation Front was to establish itself as a provisional government in Communist-controlled territory north of Kontum in the Central Vietnamese highlands.   No attempt has thus far been made to do this.   In fact, the Front softened its avowed goal of overthrow in a declaration issued by its central committee on July 20, 1962 — the anniversary of the Geneva Agreements.   Although it once more called for the formation of a national coalition government, the withdrawal of American troops, and neutrality in foreign affairs, the Front said not a word about replacing Ngo Dinh Diem or

[30] Department of State, *A Threat to the Peace,* Part II, p. 2.

[31] See, for example, Luu Quy Ky, "Necessity to Overthrow the Extremely Reactionary State Machine of the U.S.-Diemists," *Hoc Tap* (Hanoi), Issue No. 7, July, 1961.

[32] Information about the composition of the Front was given by Hieu in a press conference during his visit to Moscow, reported in the *New York Times,* July 9, 1962, p. 2.

reunification; it asked simply that the "concerned parties" stop the war and that the proposed coalition government have a new National Assembly elected. This new gambit may have been inspired by the Laotian settlement; the Vietnamese government interpreted it to mean that the war was going badly for the National Liberation Front.

Only a small portion of the Communist military units and agents operating within the Republic of Vietnam has been sent from North Vietnam, and nearly all of these have been Southerners who withdrew to the North after the Geneva Agreements. It does appear that infiltration from the North has increased since 1960 as Communist forces sustained heavier losses and as their scale of activity increased. The long, unguarded coastline and Laotian and Cambodian frontiers make penetration of the South easy, and the extension of Pathet Lao control over the eastern corridor of Laos has opened a direct supply route between North Vietnam and the Central highlands of the South. Communist military personnel and supplies are known to have passed along this route since the Laotian cease-fire of May, 1961, and there have been reliable reports of guerrilla bases and training camps in Laos for the use of troops operating on the Vietnamese side of the border. It appears, however, that the main infusion of personnel from North Vietnam has consisted of political cadres and military officers, though in some instances entire military units of Northern-trained Southerners may have been sent in. The South Vietnamese government's claim of massive infiltration does not appear to be supported by the available evidence, and its charge in May, 1962, that 12,000 troops had entered South Vietnam over an 18-month period is almost certainly greatly exaggerated.[33] Similarly, most of the weapons and other supplies available to the Communist forces in the South have been obtained there by raids on military posts, hospitals, and the like, and by direct levies on the population, purchases made possible through the taxation of peasants, plantation owners, and businessmen, and by related tactics. Communist military units are frequently short of arms, medicines, and other supplies, and the objective of many of their military attacks has been the seizure of much-needed commodities. Many Communist weapons have been made in small jungle arsenals.

Russian and Chinese involvement in the Vietnamese hostilities has thus far been indirect. Premier Pham Van Dong and other high government officials visited various members of the Communist bloc between June and August, 1961. A major purpose of their visit may have been to obtain increased military aid for the North and political support for its guerrilla war in the South. While Communist-made arms, medical supplies, and other materiel have been found only in

[33] *Ibid.*, May 30, 1962, pp. 1, 4.

very small amounts in the South, it is quite possible that, as the North has rearmed with modern weapons, it has sent older materiel, of French and American manufacture, to the guerrilla forces. Both the Russians and the Chinese have warned the United States to halt its military support of the Republic of Vietnam. In late February, 1962, the Soviets stated that North Vietnam's appeal for international support against "U.S. aggression" would be heard, and the Chinese, in terms similar to their utterances prior to their entering the Korean War, said that United States military aid to the Diem government seriously affected their security and "could not be allowed to continue."[34] At the same time, the Soviet Union has apparently taken a more moderate position than China in this instance, just as it did in the Laotian fighting a year earlier. The Soviets — but not the Chinese — reportedly counseled Hanoi in February, 1962, against tactics that could embroil the major powers in a war over Vietnam.[35] Washington has evidently discounted the chances of direct Communist intervention in Vietnam,[36] but it remains to be seen what effect the Soviet-Chinese split will have on North Vietnam's guerrilla war strategy. The North Vietnamese have thus far straddled the fence. If, for example, they have attacked Yugoslav revisionism one month, they have the following month declared their support for a policy of peaceful co-existence.[37]

Thus far, it appears that North Vietnam and its allies, particularly the Soviet Union, do not want the renewed war in Vietnam to get out of hand. They seem to prefer a war acted out according to their rules: a guerrilla war, confined to the South, fought only by Vietnamese. Internationalization of the conflict would not only bring help to the forces of the South Vietnamese government, which needs direct assistance more than the insurgent army does, but would threaten to spread the war to North Vietnam itself, and perhaps further. In late 1961, the United States, in deciding to increase its military advisory mission and the kinds and quantity of its military aid, determined that it would no longer accept the Communist rules.

But the Communist side has not played strictly according to these rules, either. As we have seen, the war against the Ngo Dinh Diem regime was launched and has been directed from North Vietnam, though it has until now depended mainly upon Southern sources for recruitment and supplies. However, it is rather doubtful that the war could be carried to successful completion without a significant inter-

[34] *Ibid.,* February 25, 1962, p. 1, and February 28, 1962, pp. 1, 5.
[35] *Ibid.,* March 2, 1962, p. 6.
[36] *Ibid.,* February 26, 1962, p. 1.
[37] *Nhan Dan* (Hanoi), December 5, 1962; *Washington Post,* January 30, 1963, p. A 17.

vention on the part of the North. Guerrilla forces can wreak serious damage by their own efforts, but to mount a large offensive requires arms and supplies they don't have. Outside assistance was an important factor in the ability of the Viet Minh to step up their war against the French, as North Vietnamese sources, generally reticent about their dependence on the outside, have conceded. Vo Nguyen Giap, for example, acknowledges that the triumph of the Communist Chinese in 1949 exerted "a considerable influence" on the Indochina War, opening a "new phase" in which the Viet Minh were able to wrest from the French three provinces bordering on China, and paving the way for a series of offensive operations in the Red River delta.[38] The increase since late 1961 in the number of men and the quantity of supplies poured into South Vietnam through Laos testifies to the importance of external aid in the heightened struggle to overthrow the Republic of Vietnam.

The Communist bloc has reason to be concerned with the American build-up in South Vietnam. On May 4, 1961, Senator J. W. Fulbright announced, after a meeting with President Kennedy, that the Administration was considering military intervention in Vietnam.[39] The sending of American troops was one of the questions raised by Vice-President Lyndon Johnson in his visit to Saigon several days later, but this offer was rejected by President Diem on the grounds it would be contrary to the Geneva Agreements and would provide strong propaganda to the Communists. Instead, the Vietnamese government sought and obtained from Johnson a promise of increased aid to an enlarged Vietnamese army and the training and equipping of the Civil Guard and Self-Defense Corps. This decision did not settle the question of American military intervention, for in mid-October, just prior to the arrival in Saigon of the study mission headed by General Maxwell D. Taylor, Joseph Alsop reported that "quiet but serious consideration" was being given in Washington to sending a small force of American troops to Vietnam "in order to have a reserve locally available in case of intensified Communist aggression."[40] While General Taylor said on his arrival that he was not assuming that American troops would be sent to Vietnam as a result of his assessment of the situation there, he was later reported to have assured President Kennedy that victory could be won without committing "sizeable" American forces.[41]

Instead of entering the war directly, the United States backed into it.

[38] *People's War, People's Army*, p. 22.
[39] *New York Times*, May 5, 1961, p. 1.
[40] *Times of Vietnam*, October 13, 1961.
[41] *Vietnam Press* (English edition), October 18, 1961 (morning issue), p. H-9; *New York Times*, February 12, 1962, p. 3.

In November, 1961, its Military Assistance Advisory Group numbered about 685 personnel. As additional personnel were poured into the country, this agency was absorbed into a Military Assistance Command headed by a full general. The purpose of the new Command was to separate the operational part of American military activities from the aid and advisory activities, and also to provide the organizational framework for possible large-scale military intervention.[42] By spring of 1963 the American military contingent had swelled to about 12,000 officers and men. American "advisers" accompanied Vietnamese troops in anti-guerrilla patrols, American crews transported Vietnamese troops to the scenes of battle by helicopter, American fighter pilots participated in air strikes, American warships patrolled the waters below the seventeenth parallel, American military technicians handled communications equipment in combat operations.[43] It matters little that American military personnel were called advisers and trainers or that they were instructed to fire on the enemy only when fired upon. They were decidedly involved in combat activities and, when confronted by the enemy, could not be expected to allow him to shoot first. The reality of American involvement in the war was testified to by the 73 American military personnel killed in Vietnam between late 1961 and May, 1963. All that can be said about the military intervention of the United States in Vietnam is that it is not yet on a massive scale.

There are two ways in which the present war might be carried to North Vietnam. One is through invasion in force. This would require the commitment of large American land, sea, and air units and, while there appears to be some military sentiment in favor of this course, it is doubtful that it would be undertaken unless the North should engage in direct attack. The other way is by extending guerrilla warfare into North Vietnam. This has been attempted by the South, though its extent is hidden in official secrecy. As early as April, 1959, North Vietnamese authorities announced the sentencing of "U.S.-Diem" agents, and in October, 1961, Radio Hanoi claimed the South had recently intensified its efforts to send spies and Rangers into Northern territory. The North, it stated, had organized security groups in over 90 per cent of its villages in order to combat these activities.[44] There appears to be some justification for this concern. A Hanoi newspaper in early October, 1961, reported that a number of

[42] *New York Times,* February 9, 1962, pp. 1, 3, and February 11, 1962, p. 16.

[43] See, for example, *ibid.,* December 12, 1961, p. 21, December 13, 1961, p. 2, February 14, 1962, p. 6; and *Washington Post,* February 9, 1962, pp. A-1, A-5.

[44] Hanoi radio broadcast, October 29, 1961, reprinted in FBIS, *Press and Radio Highlights* (Saigon), October 30, 1961.

fires in factories, warehouses, and crowded localities were caused by enemy sabotage;[45] in July of the same year a South Vietnamese plane was shot down over Northern territory, and its occupants put on trial; and foreign sources in Hanoi have reported rumors of various acts of subversion and sabotage, including the destruction of a number of tanks and trucks destined for Laos, at Hoa Binh in early July.[46] The North acknowledges that penetrations of its frontier have occurred "on many occasions" and that the infiltrators have been able to link up with local agents and "other counter-revolutionaries" in carrying out their "wicked schemes."[47]

Although Southern subversion in the North has inconvenienced the Communist regime and has gained support from some elements of the population there,[48] it is not likely that it will achieve any serious effects. For one thing, the North has much better control over its population than the South has over its people. Also, the South lacks the ready organization and the years of groundwork which preceded the North's campaign on the territory of the Republic of Vietnam. Moreover, the Southern government lacks the ideological foundations and the organizational theory necessary to sustain a subversive movement of any dimensions. It is the Communist North, not the middle-class, conservative Southern regime, which is able to set loose subversives to live among the peasant population.

The International Control Commission

The International Commission for Supervision and Control in Vietnam has had the unenviable task of trying to keep the peace in the nation. It was not intended that the Commission should function beyond July, 1956, when unification elections were expected to end its supervision of the Geneva cease-fire arrangements. The Commission has continued to operate beyond the election deadline at the request of the co-chairmen of the Geneva Conference, Great Britain and the Soviet Union. The Commission was able to carry out its immediate functions following the cease-fire because both the French and Viet Minh wanted to bring an orderly end to hostilities, but it has since encountered continual and increasing frustration in attempting to fulfill its responsibilities. It faced numerous obstacles, especially from the Northern authorities, in its efforts to supervise the free

[45] *Nhan Dan* (Hanoi), October 6, 1961.
[46] This is based on confidential information.
[47] *Nhan Dan* (Hanoi), August 7, 1962.
[48] *Hoc Tap* (Hanoi), April, 1962.

movement of refugees between zones, and this phase of the armistice succeeded as well as it did only because French forces continued until the spring of 1955 to occupy areas of the North, and because the Northern authorities had underestimated the number of people who would choose to move to the other zone. Following the refugee phase of its activities, the Commission found itself blocked by the refusal of the Southern government to agree to unification elections, or even to discuss the subject with the North. Indeed, the South has refused to maintain any official contacts with the Communist half of Vietnam. When the French ended their liaison mission with the ICC, on August 15, 1956, following the withdrawal of the French High Command from the country, the Southern government informed the ICC that, while it was prepared to cooperate with the Commission, it was not prepared to assume France's responsibility for implementing the Geneva Agreements within its borders. The ICC had relied on a Joint Commission consisting of an equal number of representatives from the two military high commands for resolving many disputes. This special commission died when the South Vietnamese refused to appoint representatives to it.

The ICC has had two major responsibilities since 1956. One has been to ensure the safety of persons from reprisal or discrimination by either government for their activities during the hostilities. The other responsibility has been the execution of the military provisions of the Geneva settlement, according to which both sides were forbidden to add to their military capabilities by increasing the size of their armed forces, establishing new military bases, permitting foreign powers to establish bases on their soil, reinforcing their armaments or adding new weapons, or increasing the number of foreign military personnel. The rotation of personnel and the replacement of matériel were, however, permitted.

In order to carry out its responsibilities, the Commission maintains, as its eyes and ears, ten fixed-team locations at important ports of entry, and uses a number of mobile teams to conduct investigations where and when needed. The fixed-team sites are presently at Dong Dan, Lao Kay, Haiphong, Vinh, and Muong Sen in North Vietnam, and at Saigon, Cap St Jacques, Danang, Qui Nhon, and Nha Trang in South Vietnam.[49] There is, in addition, a team located at Gio Linh, at the seventeenth parallel, which is charged with supervising conditions within the three-mile demilitarized zone established along the line of the parallel. The three-member Commission itself is located at Saigon and maintains a sub-office at Hanoi where, until April, 1958, its headquarters were. All of the Commission's teams are composed

[49] Four other fixed team sites were abolished in December, 1960.

equally of Canadians, Indians, and Poles, and nearly all of its decisions are made by majority vote. Except for its regular checkpoints for watching over the arrival of ships and aircraft from abroad, ICC investigations are undertaken upon receipt of complaints filed by private parties or through the liaison agencies of the two governments.

Some of the Commission's problems stem from its lack of enforcement powers. It can only suggest appropriate behavior to a derelict party, then recommend action, and finally cite that party for a violation of a provision of the Agreement on the Cessation of Hostilities. The infraction is reported to the British and Soviet governments for any action they may be able to agree upon, which could at the most lead to an official remonstration. Thus, the ICC has at its disposal only moral sanctions, or whatever pressure may be aroused through international opinion. Some of the problems of the Commission result directly from its composition, which places the Indians in a position of hopeful mediators between the pro-Northern Poles and the pro-Southern Canadians. It should be added that the Canadian representative to the ICC has generally tried to follow an impartial course, and he has joined on a number of occasions with his Indian and Polish colleagues to cite the South for infractions. The Polish representative has never reciprocated this impartiality and, in fact, the Poles keep the Northern authorities fully apprised of what happens within the ICC; the Indian representative has frequently been unwilling to take stands on issues unless the Polish and Canadian members are in agreement. As a consequence, the general leaning of the ICC has been to the advantage of the North. As if all this were not enough, neither the North nor the South has been willing to accept the Commission's authority in matters touching upon important interests, and both governments have freely substituted their own interpretations of the armistice terms for those established by the ICC. Both governments have obstructed the free movement of Commission teams, have evaded its requests and inquiries, and have denied it information necessary for the formation of judgments.

According to the number of officially-cited infractions, South Vietnam has violated the cease-fire agreement much more frequently than has North Vietnam. It appears from the International Control Commission's reports that through February 28, 1961, about 154 violations had been registered against the South and only one violation against the North.[50] But, as the Canadian and Indian representatives

[50] International Commission for Supervision and Control in Vietnam, *Interim Reports* (First through Eleventh) (London: Her Majesty's Stationery Office). It is not easy to tabulate specific violations from the presentations contained in these reports.

have been constrained to point out, "the number of formal citations in itself is no fair measure of the degree of cooperation received from either party."[51] In addition to the advantage to the North of the strong partisanship of the Polish representative on the ICC, the Northern authorities have been much more astute, or devious, than their Southern counterparts in avoiding overt disobedience of Commission requests. The inability of ICC teams to perform their duties due to roads professed to be washed out, unavailable transportation, and administrative delays is much greater in North than in South Vietnam. Many of the citations which the South has received have involved persons alleged by the North to be former resistance fighters. The Southern government, claiming that such persons have been acted against for their post-Geneva behavior, has denied the Commission jurisdiction over them. Also, the North has much better intelligence about happenings in the South, including ship and plane movements and additions to the American military advisory group, than the South has of activities within the North. And, while most foreign aid comes into South Vietnam by way of a few ports and airfields which can be kept more or less under scrutiny by fixed teams, it is impossible for the International Control Commission to control most of the possible points of access to North Vietnam along the broad Chinese frontier.

It is easy to understand why the ICC has tended to avoid major decisions and has procrastinated on many others. It is internally divided, its fixed teams are denied much information concerning ship and air movements, its mobile teams are not allowed free movement in the field, and the good-will upon which its effectiveness depends, which was never high, is rapidly disappearing. Both the North and the South have been more interested in manipulating the Commission to their political advantage than in resolving disputes, and the North especially has subjected the ICC to strong and continuous pressure. During the single month of June, 1961, for example, 80 delegations paraded before the Commission's Hanoi office to protest against its policies, and on one occasion alone 99 petitions containing 20,000 signatures were deposited at this office. The North is particularly incensed with the Commission's special report of June 2, 1962, which, while finding that the South had violated the Agreements by receiving increased military aid from the United States and by establishing a "factual military alliance" with it, saw these violations in the light of Northern aggression against the Republic of Vietnam. The North had, according to the Commission majority — the Polish representative

[51] *Ibid., Eleventh Interim Report, February 1, 1960 to February 28, 1961,* p. 25.

dissenting — sent men, arms, and other supplies into the South for hostile purposes and had incited activities aimed at the overthrow of the Diem regime.[52] The North has consistently denied any connection with the National Liberation Front, but has put forward the interesting argument that the Front is actually supporting the Geneva Agreements, inasmuch as its objective is the reunification of Vietnam.[53]

The open and flagrant violations of the Geneva Agreements and the increasing defiance of the International Control Commission have made the future of this body uncertain. A few days after the American military build-up got underway in December, 1961, it was reported that the Commission was considering the advisability of continuing to function in Vietnam, and the Commission's June, 1962, report referred to "a near-complete breakdown" in its functions.[54] Despite its ineffectiveness as a keeper of the peace, the withdrawal of the ICC would be unfortunate, for the Commission, to use its own words, "has tried to play the role of a catalyst and has provided a forum and link for both parties."[55] It has done these things not only through its official activities but also through the informal relations which some of its members have established with leaders of the opposing governments. In a situation where no other contact exists, this slender bridge connecting the divided country is sufficient justification for the continued existence of the International Control Commission.

Conclusion

The war being waged in Vietnam is a continuation of the struggle which the Communist-led Viet Minh initiated in September, 1945, with the proclamation of a Democratic Republic. It has been, on the Communist side, a twofold struggle. On one hand, the Communist objective has been the nationalist one of restoring Vietnam to independence by the expulsion of colonialist control. On the other hand, its objective has been to create a socialist society, on the Leninist model, controlled by the Communist Party. The relative appeal of the two objectives for the Vietnamese people is reflected in the Communist movement's constant presentation of itself in nationalist guise and the consistent success with which Communist propaganda has evoked nationalist and related sentiments: independence, democracy, prosperity, and peace. It was only after the Communists had securely

[52] *Ibid., Special Report to the Co-Chairmen of the Geneva Conference on Indochina* (June 2, 1962).
[53] See Ky, *Hoc Tap* (Hanoi), July, 1961.
[54] *New York Times,* December 13, 1961, p. 2; *ibid.,* June 26, 1962, p. 8.
[55] *Eleventh Interim Report,* p. 27.

established themselves in power in North Vietnam, and after hopes of peaceful reunification were given up, that the Communist leaders embarked on the collectivization of agriculture and other economic activity. Indeed, the Communist party does not formally exist in Vietnam, even in the Democratic Republic of the North.

This is not to say that Ho Chi Minh and his colleagues are hypocrites when they speak of nationalism; the evidence is persuasive that they are Vietnamese nationalists as well as Vietnamese Communists. But they have disguised their Communist program because that program would not have attracted the necessary support to their movement. Also, because they are Communists, they have not scrupled to attack competing nationalist forces. During the Indochina war they assassinated, intimidated, discredited, and even betrayed to the French those who challenged Communist leadership of the nationalist movement in Vietnam.[56] Rather than deploring such brutality against the nationalist opposition, one Northern leader, writing years later, regretted only that the Viet Minh had not acted more firmly to eliminate its non-Communist competitors.[57] And when Ho Chi Minh was asked by a French reporter in 1946 about the execution of Ta Thu Thau, a well-known Trotskyite, by the Viet Minh, Ho was able to call his deceased rival "a great patriot" for whom all of Vietnam wept, but he was candid enough to add that those who did not follow his own line would be crushed.[58] In their determination to destroy their new nationalist rival, the government of Ngo Dinh Diem, the Communists have not only been willing to spill the blood of patriotic Vietnamese but to wreck those programs of the Diem government which show promise of improving the lot of the Vietnamese people.

In their efforts to win popular support against the Republic of Vietnam, the Communists operate under two handicaps which did not exist prior to 1954. One is the clearly collectivist character which the Democratic Republic of Vietnam has assumed, and the political repressions and economic deprivations that have been imposed on the Northern population. The other is the establishment of a nationalist regime in the South, which, whatever its weaknesses, is an independent government managed by Vietnamese. While both of these factors have weakened the Communist appeal for the Southern people, their importance should not be exaggerated. The Communist movement in

[56] Philippe Devillers, "Vietnamese Nationalism and French Policies," in William L. Holland (editor), *Asian Nationalism and the West* (New York: Macmillan, 1953), pp. 214–15.

[57] Truong Chinh, *The August Revolution* (Hanoi: Foreign Languages Publishing House, 1958), p. 41.

[58] Cited in Jean Lacouture, *Cinq hommes et la France* (Paris: Éditions du Seuil, 1961), p. 73.

South Vietnam is not based on the record of socialism in the North. Except for the refugees, very few Vietnamese have actually lived under Communism, and the refugees left North Vietnam before the Communist regime began showing its tough side. Thus, most of the Southern population knows post-1955 Northern society only from the propaganda of its government, and government propaganda has not only been crude but has contradicted general peasant experience with the Viet Minh and, more recently, with Communist agents and guerrillas operating in their midst.

In order to offset the nationalist appeal of the Ngo Dinh Diem government, the Communists have assiduously attempted to fit it into the mold of the colonial past. Colonialism, the people are told, still exists in Vietnam under a new guise. The puppet Associate State of Vietnam has simply been replaced by the puppet Republic of Vietnam, Ngo Dinh Diem has assumed the place of Bao Dai, and the Americans have succeeded to the imperialist role formerly played by the French. So deeply has the *My-Diem* (American-Diem) relationship been established in the minds of the peasants that Vietnamese government officials have been addressed, with all respect, as *My-Diem* by peasants doing business with them. The Communists have also succeeded in establishing themselves as the proponents of reunification, with the Southern government as the obstacle to reunification. It has been North Vietnam which has put forward all proposals for reunifying Vietnam and, short of reunification, for establishing normal trade and other relations between the two zones. The Southern government has consistently rejected all such overtures, but has not offered anything positive in their place. The French had carved three artificial states from the territory of Vietnam, and the South Vietnamese government has been maneuvered into the position of seeming to wish to perpetuate a divided country. Thus, it is North Vietnam and its National Liberation Front which appear to favor reunification and the cause of Vietnamese nationalism.

It would be a serious mistake to consider Communist power in South Vietnam as based predominantly on terrorism or military strength, or even upon the indifference of an ignorant peasantry. In 1949 Paul Mus, who had negotiated with the Viet Minh on behalf of the French government, warned the outside world of the nature of Viet Minh power. "It is essential," he said, "to discard at once any notion that in Vietnam the French are dealing with nothing more than a mass of apathetic peasants who have been terrorized by their [Viet Minh] leaders. When the writer had occasion two years ago to travel behind the Viet Minh lines, he found widespread evidence of an organized popular movement both at the front and in the rear."[59] There is no evidence that the situation today has substantially changed in those areas of South Vietnam which are under strong Communist influence. Terrorism is the negative part of the Communist program to win popular support; moreover, it affects only a very small portion of rural inhabitants, and it is often directed against unpopular officials in the guise of protecting the peasantry. The fact is that Communism, in the dress of nationalism and in its advocacy of land to the peasants, represents a powerful force in South Vietnam, and one which receives widespread support from the peasant population. It has little trouble recruiting its partisans from among young villagers and, once recruited, these peasant-soldiers fight bravely and tenaciously and very seldom desert to the other side despite the rigors of guerrilla existence. The peasantry is not so much a pawn or a prize as it is the arbiter in the struggle between Communist and anti-Communist nationalism. While the outcome of the struggle will depend upon the force of arms, military strength itself is closely related to the winning of peasant allegiance. That side will win peasant support which can demonstrate that it represents the cause of Vietnamese nationalism and the vague aspirations of a new life which form part of its appeal.

[59] Paul Mus, "The Role of the Village in Vietnamese Politics," *Pacific Affairs,* 22 (September, 1949), 265.

7

Anti-Communism and Popular Freedom

The revolutionary strategy pursued by Vietnamese Communism has been curiously paralleled by the anti-Communist policies of the Vietnamese government. Like the Communists, the Diem government until about 1959 bent its main efforts to winning political support from the people and to eradicating enemy influence in the countryside by non-military means. Like the Communists, it frequently used coercion or selective terrorism in dealing with those who supported the enemy. And like the Communists, the government placed its major military reliance upon locally recruited armed forces. The village-based Self-Defense Corps wore the same simple black clothing as the village-based guerrillas (indeed, as the villagers themselves); they were not much better equipped; and their spare time was similarly spent in tending their fields or in other non-military work. Matching the Communist regional troops was the Civil Guard which operated, under the command of the province chiefs, like its enemy counterpart, inside of particular districts or within a single province. The Vietnamese army was held aloof from military operations after its rout of the sects and the Binh Xuyen in 1955. Subversive activity was too small-scale to warrant its employment and, besides, it was being rebuilt as a conventional military organization during this early period. At the same time, the Communists were slowly developing their own regular military units.

After the Communists began their military offensive in late 1959, the government was compelled to turn increasingly to military counter-active measures. Three elements in the government's new response may be noted. First, the army has been put into action and has been transformed in the process from a conventional to an increasingly anti-

160

guerrilla fighting force. In other words, the government has acknowledged the inability of either the Self-Defense and Civil Guard forces or of a conventional army to cope with Communist insurgency. Second, the Self-Defense Corps and Civil Guard have been considerably strengthened, and additional militia forces, based on the hamlet, have been added to them as local defense organizations. Finally, Vietnamese society as a whole has undergone a change which can best be described as the militarization of the population. The public bureaucracy, particularly at the local levels, has been shaped into a military machine, and a massive effort is now under way to convert most of Vietnam's hamlets into armed bastions, whose peasant occupants will defend themselves against the Communist infestation of the surrounding countryside.

The government's anti-Communist efforts since 1959 must, as in the earlier period, be seen in relation to their close parallel of Communist developments. The government's commitment of regular army units reflects the great increase in the size of regular Communist units and their commitment to military operations. The upgrading of the Self-Defense and Civil Guard forces has followed the upgrading of Communist regional and local guerrilla forces. The conversion of government-controlled territory into separate armed camps has been matched by a similar conversion of Communist-controlled territory, in which the government's "strategic hamlets" confront the "fighting hamlets" of the National Liberation Front.

This deadly parallel between government and Communist military strategy should not be carried too far. For one thing, it should be noted that the government has made its efforts on behalf of the legitimate public authority, while Communist efforts have been aimed at subverting that authority — though it is also possible to view the present struggle as one between competing claims of legitimacy. Also, it should be observed that government treatment of pro-Communists, though at times brutal enough, is less ruthless than the practices used by the Communists against pro-nationalists. Another difference between the two sides lies in the superiority which the government enjoys in the size, equipment, and logistic support of its armed forces, though it is improbable that it enjoys even equality in morale and dedication. Finally, to pursue the comparison no further, the bases of government power are the cities and towns, while the Communist foe has his most secure bases in the mountains, swamps, and other sparsely inhabited areas, with his power extending from there into surrounding rural areas. The geographic difference in foci of power strongly affects the military strategy of both sides. This difference was succinctly expressed by a veteran journalist of the Indochina War period after he had observed a Vietnamese army operation in the Mekong delta in 1961. "Once again," he said, "it was an army that thought in terms of towns and roads — and an enemy that thought in terms of people and countryside."[1]

The Military Effort

It is fortunate for the South Vietnamese government that the North made no military moves against it during the first years of independence, because it is very doubtful that the South could then have withstood them. The Ngo Dinh Diem government inherited about 250,000 troops when it took power in 1954, but it inherited little else. The morale of the Vietnamese who fought with the French had been low and desertions very high, especially among non-commissioned officers. The army in 1954 had almost no staff, artillery, heavy armor, engineering sections, or communications. It was woefully weak in officers, few of whom were above the rank of major, because the French, when they transferred their Vietnamese troops to the newly created national army in 1953, retained practically all the higher staff and command positions. In fact, administrative responsibility for the Vietnamese armed forces was not turned over to the Vietnamese government until February, 1955, and the chief of staff of the army during the first months of the Diem regime, General Nguyen Van Hinh, was an outspoken critic of his civilian leader and a French citizen. The national troops included many supplementary and militia units which had been used only in static defense positions to relieve the French Expeditionary Corps, and in training and equipment they were much inferior to the regular Vietnamese units, whose preparation for combat was in general poor enough.

The government's first task was to reorganize — more accurately, to integrate, train and properly equip — the fighting forces inherited from the colonial period. The task was undertaken with American and, until the spring of 1956, French army advisers. The most important contributions of the United States Military Assistance Advisory Group have been in equipping the army, paying its wages and most other expenses, assisting in its training, and advising in the development of logistical and other auxiliary services. Probably the greatest American impact on Vietnamese military thinking has been achieved through sending hundreds of young officers to the United States, Okinawa, and the Philippines for training. In an army where company commanders were assigned to head hastily formed regiments and even divisions,

[1] Dennis Warner, "The Invisible Front Lines of South Vietnam," *The Reporter,* August 17, 1961, p. 30.

where lieutenants found themselves commanding battalions, and non-commissioned officers were put in charge of companies and platoons, special military training was a prime necessity and the United States military support program has helped to meet it.[2] The Vietnamese army was cut back to 150,000 men — the size that the United States was willing to support.

In one crucial respect the new Vietnamese army bore a strong resemblance to that of the pre-independence period. It was a conventional military force oriented to positional warfare and static defense. This was due in part to the military backgrounds of the officers corps, particularly the senior officers, who had come less under the influence of American military thinking. But American military policy was also responsible, for while it tried to break the Vietnamese army of its obsession with entrenched military posts, it viewed that army primarily as a deterrent to an invasion in force from North Vietnam. South Vietnam was precluded by the Geneva Agreements from membership in the South East Asia Treaty Organization, but its army was largely organized, equipped, and trained to stop or slow down an invasion until SEATO forces could come to its aid. The officer responsible for implementing American military policy in Vietnam, Lt. Gen. Samuel T. Williams, expressed the American view of the military threat to South Vietnam on the occasion of his retirement in August, 1960, after five years as Chief of MAAG. "In 1954," he said, "the Communist army of North Vietnam could have crossed the seventeenth parallel and walked into Saigon standing up. Today if they tried it, they would have one nasty fight on their hands."[3]

The direction given to the Vietnamese army was not intended to leave the country without internal security forces. The Civil Guard and Self-Defense Corps were assigned primary responsibility for dealing with the various rebel groups operating in the countryside after the Geneva armistice. Most of the personnel in both security forces had served with similar supplemental military organizations during the Indochina War. The American Military Assistance Advisory Group assisted the Self-Defense Corps, which was attached to the Department of National Defense and headed by regular army officers, but American support during the first years after independence was almost entirely restricted to furnishing most of the payroll of the Self-Defense Corps and turning over to it a small amount of old weapons. The

---

[2] An informative, though approved, version of American military assistance to the Vietnamese armed forces is contained in Judson J. Conner, "Teeth for the Free World Dragon," *Army Information Digest,* November, 1960 pp. 32–43.

[3] *Ibid.,* p. 43.

training of the approximately 40,000 members of the Corps came from the Vietnamese army and was rudimentary; often its weapons were sticks, clubs and other such makeshifts. As a result, it was hardly adequate to the task of defending villages, roads, and other local strategic points against armed attacks by Communist guerrillas. The Civil Guard, which numbered about 50,000 officers and men, was organizationally separate from the army but most of its officers, including its leadership, were regular army personnel. The shortcomings in the Civil Guard stemmed to a considerable extent from a protracted dispute between Vietnamese and American authorities over the nature of the organization. Michigan State University, under contracts with the two governments, was responsible for assisting in the training and equipping of the Civil Guard, which it viewed as a rural police organization; its inability to reach an agreement with the Vietnamese government (which perceived the Civil Guard, in effect, as a supplement to the army) led to the withholding in 1957 of most projected American aid. In addition, the Vietnamese government did little to improve the efficiency or morale of the Guard during this period, using it as a dumping ground for inferior army officers. The organization — poorly trained, poorly led, and lacking needed armament, transport, and communications — was faced with the increasingly difficult job of maintaining security in an increasingly insecure countryside. The instability of the Civil Guard is indicated by the rapid turnover in its top administrative spot: five persons held the post of general director between 1955 and 1958.

By 1959, the total military forces of Vietnam were grossly superior both in number and in firepower to those of the Communist guerrillas; however, this superiority was being counterbalanced by rising enemy strength and offset in good part by the Communist extension of political control over ever-larger portions of the countryside, and by the advantages which guerrilla fighters enjoy in initiating action. The quality of the government forces — a roadbound, mechanized, defense-minded army, supplemented by an ill-trained and under-armed bedraggled Civil Guard and Self-Defense Corps — added to the enemy's advantage. The government's military picture slowly began to change in 1959. First, assistance to the Civil Guard began to arrive after the middle of the year, following a long-delayed decision in Washington to support a multi-million dollar program to train and equip it, largely on the Vietnamese government's terms. The concomitant shift in function of the Civil Guard led the Michigan State University Group to withdraw from its advisory and training role, and, on July 1, the Civil Guard became the responsibility of the United States economic aid mission. The nature of the Civil Guard became clear in November, 1960, when it was transferred from the Department of Interior to the Department of National Defense, and in early December the American military mission assumed responsibility for its training and equipment. In contrast to the civil instruction which Michigan State and the economic aid mission had given this paramilitary organization, the military mission embarked on a two-year program to retrain its members in both conventional and anti-guerrilla warfare.

The first stirring of change in the Vietnamese army appeared in mid-1960 with the creation of small, flexible anti-guerrilla teams patterned after the Ranger units of the American army.[4] The first group of American military advisers trained in anti-guerrilla warfare arrived in Vietnam in the early part of that year. With the strong support of President Diem, the development of these special hunt-and-kill forces picked up momentum during 1961, and there were about 86 companies in the field by early 1962. The army as a whole underwent expansion beyond its 150,000-man ceiling during 1961 with the calling up of reserve officers and enlisted men and then, in August, 1961, with a general draft of all high school graduates between the ages of 25 and 33. In negotiations concluded in December, 1961, the United States agreed to support most of the increase, which has brought army strength to 210,000. The United States also increased the delivery of war materials as well as the size of its military group in Vietnam. In addition to conventional arms, the United States has provided Vietnam with large quantities of helicopters and patrol vessels with American crews to man them, light bombers and fighter planes, communications equipment, and chemicals for destroying crops grown in Communist areas and for destroying foliage cover along the Laotian frontier and along Communist-harassed highways. The Civil Guard and, to a lesser extent, the Self-Defense Corps began to feel the impact of increased American military aid during late 1961 and during 1962. By the middle of 1963, their strengths had been increased to 72,000 and 80,000 men, respectively.

Along with strengthening its military forces and adapting them to guerrilla warfare, the Vietnamese government has to a great extent militarized its regular government administration since 1959 in response to the growing Communist threat. The military evolution of the Civil Guard, which had been aided and viewed, at least by the Americans, as a civil police organization, has already been described. The General Directorate of Police and Security, which contains the regular and security police services, also began to assume a strong

[4] *The Times of Vietnam Magazine* reported on November 12, 1960, pp. 5, 17, that three Ranger training camps were being operated by personnel trained in the United States, Malaya, and the Philippines.

military posture after 1959. The heads of the Police and Security Services and other high officials have, since 1956, always been military officers, but after 1959 military penetration of other positions, including provincial and district commands, proceeded rapidly. Even the Saigon police department has not escaped this trend, and all of its new district police chiefs appointed in 1960 were military officers. The General Directorate of Police and Security has assigned local security agents to military-type patrolling and has continually sought more and more military equipment. The primary concern of provincial security officers, the great majority of whom are now military personnel, is to defeat Communism, with a commensurate diminution of interest in conventional police activities.

The regular government structure in the provinces has likewise been affected by the trend towards militarization. In 1958, 13 of the then 36 province chiefs were military officers, and it was planned to replace most of them with civilians in the near future. By September, 1960, there were 21 military and 17 civilian province chiefs, and by August, 1962, the ratio had jumped to 36 military officers and 5 civilians in an expanded 41 provinces. Significantly, four of the five remaining civilians were assigned to the Central Vietnamese lowlands, the area still least disturbed by guerrilla forays. The district chiefs serving within provincial jurisdictions today are primarily junior military officers, and the entire administrative process at the province and district levels has become saturated with military concerns. "The pattern of local administration in rural areas," in the words of one observer, "resembles the pattern in enemy-occupied territory during wartime. . . . [Officials] operate in garrison-like quarters surrounded by barbed-wire barricades, and travel into the countryside only under heavy guard."[5] Health, education, and agricultural authorities tend to confine their work largely to provincial and district seats rather than move into the dangerous surrounding countryside.[6] The most active organizations at the district and village levels are directly concerned with security. In addition to any army detachments which may be located in the area, each district invariably has a Civil Guard unit, which may patrol the villages of the district during the day, but whose main purpose is to protect the district headquarters and its official missions. Security agents also operate from the district headquarters, and

[5] Joseph J. Zasloff, "The Problem of South Vietnam," *Commentary,* February, 1962, p. 132.

[6] For a discussion of government administration in 1960 in a Vietnamese village, which also served as a district seat, see John D. Donoghue and Vo Hong Phuc, *My Thuan: The Study of a Delta Village in South Vietnam* (Saigon: Michigan State University Vietnam Advisory Group, May, 1961).

small groups of rural police and Self-Defense militia aid in protecting the district town. Most of the militia, where they have not been driven out, are assigned to village defense. Under the command of the village police chief they patrol the village area, escort officials on trips outside village compounds, man local defense posts, and guard public buildings and bridges. Important local government officials — district chiefs, security heads, civic action cadres, village chiefs, National Revolutionary Movement leaders — have their own intelligence networks consisting of local inhabitants and sometimes, it is said, Communist double agents.

The Political Campaign

In the first years of independence, the Vietnamese government relied largely on political weapons for dealing with its internal Communist problem. It was initially concerned with disinfecting the population of Communist and other anti-regime sentiments, and the agency charged with this mission was the Department of Information and Youth. This Department was, from a certain point of view, admirably qualified for the job. Its head, Tran Chanh Thanh, and many of its cadres had learned the art of political propaganda in earlier service with the Viet Minh. As government troops occupied Viet Minh and sect-controlled areas in the spring and summer of 1955, Information agents swarmed in their wake denouncing the triple evils of Communism, colonialism, and feudalism, and extolling the Ngo Dinh Diem government. These themes were pounded home in posters, banners, leaflets, radio messages, and rallies. Particularly noticeable in this propaganda barrage was the effort made to replace the well-known image of "Uncle Ho" with that of the unfamiliar Ngo Dinh Diem.

Perhaps the most important — certainly the most flamboyant — propaganda vehicle for the government was the Anti-Communist Denunciation Campaign launched about the middle of 1955. In a typical denunciation ceremony, Viet Minh cadres and sympathizers would swear their disavowal of Communism before a large audience; the repentants would recount the atrocities of the Viet Minh and, as a climax to their performance, would rip or trample upon the Viet Minh flag and pledge their loyalty to Ngo Dinh Diem.[7] The early results of the Denunciation Campaign, by Tran Chanh Thanh's accounting, were

[7] In what was reported as the largest Communist denunciation rally to date, tens of thousands of Saigon residents were witnesses to the conversion of 2,000 former Viet Minh cadres in late February, 1956. See *Vietnam Press* (French edition), February 28, 1956 (morning issue), pp. 1–4, for a full description of the rite.

impressive. In May, 1956, he announced that the campaign had in a period of about ten months "entirely destroyed the predominant Communist influence of the previous nine years." According to Thanh, in this short period 94,041 former Communist cadres had rallied to the government, 5,613 other cadres had surrendered to government forces, 119,954 weapons had been captured, and 75 tons of documents and 707 underground arms caches had been discovered.[8]

It is true that a considerable number of Viet Minh supporters broke with the Communist-controlled movement after Geneva, but it is highly questionable whether the programs of the Department of Information and Youth were an important factor in their decisions. It is much more likely that the agency's ubiquitous, heavy-handed propaganda antagonized more people than it attracted. It is even more clear that the Anti-Communist Denunciation Campaign gave an exaggerated picture of the agency's achievements. To give but one example, the Vietnamese government in 1958 notified the International Control Commission that it had, since 1954, discovered 225 arms caches on its territory[9] — many fewer than Tran Chanh Thanh claimed his Campaign had found in ten short months. The antics of the Communist Denunciation Campaign piqued one Saigon newspaper into risking — and incurring — inspired mob action and government shutdown by calling it a "puppet show."[10] The experiment in defeating Communism by boisterous Communist propaganda methods gradually lost impetus, and in 1960 Tran Chanh Thanh was assigned to serve his country's interests as ambassador to Tunisia, and his department was reduced to non-Cabinet status and then, in 1961, absorbed by the Department of Civic Action.

Related to the anti-Communist campaign led by the Department of Information have been the activities of the mass government party, the National Revolutionary Movement, and its administrative counterpart, the National Revolutionary Civil Servants League. Tran Chanh Thanh was chairman of the NRM until 1958, and his department prepared the political topics for discussion in the regular meetings held throughout the public service under the auspices of the Civil Servants League. These meetings, the most important function of the League, had as a major purpose the political indoctrination of civil servants. The NRM has had more varied tasks that include participation in the election process, but most of its activities at the district and village

[8] U.S. Operations Mission to Vietnam, *Saigon Daily News Round-Up,* May 14, 1956, p. 3.

[9] *Note d'étude sur les violations de l'accord de Genève par le Viet Minh* (Saigon, March 1958), p. 9. (Mimeographed.)

[10] USOM, *Saigon Daily News Round-Up,* May 18, 1956, p. 3.

levels have been devoted to anti-Communism in intimate relationship with the official administrative structure. District information chiefs, who handle anti-Communist propaganda in their localities, have usually served as district chairmen of the National Revolutionary Movement and, by presidential decree, the village chairmen of the Movement have served as village political commissioners. In addition to its propaganda role, the NRM has served as a counter-intelligence and security organization in the countryside, providing information on subversive activities and helping track down Communist agents and sympathizers.[11] As a result, local leaders and agents of the Movement have been prime targets of Communist terrorism.

A more positive approach to the Communist problem in the countryside during the early independence period was that taken by the General Commissariat for Civic Action. Its program for village Vietnam originated in early military efforts to stimulate and assist the peasants in rebuilding war-damaged facilities. This effort developed into a community-action program in 1955, directed by the Civic Action agency and executed by 1,400 agents operating in small mobile teams. Civic Action personnel, to be sure, propagandized for the government, but they also distributed drugs and medicines, gave seeds and advice to the peasants, and worked with them in the rice fields. Most of them were young volunteers without previous government experience, and they did what very few other government officials have done: they dressed and lived like the rural people and they adopted a severe code of ethics to go with their austere life. Because of the jealousies of the province chiefs and the departments of Health, Information, and Agriculture, who felt that Civic Action had intruded into their jurisdictions, this program was curtailed at the end of 1956.[12] It was not until mid-1961 that Civic Action, elevated to departmental status, resumed its mission of carrying the central government to the rural people.

Another of the government's political efforts to contain Communism has been its attempt to organize the Vietnamese people into neighborhood-control groups. This program, called the Mutual Aid

[11] In early 1959, for example, the information chief of An Xuyen province reported that a five-week anti-Communist campaign conducted by the provincial National Revolutionary Movement had resulted in the surrender of 8,125 Communist agents and the denunciation of 9,806 other agents and of 29,978 sympathizers. (USOM, *Saigon Daily News Round-Up,* February 28, 1959, pp. 4–5.)

[12] See John D. Montgomery, *The Politics of Foreign Aid* (New York: Praeger, 1962), pp. 70–71; Michigan State University Vietnam Advisory Group, *Report on the Organization of the Special Commissariat for Civic Action* (Saigon, June, 1957), pp. 3–8.

Family Group (*Lien Gia Tuong Tro*), is another device borrowed from the Viet Minh, though it appears to have roots in traditional Vietnamese administration. The Viet Minh used it to administer and control the people under their authority during the Indochina War; the government distinguishes its own adaptation by pointing to its supposed mutual-aid objectives and the fact that — in theory at least — it is voluntary.[13] Actually, there seems to be little difference between the Communist and nationalist versions. Emphatically, the government's system is not voluntary. Each household in Vietnam is combined with several others, usually in groups of five to seven families, to form a family group (*lien gia*). A like number of family groups form an agglomeration (*khom*). Each family group and each agglomeration has its appointed chief who is responsible to local officials for the activities of his group. The family groups perform a number of functions. They furnish free labor for public projects, settle petty disputes, and disseminate information from higher authority. Most of all, however, they function as security cells. It is the responsibility of each family group to control the behavior of its members and to report any irregularities, including the presence of visitors or other strangers, to village or city security officers. In order to facilitate control over personal movements, every house in Vietnam must indicate on an outside plaque the number and sex of all its occupants.[14]

The Vietnamese government has not lacked legal means of coping with its Communist challenge. It early established a system of political re-education centers for Communists and active supporters who were not amenable to lesser forms of persuasion. The legal basis of the centers is a presidential ordinance of January, 1956, which permits the arrest and detention of any person deemed dangerous to the safety of the state, though the camps existed prior to that time. The general practice has been to assign political prisoners to the Saigon or provincial prisons for the first step in their re-education, and then to transfer them to special camps located at Thu Dau Mot, Thu Duc, Rach Gia, and Thang Tan. Those who have shown sufficient progress are finally placed in centers close to their homes, from which they are gradually released.[15] Estimates vary widely as to the number of persons who have been held in these camps, as well as to the number who actually

[13] See, for example, *Vietnam Press,* week ending February 7, 1960, p. 7.
[14] See Donoghue and Phuc, *My Thuan,* Appendix A, for a translation of instructions concerning the organization of family groups, dated March 13, 1957, sent by the Secretary of State at the Presidency to all province chiefs and municipal heads.
[15] Press conference given by the Secretary of State for Civic Action, Saigon, August 21, 1961.

had Communist associations. The Secretary of State for Information stated in 1956 that between 15,000 and 20,000 Communists and active sympathizers had been held in political re-education centers since 1954.[16] This figure was probably low at the time; at any rate, the population of the camps has since increased considerably. The composition of the camps is also open to speculation. Although it appears that the government is interested mainly in rounding up Communists and the Communist-infected, one writer, on the basis of talks with former inmates, has reported that "the consensus of the opinions expressed by these people is that . . . the majority of the detainees are neither Communists nor pro-Communists."[17] At least some of the people favorably disposed toward the government have considered this method of dealing with subversion to be too gentle.[18]

A far less gentle way of handling subversives has been to bring them before military tribunals under charges of crimes against national security. Three such courts were established by law in May, 1959, and additional courts were established by executive decree in May, 1962, to handle crimes committed in "front line" areas. Both civilians and military personnel are subject to the jurisdiction of these military courts, and there is no appeal from their decisions except in cases of capital punishment. In such instances, the President may grant clemency. The government has thus far confined its use of military justice to clear-cut cases of terrorism whereby it could dramatize its struggle against the enemy, and most such cases have involved the death penalty. For the great majority of political prisoners, the penalty has been incarceration without trial in re-education centers.

The Vietnamese Constitution permits the President, by declaring a state of emergency, to suspend the application of laws as necessary in any part of the country. President Diem issued such a declaration on October 18, 1961, and the National Assembly quickly followed by delegating extraordinary powers to him in order to cope with the emergency. These actions emphasized the seriousness with which the government regarded the security situation, but they otherwise did no more than give legal sanction to powers which the President was already exercising. For example, the launching in 1959 of a massive and widely heralded program of regrouping the peasantry into agro-

[16] John Osborne, "The Tough Miracle Man of Vietnam," Life, May 13, 1957, p. 168.
[17] P. J. Honey, "The Problem of Democracy in Vietnam," The World Today, 16 (February, 1960), 73.
[18] See Wesley R. Fishel, "Vietnam's War of Attrition," The New Leader, December 7, 1959, p. 20.

villes, or rural cities, was not authorized by legislation or even executive decree.[19] The main restraints on the government in its non-military campaign against Communist insurgency have been those imposed by itself and by Communist power.

The Government and the People

We have thus far in this chapter focused attention on the Vietnamese government's efforts to combat its internal Communist threat. It is appropriate at this point to turn to the government's relations with its people generally. The two subjects are related. The government's anti-Communist policies have inevitably led to, or been the justification for, various restraints on the liberties of the Vietnamese people; and these restraints, while giving the government a certain short-run security, have made pursuance of its anti-Communist crusade more difficult. Its control over political activity has already been described; we shall consider here other aspects of its relationship to the people.

The striking feature of private organizations in Vietnam is that so many have been created by the government and so many others brought under its control. Voluntary formal organizations are few, and even these few tend to seek government support for their activities. It is worth noting that the National Union Front looked to the Presidency for subsidies which included purchase of a headquarters building. Even Phan Quang Dan was not above seeking governmental blessing: when he set out to oppose the 1956 elections on the charge that the regime was employing dictatorial methods, Dan wrote to ask Diem's encouragement in his struggle.[20] Private religious groups such as the Catholic Church and the Hoa Hao and Cao Dai sects seem to seek government assistance also, finding their effectiveness impaired without it.

The weakness of voluntary associational life is particularly noticeable in rural Vietnam. Almost all so-called voluntary organizations in the countryside are actually government creations, directed by government agencies, with their executive committees made up of village council members and perhaps a few village notables. In one village, for example, the village chief was also the chairman of the Farmers Association, the Farmers Cooperative, the Farmers Union, the Stu-

[19] The only legal recognition of the program was a brief presidential order dated November 20, 1959, setting up a special extrabudgetary account for agroville construction.

[20] This was expressed in a letter to the President, dated February 16, 1956, copies of which were circulated in mimeographed form.

dent-Parent Association, the Republican Youth group, the Women's Solidarity Movement, and the National Revolutionary Civil Servants League, in addition to heading such frankly governmental groups as the Agricultural Affairs Committee, the Social Welfare Committee, and the Rural Development Committee.[21] This pattern, with minor variations, extends throughout all the part of Vietnam which is under government control.

Among the government-created organizations, the Republican Youth (*Thanh Nien Cong Hoa*) deserves special notice. Established in early 1960 by the Civic Action agency, this organization seeks nothing short of mobilizing the entire population, or so much of it as remains under government control, in the anti-Communist struggle. It has grown rapidly and appears to have largely eclipsed the two other mass political instruments, the Civil Servants League and the National Revolutionary Movement. Like the League, membership in the Republican Youth is practically a concomitant of public employment for lower-level civil servants but, unlike the League, the new association adorns its members with uniforms which they wear to work one day a week, teaches them to drill, occasionally involves them in civic construction projects, and sets them on guard duty before public buildings in the evenings, thereby freeing military personnel for more important business. Outside of government agencies, the Republican Youth is best organized among the rural population and, in areas under government control, takes in nearly all able-bodied men between 18 and 50. The movement in rural Vietnam is much more militaristic than in the cities, and functions as a hamlet defense force; its members stand guard duty at night and assemble in force to repel Communist incursions. Men between 18 and 35 and between 36 and 50 are usually organized into different companies, but their functions appear to be the same. These amateur defense groups are commanded by the village police chiefs, who have often had some military experience, or by non-commissioned officers assigned from the army. The village commanders, assisted by the hamlet chiefs, give the groups some training in guerrilla warfare and surveillance. The standard weapon of the Republican Youth is a long blade mounted on a pole, but local defense groups in loyal villages are now being armed with rifles and grenades.

The Vietnamese government has not overlooked other groups in the population. For women there is the Women's Solidarity Movement, directed by Mme Ngo Dinh Nhu, which gets logistical support from the Department of Civic Action. Until March, 1962, this organization was nominally under the wing of the Civil Servants League and bears the mark of this early association, for its central, provincial,

[21] See Donoghue and Phuc, *My Thuan,* pp. 23–38.

and district directing committees are composed largely of the wives of government officials on the same levels. Most of the Movement's urban members appear to consider their affiliation a prudent concomitant of their husbands' employment, but some apparently share Mme Nhu's determined feminism and are interested in participating in charitable and other activities in aid of their sex. Since 1961, young women have had the opportunity of joining Mme Nhu's women's paramilitary corps, a volunteer group which provides training in gun-handling, first aid, and morality for high school-age and other women. For students there are several organizations, all closely supervised by the government. The most important is the National Students Union of Saigon University, which the regime controls to the point of manipulating the elections of its officers. For businessmen there is more freedom and, except for the quasi-official Chamber of Commerce, business groups are left more or less to their own devices so long as these do not embrace politics.

The associations mentioned so far have been created by the government and are effectively under its control. Two other institutions, the press and the trade union movement, share a somewhat greater measure of autonomy. Both existed before the Diem regime, in contrast to the organizations just discussed, and both preserve an uncertain balance between control and freedom. Of the two, the press is much more narrowly circumscribed. For one thing, the foreign-language press (consisting of one English, three French, and about ten Chinese daily and weekly newspapers) is subject to prior censorship. Secondly, the Vietnamese-language press, while it was freed from official censorship in February, 1956, has been brought under an effective system of informal censorship. The General Directorate of Information and Press distributes daily and weekly guidelines to all editors, suggesting what news they should print and what news they should not use. For example, in January, 1959, editors were advised not to report the trial of students who had participated in a demonstration; in March, 1959, they were requested to halt discussion of the disappearance of a city official who was suspected of having embezzled a large sum of money; in April, 1960, they were requested to continue the criticism of the National Assembly election campaign being carried on in the North, to avoid foreign press agency dispatches reporting on Russia's third Sputnik, and to ignore Senator Stuart Symington's statement that Communist China would have to be reckoned with in diplomatic relations. The guidance sheets often recommend the use of Vietnam Press material; the Vietnam Press, the official and only news agency, itself receives guidance from the head of the information agency and, on occasion, from the President himself. All Vietnamese newspapers, to play safe, depend on the Vietnam Press for most of their stories, and generally submit any self-generated stories on possibly sensitive subjects to the General Directorate of Information and Press for advance clearance.

The press has good reason to be cautious. With the one exception of a government newspaper published in Hue, all newspapers are published in Saigon where they can easily be controlled by the government. There are several sanctions available for use. First, most Vietnamese newspapers receive government subsidies in the form of bulk purchases of their daily output, and some of them, especially the openly government papers like the *Cach Mang Quoc Gia,* which are not popular, could not survive without this assistance. Second, the government controls the distribution of all papers through an officially created organization called the United Distribution Agency. In the days when there was still an opposition press, the Agency could prevent opposition sales outside Saigon and make distribution difficult within the city. Today it serves as a check on papers caught in momentary error, furnishing means for government seizure of the offending issues before they reach the newsstands. Sometimes this limited economic sanction is imposed for rather surprising reasons, as when an issue of the *Dong Nai,* a pro-government paper, was impounded for criticizing the French attack on the Tunisian town of Bizerte in the summer of 1961. There is a third, veiled, sanction against the press, the loosing of mob attacks on non-conforming newspaper offices and plants, which has been used on a number of occasions. Mob action is always viewed by the government as spontaneous action by some patriotic segment of the population, and in all cases the police arrive too late to prevent damage. Finally, the government may institute legal action against offending members of the press. Presidential Decree No. 13, issued February 20, 1956, just one day after censorship was abolished, made editors and journalists liable to fines, prison sentences up to five years, and suspension of publishing rights for a number of crimes including the printing of stories which aid the Communist cause or defame the republican regime. The government's definition of these trespasses has been quite loose. The priest-editor of the *Duong Song* had his paper closed and was himself given an eighteen months' jail term for editorially praying God in March, 1957, "to keep the President in good health and clearsighted so that the confidence of the early beginnings [could] be *regained.*"[22] The *Dan Chu* and its editor suffered the same fate for reprinting this editorial.

The most celebrated case of press suspension was that of the *Thoi*

[22] Emphasis added. See the account of this and other early press episodes in J. A. C. Grant, "The Vietnam Constitution of 1956," *American Political Science Review,* 52 (June, 1958), 458–62.

Luan. Started in May, 1957, as a frankly opposition newspaper, the *Thoi Luan's* presses were temporarily stopped in September, 1957, by mob action. In March, 1958, the newspaper was permanently closed by court decree. The government had tolerated a series of critical reviews of its policies anonymously written under the dedication, "Letter to My Deputy," but the March 2 Letter went too far. This was a long, blistering attack on the constitutional foundations, policies, and leadership of the regime, said to be distinguished from Communist and Fascist rule only by the absence of ideology and organization. The republican Constitution was declared to be inferior even to those of Communist states and republican elections were said to be even more dubiously legal than those of the Bao Dai period. In addition to losing his newspaper, editor Nghiem Xuan Thien was given a suspended prison sentence and fined about $1,400.[23]

During its brief history, the *Thoi Luan* had become the best-selling newspaper in Vietnam, with a circulation of about 80,000 copies. There has been no newspaper like it since 1958, for the government has refused to authorize any further opposition papers and has closely watched over the existing ones to ensure that none is tempted to emulate the *Thoi Luan's* immense, if brief, popularity. Given the government's attitude toward the press, it is difficult to understand why the *Thoi Luan* was allowed to publish so long. The President feels that newspapermen concoct their stories through a combination of opium, drink, and idle rumor; the head of the Information and Press agency adds a conviction that they have little education and that their chief interest is money; and a Vietnamese judge, lecturing local newspapermen in May, 1959, told them that "those who are incapable of seeking another trade engage in the career of journalist." At various government levels there is an expressed concern that Communists may infiltrate the press or otherwise use it for their ends, and there is considerable talk of the need to improve the quality of Vietnamese journalism as a precondition to permitting a free press.

The government's attitudes and policies have resulted in a largely docile press. This is not to say that the Saigon newspapers do not criticize the government. However, if criticism extends beyond minor officials and issues, one can be quite sure that it will either have been inspired by the top leadership, or it will be filtered through a screen of vagueness. As an example of the latter, we may take the long criticism of press repression which appeared in the cautiously critical *Tan Dan* a few years ago. It attacked the burning of opposition newspapers, the use of "temporary" controls to muzzle the press, the compulsion of

[23] The *Tu Do,* March 14 and 15, 1958, carried long reports of the trial, including Nghiem Xuan Thien's forthright defense of his editorial views.

following the party line, and the suppression of unpalatable news — within Communist countries.[24] Most Vietnamese newspapers avoid politics, beyond accepting the government's line, and those which take strong political positions are now safely pro-government, anti-Communist, and government-subsidized. Oppositionism still lurks in the Vietnamese press, but it is seldom apparent. Typical of the press's caution in the last few years was its handling of President Sukarno of Indonesia's emergency airplane stop in Saigon when returning from a visit to Hanoi. No paper dared mention where he had been, and at least one newspaper reported that he was en route from Cambodia.[25]

Trade unions came upon the Vietnamese scene after the emergence of a national press. The first Vietnamese newspaper was apparently the *Tribune Indochinoise,* established in 1923 as the organ of the Constitutionalist Party, and this and *La Lutte,* the Trotskyite paper started in 1933, were the precursors of a vigorous, if erratic, national press which sprang up after the Second World War. The French-controlled press, incidentally, enjoyed more freedom than has since been allowed under the Republic. But laboring people were not permitted to form associations until 1947, and regular trade unions did not make their appearance until November, 1952, with the promulgation of basic regulations, still in effect, which grant workers the right to form their own unions and run their internal affairs. The republican Constitution affirms these basic rights, except that civil servants may not engage in strikes, but makes their exercise subject to conditions prescribed by law.

The size of the Vietnamese work force was estimated at 5,600,000 in 1962, of which about 80 per cent was engaged in agriculture and fishing.[26] Trade union membership is claimed for about 10 per cent of the work force, but this, like other membership figures, appears to be greatly inflated. Most union members are concentrated in the larger urban enterprises and the rubber plantations, and are organized into three labor federations, of which the Vietnamese Federation of Workers (*Lien Doan Lao Dong Viet Nam*) is decidedly the most important. It is headed by Tran Quoc Buu, a longtime associate of Ngo Dinh Nhu, and it receives technical and other aid from the International Federation of Christian Trade Unions. All three federations benefit from government subsidies, mainly in the form of business concessions such as the operation of warehouses and insurance companies.[27] As with other organizations, the government seeks to con-

[24] *Tan Dan,* March 22, 1958.
[25] *Times of Vietnam,* July 2, 1959, p. 1.
[26] *Times of Vietnam Magazine,* May 13, 1962, p. 5.
[27] *Christian Science Monitor,* February 16, 1962.

trol the activities of the trade union movement and occasionally interferes in specific matters. The government has the right to reject
applications to form unions, to interject itself in union-management
negotiations, to expel union members, and it must be notified of all
union meetings. The government's main concern is with Communist
infiltration of unions, of which there has been some, and with union
engagement in politics. In 1956, the government took alarm at reported Communist infiltration of rubber plantation workers' organizations in Binh Duong province and arrested a number of the union
leaders there. In 1961, it engineered new elections in the railway
workers union to depose leaders who were "too energetic," and it has
sought to manipulate the internal affairs of the trade unions in
numerous other ways.

Government control over the union movement is, however, incomplete. The leaders of the three federations follow the government line
and avoid any appearance of independent political activity, but do not
themselves have effective control over many of their constituent unions.
Of all private associations functioning in the nationalist camp, only the
trade union movement has the mass base and sufficient autonomy to
constitute a potential threat to the Ngo Dinh Diem government.

Thus far we have considered the Vietnamese government's efforts to
control its people. We should consider now its massive effort to cut
them off physically from the Communist forces operating in the
countryside. This effort has taken the form both of regrouping the
peasantry and of creating a vast network of compact armed forts
throughout rural Vietnam. The consequence of these programs,
should they succeed, will go far beyond their immediate security objectives, for they involve nothing less than a transformation in the
whole style of rural living. The idea of regrouping Vietnam's peasant
population into islands of rural security did not originate with the Diem
regime; the French had carried out similar measures on a small scale in
the Tonkin delta in 1953. The present programs are, however, much
more far-reaching, and are intended to encompass most of the population of rural Vietnam.

The regrouping of peasants began quietly about February, 1959, in
areas of the southwest which had been strongly infected by the Viet
Minh.[28] In this initial effort, peasants were regrouped into two types

[28] For information concerning the Vietnamese government's regroupment
policies between 1959 and 1960, the writer is indebted to the Michigan
State University Vietnam Advisory Group for having opened its research
files on the subject to him and, especially, to the excellent unpublished study
by Nguyen Khac Nhan, *La construction des agglomérations rurales charn-
ières au Sud Viet-Nam* (Université de Paris, Faculté de droit et des sciences
politiques, 1961).

of centers which, usually created side by side, were distinguished mainly by the politics imputed to their occupants. One type of center was for families who, because one of their members had moved to North Vietnam with the Viet Minh in 1954–1955, were considered favorably disposed, or at least vulnerable, to Communist guerrilla activities. The other type of center was established for the opposite purpose: to protect loyal peasants from Communist reprisals. Security was the only consideration in the regrouping. Peasants were transported from their regular homesteads to a new place where, often far from their rice fields, they were expected to re-establish their lives with only minimal assistance from the government. The reaction of both loyal and "Communist-contaminated" peasants was unanimously bitter, and the hastily conceived program was suspended about March, 1959.

Regroupment took a new form and received public acknowledgment in President Diem's announcement, on July 7, 1959, that the government was undertaking to improve the standard of living and the security of its rural people through the creation of "prosperity and density centers" (*khu tru mat*). Eighty agrovilles, as these centers came to be called, were planned by the end of 1963, each containing about 400 families, or between 2,000 and 3,000 persons. In addition, perhaps 400 smaller agrovilles (*ap tru mat*), each holding about 120 families, were projected, to be clustered as satellites around the larger centers. Each agroville was to be divided into residential, commercial, and governmental quarters, laid out according to a master plan. In the government's view, the agroville's attractions were sure to win peasant support: the peasants would enjoy security, and they would have many of the advantages of urban life including electricity, a school, a maternity hospital, a market center, even a public garden.

Most peasants, however, saw the agroville program quite differently, whether they were included in the new settlement or not. They had to prepare the sites, without pay and often providing their own tools, which meant building access roads, digging wide surrounding canals and interior interlacing canals, and distributing the vast amount of earth thus removed so as to provide raised foundations for houses and other buildings. At the Vi Thanh agroville site, located in what was then part of Phong Dinh province, 20,000 peasants from four neighboring districts were brought in to begin construction. At the Thanh Thoi agroville, in Kien Hoa province, 3,000 Republican Youth from eight southwestern provinces joined with 2,000 other Republican Youth of the province to help the local population in their efforts. Since the number of people who could be moved into the total number of planned agrovilles did not exceed 500,000, it was obvious that most of those forced to work on the sites would not profit from their labor.

The government, moreover, was wrong in assuming that those selected to live in the agrovilles would willingly do so. The peasant was asked or, in most cases, compelled to abandon his old homestead with its ancestral tomb, small garden, and fruit and shade trees, for a desolate plot of ground in a strange place. He had to build his new house from materials taken from his old one, and his only help from the government was the gift of about $5.50 and the offer of an agricultural loan. The loan was necessary, because the peasant had to pay for the acre and a half of land he had been allotted. Whatever he thought of having neighbors and administrative services close at hand, he did not like the long distance which he generally had to walk to his rice fields. Many people resisted entering the agrovilles or went into them with great reluctance.

Communist attacks on some of the construction sites and intensive Communist propaganda against the program seriously added to the government's problems. The Communists' motives were clear, for the agrovilles, besides preventing access to the peasantry, were established in strategic areas, usually along a main road or water axis, which obstructed their free movement. So important was the strategic consideration that the President himself approved all proposed locations. Another difficulty was the ambitious scope of the program. It required detailed planning, the commitment of a considerable number of government personnel, and fairly substantial expenditures for public buildings, all of which the Vietnamese government had to sustain from its own revenues. For these various reasons, the program came virtually to a halt in early 1961, with about 22 agrovilles actually completed.

The limited plan of regrouping loyal and Communist-contaminated peasant families had given way in mid-1959 to the grandiose agroville scheme. The agroville program in its turn gave way to a new rural security program in late 1961: the establishment of strategic hamlets. The strategic hamlet program is at once both more modest and more ambitious than its predecessor. Unlike the agrovilles, it does not seek to create peasant cities in new locations according to a master plan drawn in Saigon, and thus it does not require the same heavy expenditures in money, supervisory personnel, and forced peasant labor. The aim of the strategic hamlet plan is to fortify existing villages. Nor does the strategic hamlet program, at least in conception, try to create its rural fortresses in the heart of enemy territory, as was the practice in the establishment of the agrovilles. Rather, those areas first selected for strengthening are the ones where government control is fairly strong; strategic hamlets are then extended from this secure base as government forces push back Communist power.

There are two variations of the strategic hamlet program, according to the degree of effective government control in an area. Where it is secure, the existing hamlets of a village — a typical village will include about four or five — are separately developed. Hedges, ditches, fences of sharpened bamboo stakes, and other barriers are built in a triangular or square pattern around the more populous part of the hamlet. Those living outside this perimeter are asked to move inside (at the risk of being considered hostile if they refuse), or they may be forced to move in. Special teams reorganize the local administration, sift the loyalties of the inhabitants, re-establish where necessary the various government-sponsored associations and see that the local people join those appropriate to their sex, age, and status, and train the young men to take over the defense of their hamlet. Democracy in also introduced to the strategic hamlet in the form of controlled elections of hamlet committees and councils.

Where government control of an area is not secure, or where the existing location of a hamlet is not defensible, the hamlet is destroyed and its inhabitants transferred to a more secure place. In these heavily influenced Communist areas the main emphasis is on military security, and political and social objectives are largely ignored. The entire male population is often militarized unless it is distrusted by the government, and here control over personal movement is more severe. Such hamlets are sometimes called combat hamlets, and it has been necessary to maintain larger government forces in or near them in order to ensure their survival.

The ambitiousness of the strategic hamlet program lies in its scope. The Vietnamese government planned in late 1961 to fortify over 11,000, or two-thirds, of the country's hamlets by 1963. Actual construction has proceeded pretty much on schedule and the government was able to report that 7,205 hamlets, containing two-thirds of the country's population, had been fortified by the end of June, 1963, and that an additional 2,398 hamlets were under construction.[29] An attempt is being made to provide health, educational, and other facilities to each fortified place, in addition to armaments and communication systems. By any measure, this is a vast undertaking. Also, it is not without its complexities, for, while it is under basic military direction, it requires the coordination of the army, Civil Guard, Civic Action, police and security, and other government organizations.

The fortification and regrouping program for the Central highlands has varied somewhat from that in other areas. In the first place, practically all the rural Vietnamese living in the highlands were transplanted there from the Central coastlands in the land development

[29] *Times of Vietnam Magazine,* July 14, 1963, p. 10.

program initiated in 1957. These people were settled, with considerable government assistance, in compact centers distributed through Kontum, Pleiku, and Darlac provinces. Except for a few centers established for former political dissidents which have been kept under armed guard, the land development program was voluntary. As the security situation worsened in the highlands after 1960, the government began strengthening these places and giving their inhabitants the means of self-defense. For the tribal people of the highlands the approach has been again different. These people live in hundreds of small communities scattered throughout the area, often in places difficult of access. Their vulnerability to Communist influence has been high, as a result of their distrust of Vietnamese settlers and government officials and the astute efforts of Communist agents to win their favor. These agents have adopted tribal customs, often speak the tribal dialects, have married tribal women, and have in many cases lived and worked for years among the tribal people. Young tribesmen have been sent to North Vietnam for political and guerrilla training and have come back home. The tribal peoples have been promised regional autonomy — a promise which has a strong appeal. As they have elsewhere, Vietnamese Communists have mixed compulsion and terror with persuasion and good works.

The Vietnamese government began regrouping and consolidating tribal communities in 1959, but it was not until mid-1961 when the balance of power began teetering dangerously in the highlands that it pursued its program with vigor. In the fall of 1961, the government undertook to regroup 35,000 tribesmen in Kontum province, about half the total tribal population there, and launched similar efforts in other provinces bordering on Laos. Although there has been some resistance to the program, with resettled groups drifting back into the forested hill country, it has met with a fair degree of success.

The Vietnamese government's rural-control programs, whatever they have been called, have had common objectives. First, they have sought to cut the link between the villages and the Communist guerrilla forces. To the extent that rural localities are pro-Communist, this means exterminating or at least subduing hostile sentiment within them; to the extent they are anti-Communist or neutral, it means providing security against the Communists. In either case it means depriving the guerrilla movement of its nourishment of taxes, food, manpower, and shelter from the villages. Second, the programs have sought to force the guerrillas into open engagements or back into uninhabited swamp and mountain retreats. This would not only enable the government to deal with the enemy in pitched encounters, but would also create "kill zones" outside of the fortified areas in which nationalist land, artillery, and air attacks need not worry about killing friend along with foe. Finally, the programs seek to divide defense functions between local forces, such as the Republican Youth, Self-Defense Corps, and Civil Guard, which will be primarily concerned with defending strategic hamlets and other fortified places, and the regular army, which will thus be free to engage the main Communist forces. It is no exaggeration to say that the survival of non-Communist Vietnam depends upon the success of its strategic hamlets.

The Balance Sheet

The anti-Communist policies of the Vietnamese government have not checked the growth of Communist strength in Vietnam. Given the determination of the North, no policies could have prevented guerrilla warfare from breaking out. Given the North's advantages in the post-Geneva years, no policies could have prevented this warfare from growing to fairly serious proportions. The Democratic Republic of Vietnam, it should be recalled, emerged from the Indochina War with a strong and experienced army and administration. It had, furthermore, kept an extensive network of its agents in the South, along with hundreds of caches of weapons, and it had left the conviction in many Southerners' minds that it represented the best, certainly the most militant, interests of the Vietnamese people in the struggle for independence. The new government in the South was struggling to extract itself from the debris of French colonialism. The great influx of refugees into the South, the internal conflicts which beset it in 1954 and 1955, and the tasks of building new constitutional forms and rehabilitating a war-devastated economy placed nearly intolerable burdens upon it. To make matters worse, the 900 miles of sea frontier and the 800 miles of land frontier that it shared with Laos and Cambodia were largely unguarded and easily penetrable from North Vietnam.

As we have attempted to show in this and other chapters, certain policies of the Vietnamese government, and its American ally, have inadvertently contributed to the development of the power of Vietnamese Communism within South Vietnam. The conventional training of the army, the neglect of the Civil Guard, the negativism of anti-Communism as a propaganda theme, the neglect of the peasantry, and the behavior of government officials toward the people are among the errors of the past. It would be more useful at this point, however, to evaluate the government's anti-Communist efforts in the light of the present situation, and to this subject we now turn.

The military capability of the Vietnamese armed forces has increased greatly since the end of 1961. In addition, the government has been training and arming the Republican Youth in loyal villages and hamlets. The quality of Vietnam's fighting forces has improved as well. The Civil Guard and Self-Defense Corps quickly lost their ragamuffin status as American aid was showered upon them in 1961 and 1962, and the army has received all the equipment it needs for engaging in fast-striking offensive operations, including attack bombers, artillery, troop-carrying helicopters, amphibious assault vehicles, and communications equipment. The strategic hamlet program promises to release a significant portion of the regular troops from static defense as the peasants gain the ability to defend their fortified communities. Equally important, the strategic hamlet program, if it succeeds, will sever the nourishing link between the villagers and the guerrillas. In this connection, it should be noted that the Vietnamese government has belatedly recognized the need to remove those officials who, through their unpopularity, have contributed to the Communist cause, and the need to allow the peasants to elect their own administrative committees and village councils. This latter step is being taken only in hamlets which have been made secure; about 500 hamlets had elected officials at the end of 1962. Finally, the large exodus of highland minority peoples from their isolated forest and mountain communities, even assuming that it has not been entirely voluntary, is a hopeful sign. Without tribal support, the guerrillas operating in the highlands will have difficulty in maintaining themselves, and their safety will be imperiled if the Rhade and other tribesmen make use of the weapons which American special forces personnel have been giving them.[30]

Despite these hopeful signs, the military situation in Vietnam remained, at the time of this writing, grim and uncertain of success. For one thing, the government is limited in the extent to which it can throw its military forces into offensive operations. Much manpower must necessarily be tied down in protecting towns, bridges, military installations, and other strategic points against possible attack or sabotage — not to mention the rural areas which the government is trying to pacify. Secondly, the government has still not made use of the offensive power now at its disposal. A good part of the Self-Defense militia is consigned to static defense, manning the several thousand small mud-walled posts which dot the Vietnamese scenery. These posts are useless, since they do not hamper enemy movement in the surrounding area; indeed, they assure the enemy that he is not being sought, and they are death-traps for their occupants when the enemy decides to attack them. Yet the Vietnamese government is un-

[30] See, for example, *New York Times,* April 29, 1962, p. 1; June 25, 1962, p. 3; and August 12, 1962, p. 28.

willing to give up the illusory security which these posts foster.[31] In addition, there is a continued strong tendency to use unneeded numbers of military personnel in non-combat assignments, and there is outright waste in the frequent assignment of specially trained anti-guerrilla forces to routine guard duties.[32]

The deeper military problems of South Vietnam are really political. In the narrow sense, they relate to President Diem's strict control over the military. The President is no more able to delegate military than administrative responsibility. He is, moreover, deeply suspicious of his military officers, and his suspicions are not lessened by the close relations which American military advisors have developed with some of them. The result is that military effectiveness against the enemy has been substantially reduced by the regime's need to buttress its own security. Thus, the President has elevated personal loyalty over military ability in the promotion and assignment of officers, has made use of informers within the military services, and has shifted officers who appeared to be too popular with their men or too close to the Americans. He interferes closely with combat planning; indeed, one correspondent has claimed that "not even a battalion [can] move without first consulting the President."[33] Because of Presidential interference, the Vietnamese military command structure is badly split and confused. Only six of the army's eighteen generals actually command troops; some of the others are not very competent, and some are politically suspect. All are regarded as junior subordinates by the President, who has taken upon himself the main responsibility for running the war.

The Vietnamese government has fought the war under the theme of advancing the cause of freedom against Communism. In this theme lie two other deep problems. First, the anti-Communist theme might succeed if the guerrillas were willing to join issue on this ground, or if the peasants were willing to believe that the guerrillas were Communists representing what the government tells them Communism stands for. But the guerrillas present themselves, and are widely regarded, as nationalists continuing the war against the foreigners and their lackeys. They fight in the name of the National Liberation Front, and they preach, not Communism, but "real" independence, peace, a neutral Vietnam, political freedom, extensive land reform, and other popularistic economic policies. Thus, it is not surprising that much of the government's anti-propaganda is wide of the mark. The negativism

[31] See *ibid.*, July 27, 1962, p. 4.
[32] *Ibid.*, July 8, 1962, p. 15; *Newsweek,* November 6, 1961, p. 46.
[33] Don Schanche, "Last Chance for Vietnam," *Saturday Evening Post,* January 6, 1962, p. 18.

of much of its policy has contributed to its failure to attach the Communist onus to the guerrilla movement. Its administration has been staffed, down to the lowest levels, with officials who served the colonialists prior to independence. It has refused to permit elections to reunify the country or even to counter Northern proposals for establishing relations between the two zones with proposals of its own. It has shown itself more concerned with the legalities of land ownership in the countryside than with the realities of a revolutionary situation. It has, in short, rendered its own nationalist credentials suspect.

Second, the Vietnamese government has not been able effectively to place its struggle under the banner of freedom. Even before the security situation deteriorated into widespread armed rebellion in 1959, the Vietnamese leadership had been progressively curtailing the political liberties of its people. Its control over the press, trade unions, and other organizations, and its manipulation of elections and its harassment of nationalist critics all existed prior to that time. Some new controls, such as the Republican Youth, the Women's Solidarity Movement, and the special military courts have arisen since that time, mostly in direct response to the military crisis, but for the most part older forms of control have simply been extended and intensified. The government has not been able to resist manipulating its people even in the village and hamlet elections which it has introduced as a means of countering the Communist appeal. In special instructions, it has told local officials that the various government-created associations at the hamlet level were to choose their own leaders democratically; however, the instructions added, "if the Civic Action, Youth, and Information cadres are a bit clever, these democratic elections will not bring any unexpected disastrous results; the people will elect whom we choose." Similarly, the district chief has been informed that "with a little cleverness" he can make the people elect to the hamlet administrative committee and the village council "those whom he in his heart of hearts wants to be elected."[34]

At this place, a few words should be said about the police apparatus which serves the needs of the Vietnamese government. Actually, there are a number of political police services. There is the regular *sûreté*, attached to the Department of Interior. Several other government departments, for example, Civic Action, Information, and Defense, have their own police networks. Ngo Dinh Can in Central Vietnam has his private network. But the key secret police agency is the one located in the Presidency under the innocuous name of the Social and Political

[34] The English translation of this document is entitled "From the Strategic Hamlet to the Self-Defense Village" but bears no other identification. The document apparently was written sometime in 1962.

Research Service (*So Nghien Cuu Xa Hoi Chinh Tri*). Its leader is Dr. Tran Kim Tuyen, an able Catholic intellectual from Central Vietnam. The power of this agency derives from the great amount of data which its agents have collected on government officials, military officers, businessmen, intellectuals, students, and others, and from Tuyen's role as Nhu's right-hand man in the informal power structure within the Vietnamese government. Tuyen's files give him an important role in the decisions which Nhu and the President make concerning men in and outside the government. They also give Tuyen considerable leverage over those whose histories are in the files. In addition to being the collector and keeper of political dossiers, the Social and Political Research Service serves as an action agency. It gives orders to the government political groups, subsidizes intellectual magazines, keeps track of the opposition and, where necessary, takes measures against it, and does whatever else needs doing. Thus its assignments vary widely, from ransacking an erring newspaper's offices to manipulating National Assembly and presidential elections. If a high government official has been selected by Nhu to be drummed out of the government, Tuyen provides the ammunition; if the University students appear to be getting out of hand, Tuyen's agents move into the situation. It should be emphasized that the Social and Political Research Service does not operate on the order of the Gestapo; the peculiar family dictatorship of South Vietnam is no Nazi state. Nor is Tran Kim Tuyen unnecessarily rough in carrying out his duties; a number of Saigon oppositionists even have kind words to say about him. But it is undeniable that Tuyen and his organization are extremely important instruments in the functioning of the Diem regime and in the complex pattern of political controls which emanate from the Presidential Palace.

It cannot be said that the Vietnamese leadership's concern for its security against non-Communist opponents has lacked foundation. The short post-independence history of Vietnam has been scarred by nationalist attempts to assassinate, subvert, or overthrow those in power. In 1954 there was the defiance of Diem by General Nguyen Van Hinh, who was backed by much of the army. In 1955 there was the uprising of the sects and the Binh Xuyen. In 1956 Great Vietnam and other political elements staged a small armed revolt in Central Vietnam. In February, 1957, bullets fired by an assassin, whose identity has never been made known, just missed the President while he was attending an agricultural fair at Ban Me Thuot. In November, 1960, paratroop and other military units nearly overthrew the regime in an attempted *coup d'état,* and in February, 1962, two Vietnamese air force planes destroyed one wing of the Presidential Palace in an unsuccessful attempt on the President and the Nhus.

The aerial attack appeared to involve few persons besides the pilots of the attacking planes. The 1960 *coup,* however, was launched by three crack paratroop battalions stationed in Saigon. The rebels quickly seized control of all installations except the Palace itself on the morning of November 11. They contented themselves with negotiating for Diem's removal rather than assaulting the defended Palace gates, and appeared to have achieved victory when the President that evening agreed to dissolve his government and form a provisional military government whose members would be selected by the army generals with the approval of the Revolutionary Committee of paratroop officers and their civilian associates in the *coup.* This interim arrangement was to lead to a "national union" government, the contours of which were not described but which would, according to a rebel statement, be based on free elections.[35] The rebellion collapsed as quickly as it had begun. Even while President Diem's concessions were being broadcast to the public on the morning of November 12, loyal troops from My Tho and Bien Hoa were moving against the rebel positions in the city. By late afternoon of that day, loyal forces had taken over and the surviving *coup* leaders were on their way to Cambodia aboard a military aircraft.

The planning of the *coup* was in the hands of a small number of military and civilian conspirators led by Hoang Co Thuy, a wealthy Saigon lawyer; Lieutenant Colonel Nguyen Trieu Hong, Thuy's nephew; Lieutenant Colonel Vuong Van Dong, Hong's brother-in-law; and Colonel Nguyen Chanh Thi, the commander of the paratroopers, who was brought in after the plot had been hatched. The *coup* seems to have engaged the active partisanship of only a small minority of the army and population. Considerably more of the military showed itself opposed to the rebellion than in favor of it, while considerably more civilians showed themselves in favor than in opposition. Most of the military, security, and police forces within Saigon, as well as the civil servants, remained outwardly neutral, and of these groups probably only the lower level civil servants were pro-*coup* in attitude. The bulk of the civilian population was also pro-*coup,* which feeling seemed to be strongest among students, businessmen, and commercial people. The pro-*coup* sentiment during this brief period included a hostility for the President's family and a conviction that it must be gotten rid of; some of the sentiment was quite bloodthirsty. Though there was also some critical feeling about Diem himself, the consensus seemed to be that he should be spared, and there was some active concern that he

[35] *Journal d'extrême-orient,* 12 novembre 1960; *Times of Vietnam,* November 12, 1960.

not be harmed. There was, however, a loss of confidence in Diem following the suppression of the *coup*, when he went back on his agreement to form a coalition government. However, the failure of many people to support the uprising actively would suggest that their desire for a change had not been very intense, though their passiveness could also have been due to the suddenness of the uprising and the absence of a real effort by the rebels to enlist popular support.

It is tempting to say that violent attempts to change the Vietnamese government have resulted from that government's unwillingness to permit peaceful change, but *coups d'état* have occurred in under-developed countries enjoying greater political freedom than Vietnam. On the other hand, the Ngo Dinh Diem regime has managed to survive for over eight years against recurring threats to its existence. In addition to a certain amount of plain luck, there are several reasons for the durability of Mr. Diem and his associates. First, the regime has been keenly sensitive to potential sources of danger and has taken precautionary action against them. Second, the Vietnamese middle class emerged from the Indochina War with a strong yearning for normalcy; its political apathy is only slowly wearing off. Third, the post-Geneva conflict with Vietnamese Communism has narrowed the range of political choice for many Vietnamese, leading them to accept or not actively to oppose stringent controls on their political liberty. And lastly, American backing of the Diem government, of which more will be said in the next chapter, has helped greatly to shield the regime from its would-be assailants.

If the Diem government has been able to keep itself in the saddle, it has not been able to rouse strong popular support for itself. The central problem has been leadership. Ngo Dinh Diem and his family have been convinced that they, and only they, are fit to lead Vietnam, and that leadership can be expressed through determination and example, without attempting to draw the Vietnamese people into active partnership. The people have been told what is good for them; there has been little effort to ask their opinions. It is doubtful whether Vietnam can be effectively ruled today under such mandarin prescriptions. The Communists clearly do not seek to rule on this basis; they have adapted themselves to the people's way of life when they have not come out of that life, and they have been able, where they have control, to stimulate strong popular participation while at the same time controlling its results. So long as there is an imbalance between the approaches of the government and the Communists to the Vietnamese people, the Vietnamese government will be severely handicapped in its struggle to roll back the Communist threat.

8

The Sovereign Unequals: American-Vietnamese Relations

La Présence Américaine

In 1819 a Captain John White sailed his merchant vessel up the Dong Nai river to Saigon in search of trade. Thus occurred the first American contact with Vietnam, just forty years before French warships assaulted Saigon as a first step in the French conquest of Cochinchina. Captain White did not succeed in his mission, but he did learn, as his countrymen more than a century later were to find out also, that Vietnam is governed by elaborate administrative procedures: the Vietnamese inspectors who boarded his ship drew up thirteen copies of his crew list and similarly recorded all arms carried by the vessel.[1]

Significant American involvement in Vietnam did not occur until the Second World War. At that time, President Roosevelt suggested to both Premier Stalin and Generalissimo Chiang Kai-shek that Indochina not be returned to France at war's end, for France "had done nothing to improve the natives since she had the colony." Instead, Roosevelt wanted to place the area under an international trusteeship until it should be ready for self-government.[2] The British had no liking for this anti-colonialist notion, and Roosevelt never pushed it

[1] Thai Van Kiem, "The First American in Vietnam," *Viet-My* (Saigon: The Journal of the Vietnamese-American Association), September, 1958, p. 40.

[2] Cited in Allan B. Cole and others (editors), *Conflict in Indochina and International Repercussions, 1945–1955* (Ithaca: Cornell University Press, 1956), pp. 47–48.

against their opposition. The United States did, however, give some tangible support to Vietnamese nationalism during the last stage of the war — and, inadvertently, to Vietnamese Communism. Having decided that the Viet Minh underground had the best intelligence apparatus of any of the anti-Japanese groups within Vietnam, American authorities in the Far East parachuted arms and other supplies to them. American officers operating with the Viet Minh went so far as to tell them the United States would support Vietnam's aspirations for independence once the war was ended. Indeed, the American military missions that entered Hanoi and Saigon in late summer, 1945, after the Japanese collapse, openly sympathized with the Viet Minh-created Democratic Republic of Vietnam, and some Americans addressed public meetings held under Viet Minh auspices.[3]

But American ardor for the Viet Minh quickly cooled as the Marxist nature of its leadership became apparent and as American policy accepted the return of French troops to Vietnam in the fall of 1945. From then until early 1950, the United States was mainly an outsider to the drama of guerrilla warfare between the French and the Viet Minh. In February, 1950, when Vietnam, Cambodia, and Laos were accorded the status of Associate States within the French Union, the United States quickly extended recognition to the three countries, and American military aid began to flow to the French military effort. The outbreak of the Korean War, in June of that same year, intensified American support.[4] Despite periodic pressure on the French to accord full sovereignty to the Indochinese states, the United States was willing to see the bulk of its aid channeled through French, not native, authorities.

Three events brought the United States directly into Vietnamese affairs during 1954. The first was the military crisis caused by the Viet Minh encirclement of the French military position at Dien Bien Phu. In late March the United States government decided to block the Communist conquest of Southeast Asia, even if it had to "take 'united action' with France and other countries."[5] The plan was to break the siege at Dien Bien Phu by air attacks launched from aircraft carriers against the Viet Minh positions, though consideration also was given to air and naval attacks along the Chinese coast if China did not desist

[3] See Philippe Devillers, *Histoire du Vietnam de 1940 à 1952* (Paris: Éditions du Seuil, 1952), pp. 152, 202; and Ellen J. Hammer, *The Struggle for Indochina* (Stanford: Stanford University Press, 1954), pp. 97, 130.

[4] See Agency for International Development, Statistics and Reports Division, *U.S. Foreign Assistance and Assistance from International Organizations, July 1, 1945-June 30, 1961* (revised; Washington, March 21, 1962), p. 32.

[5] James Reston, *New York Times*, March 30, 1954, p. 1.

from aiding the Viet Minh.[6] The Eisenhower administration dropped this plan when Congress and the American public were cool to it and the British objected outright.[7] The second event that drew the United States into the affairs of Vietnam was the Geneva Conference. This conference opened in late April, 1954, amid the deepening crisis at Dien Bien Phu, and ended in July. The United States was an unwilling participant at it: Secretary of State Dulles reportedly told the French ambassador in Washington on several occasions that the Conference would produce nothing, and Prime Minister Eden of Great Britain was convinced that the United States wished to bring the Conference to a speedy termination.[8] In the event it did in fact end in failure, the United States was contemplating sending three military divisions to Vietnam.[9]

The success of the Geneva Conference ushered in the third of the three events of 1954 that linked the United States to the fortunes of Vietnam. Washington quickly put aside its misgivings about the Conference's partition of Vietnam and moved to strengthen the government and economy of that part of the country which remained out of Communist hands. The small numbers of American military, technical assistance, and foreign service personnel were considerably augmented, as was American economic assistance to Vietnam. As of January 1, 1955, all American aid was given directly to the Vietnamese government, bypassing the French authorities. As American responsibility for the fate of South Vietnam assumed major proportions, French influence over Vietnamese affairs diminished. Although France retained sizeable economic investments in Vietnam — particularly in private rubber plantations — and has rendered economic and cultural assistance to the Vietnamese, France today plays a decidedly minor part in Vietnam's struggle for development and survival. It now accepts what its officials and private citizens in Vietnam denounced in 1954 and 1955 as *la présence américaine* in that country.[10]

The American presence in Vietnam is officially embodied in four major agencies: the Embassy, with about 90 employees, the U.S.

[6] Anthony Eden, *Memoirs: Full Circle* (Boston: Houghton Mifflin, 1960), pp. 106–19, Chalmers M. Roberts, "The Day We Didn't Go to War," *The Reporter,* September 14, 1954, pp. 31–35.

[7] *Ibid.* A Gallup poll taken in May, 1954, showed 36 per cent of the American people approving and 52 per cent disapproving the commitment of U.S. air and naval forces to the Indochina war. (*Los Angeles Times,* June 13, 1954, Pt. I, p. 18.)

[8] Jean Lacouture and Philippe Devillers, *La fin d'une guerre: Indochine 1954* (Paris: Éditions du Seuil, 1960), p. 83; Eden, *Memoirs,* p. 144.

[9] Eden, *Memoirs,* p. 143.

[10] The rise of American and fall of French influence in Vietnam is discussed in Bernard Fall, "La situation internationale du Sud-Vietnam," *Revue française de science politique,* 3 (September, 1958), 545–75.

Information Service (USIS), with about 35 employees, the U.S. Operations (economic aid) Mission (USOM), with about 300 employees, and the Military Assistance Command (MAC), with about 12,000 officers and enlisted personnel. The economic aid and military missions underwent heavy expansion after 1961, USOM from fewer than 200 employees and the military mission from fewer than 700. The reason for their expansion was the same: the deep commitment of the United States to counter-insurgency operations. For the USOM, this has meant a crash program to provide the Vietnamese government's strategic hamlets with social and economic necessities and the means for economic development. In addition to these four major agencies, the American government has provided Vietnam with various American groups to carry out special projects, generally under contract with USOM. Two of the more important contract groups have been the Johnson, Drake and Piper Company, which has constructed highways and bridges, and the Michigan State University Advisory Group, whose advisory and training activities have covered a broad range of Vietnamese administrative agencies and police services. Besides these "official" Americans there are perhaps 800 dependents and a handful of private businessmen and missionaries.

The American ambassador to Vietnam, like the chiefs of American diplomatic missions elsewhere, is responsible for coordinating and supervising the activities of his government in Vietnam.[11] To this end, he is the chairman of the Country Team; the other members are the chief of the military mission and the directors of USIS and USOM. The position of the ambassador is not as strong as these remarks might indicate. For one thing, he must operate within the framework of policies set in Washington that may leave him little discretion in implementation. In addition, the Saigon agencies inevitably conflict on a number of issues, usually because of their different objectives. As one director of the U.S. Operations Mission to Vietnam stated to a committee of the House of Representatives: "Naturally the MAAG (Military Assistance Advisory Group) is going to want the strongest possible military position. I am interested in economic accomplishment and the eventual economic viability of the country. The ambassador and the political officers want, by and large, to have the best political effect in the country."[12] A mission chief who finds himself countered by the Embassy or some other mission has the recourse of seeking support

[11] Executive Order 10893, dated November 10, 1960, "Functions and Responsibilities of Chiefs of United States Diplomatic Missions," *Federal Register,* vol. XXV, p. 10732.

[12] Testimony of Leland Barrows before the House Committee on Foreign Affairs. *Mutual Security Act of 1958, Hearings, March 18–20, 1958* (Washington, 1958), Part 9, p. 1232.

from his superiors outside Vietnam, and this support may be greater than that available to his rivals. The USOM, acting as the field service for the Agency for International Development, gains some advantage in Country Team discussions since it handles most of the money provided the Vietnamese government. The military mission enjoys an especially strong position in the American official community both because of its size and the high priority assigned its task. We saw in the chapter on social and economic development that the military mission has determined important economic aid priorities in Vietnam. This mission appears, moreover, to operate with only a light civilian hand upon it within the host country. The following exchange between the American ambassador to Vietnam, the chief of the American military advisory group to Vietnam, and Senator Mike Mansfield at a Senate committee hearing in 1959 is illuminating:

> *Senator Mansfield.* Have you, as Ambassador, ever directed the MAAG group to pursue or to refrain from pursuing a particular military aid project?
> *Mr. Durbrow.* Yes. . . .
> *General Williams.* Mr. Chairman, would you mind reading that question once more, please, sir?
> *Senator Mansfield.* Have you, as Ambassador, ever directed the MAAG group to pursue or to refrain from pursuing a particular military aid project?
> *General Williams.* The answer to that is "No."
> *Mr. Durbrow.* I guess you are right on that.[13]

All of the American agencies in Vietnam have their headquarters in Saigon and, until recently, the great majority of their personnel have been located there as well. The military advisory group has become the exception since 1961, with many of its augmented staff assigned to military stations throughout the country. But many American military personnel are clustered in the area around Saigon and many more are concentrated at other rear-echelon headquarters — one report has estimated that in mid-1962 there were at least five persons so located for every trainer-advisor in the field.[14] At any rate, the greatest concentration of Americans is still in the Saigon area and it is in Saigon that the American presence makes itself most strongly felt. The official Americans here enjoy a style of living generally far

---

[13] Senate Committee on Foreign Relations, Subcommittee on State Department Organization and Public Affairs, *Situation in Vietnam, Hearings, July 30 and July 31, 1959* (Washington, 1959), p. 183.

[14] *New York Times,* July 8, 1962, p. 15.

above that of the Vietnamese with whom they deal. In 1959, a Senate committee found that rents paid for American personnel in Saigon were "excessive by American standards." For about one-third of the American civilians the rents, paid by the American government, were exorbitant: including utilities, they exceeded $400 a month.[15] Most American civilians are transported to and from work and on business trips around Saigon in chauffeur-driven cars. The official American commissary sells a wide range of goods at low prices, including — at least in 1959 — rice and other products available in good quality on the local market. In short, the American community in Vietnam — except for most of the military advisors — lives far better that it would in the United States and, what is more important, in a manner which tends to cut it off from Vietnamese society.[16]

How much the Vietnamese resent these and other perquisites of the Americans is difficult to say. Perhaps most accept them as appropriate to a people coming from a different and far richer society, and the average urbanized Vietnamese appears to have a rather favorable attitude towards the Americans with whom he comes into contact.[17] Criticism of American living habits does, however, break out from time to time in the usually respectful Vietnamese press. "Americans," one complaint charges, "establish their own food and supply stores, sharing nothing with and getting nothing from the Vietnamese people. They have their own movie houses, restaurants, clubs and sports grounds completely separate from the Vietnamese people."[18] "Their living manner," states another press grievance, "creates a gap and does not help consolidate the American-Vietnamese relationship. . . . the majority still remain aloof and do not try to understand the psychology and aspirations of the local people."[19]

It would be a mistake to exaggerate the importance of the Vietnamese reaction to the way in which Americans live in Vietnam. Relations between the two countries are governed by more weighty considerations, to which we now turn.

[15] Senate Committee on Foreign Relations, *United States Aid Program in Vietnam, Report, February 26, 1960* (Washington, 1960), pp. 35–36.

[16] For the special needs of American military personnel operating with Vietnamese army units, see, for example, the *New York Times,* July 8, 1962, p. 14.

[17] See my survey of Vietnamese attitudes towards Americans, "They Work for Americans: A Study of the National Staff of an American Overseas Agency," *American Sociological Review,* 25 (October, 1960), 695–704.

[18] Article in *Dan Viet,* cited in the *New York Times,* December 1, 1961, p. 4.

[19] Article in *Nguoi Viet Tu Do,* cited in U.S. Operations Mission, *Saigon Daily News Round-Up,* June 11, 1958, p. 6. See also *Times of Vietnam,* March 5, 1958.

Mutuality and Conflict

The United States has pursued three objectives in Vietnam since 1954 — the security of Vietnam from Communist challenge, the economic development of the country, and the promotion of free if not democratic political institutions. Security has clearly been the overriding American concern. From the American point of view, a Communist take-over in Vietnam would seriously upset the balance of power in Southeast Asia and create too-favorable conditions for the extension of Communism into the whole area. As American officials are wont to say in non-public pronouncements, Vietnam is a piece of real estate that must be held by the West.

This post-Geneva concern with security is actually a continuation of American policy from the French period. The American commitment to the French military struggle in Indochina had become so strong that by 1953 American spokesmen were urging Vietnamese nationalists to moderate their demands for independence; Vice-President Nixon, who visited Saigon in the fall of that year, went so far as to preach the necessity of Vietnamese cooperation with the French.[20] Indeed, as the French showed signs of willingness to end the war by negotiation, American officials redoubled their efforts to keep the fight going. In February, 1954, Secretary of Defense Charles Wilson stated optimistically that military victory over the Viet Minh remained "possible and probable."[21] As the Viet Minh forces closed their trap around Dien Bien Phu and the gravity of the entire French position in Vietnam became palpably clear, the administration in Washington considered intervening in the war. And when France entered into negotiations with the enemy at Geneva, Secretary of State Dulles told the French ambassador to Washington that, above all, the deltas of the Red and Mekong rivers must be retained as bases from which a counterattack could recover what was lost to the Viet Minh at the conference table.[22] As one American diplomat in Saigon facetiously put the matter, "We are the last French colonialists in Indochina."[23]

America's basic policy towards Vietnam has not changed since Geneva. The importance of the security objective has been reflected

[20] Hammer, *The Struggle for Indochina*, pp. 318–19.

[21] Lacouture and Devillers, *La fin d'une guerre*, p. 52. This study contains the most detailed account of the closing phase of the Indochina war.

[22] *Ibid.*, p. 130.

[23] Cited by Hammer, *The Struggle for Indochina*, p. 319. When the English writer Graham Greene suggested to an American official in Saigon that the French might be bringing the war to a close, the response was, "Oh, no, they can't do that. . . ." (Graham Greene, "Indochina," *New Republic,* April 5, 1954, p. 13.)

in the size of the American military mission as compared to that of the economic and other groups maintained in Vietnam. It has been reflected in the large amounts of direct military assistance to Vietnam, in the use of the economic aid program to generate resources for support of the Vietnamese military budget, and in the tailoring of economic and technical aid projects to serve security purposes. And if the economic objective of American policy has had to serve military goals, the political objective has been a neglected child. Among the hundreds of Vietnamese sent to the United States on study or observation grants, an insignificant few have been journalists, members of the National Assembly, or persons connected with even the government political parties — non-government politicians have been excluded altogether. The subjects of study in the United States have been highly varied but hardly any of the Vietnamese sent by the United States government to this country have studied the machinery and functioning of political parties, elections, or legislative bodies. Similarly, American missions in Vietnam have devoted practically no resources or technical personnel to the development of the political instruments of representative government. It is true that some agencies have directed some of their efforts to these political goals. The Michigan State University Group, for example, urged the Vietnamese government to set up elective village and provincial councils and attempted to infuse its police advisory activities with democratic preachments. Many American officials have encouraged democratic behavior among Vietnamese officials with whom they have dealt; one American ambassador increased the strain in his relationship with President Diem by sharply criticizing the regime's refusal, on a legal pretext, to permit the opposition leader Phan Quang Dan to take his seat in the National Assembly in 1959. But precious little of American energies or resources has been devoted to political goals, as contrasted with the military and economic aims. Much of the American effort in Vietnam, on the other hand, has gone to strengthen the police and security forces and other institutions contributing to a modern police state.

From a certain perspective, American policies toward Vietnam have harmonized with those of the Vietnamese government. Like the United States, the Ngo Dinh Diem regime has since 1954 viewed security as its major concern. Like the United States, it has subordinated economic development to this concern, and has expressed only a meager solicitude for the fostering of democratic institutions and practices. Yet there have been important differences between the two governments as well. In part these have arisen from differing views of the means most likely to accomplish agreed-upon ends, and in part from conflicting national or more particularistic interests.

American-Vietnamese disharmony has been most apparent in the economic realm. There has been, first of all, the question of who pays how much of Vietnam's public expenditures. While the Vietnamese have been naturally interested in obtaining the maximum of American aid, the United States has as naturally wished to shift as much of this burden as possible upon the Vietnamese. There are three ways in which part of this burden might be shifted. First, the Vietnamese might finance a greater share of their imports from the large accumulation of dollars and other foreign currencies they have obtained from export sales. Second, they might substantially increase their internal taxes. Third, they might revise the exchange rate for the piaster. The piaster is officially valued at 35 to the dollar for American-financed imports, but has been generally sold at 85 to the dollar for imports financed from the Vietnamese government's own foreign reserves. Doubling the exchange rate for American-financed imports would double the amount of money generated for the jointly administered counterpart fund. It would also raise prices of the imported commodities considerably, and would also compel the Vietnamese government to reduce the level of customs duties on them. The Vietnamese have been understandably reluctant to replace American subsidies with increased internal taxation or foreign exchange earnings, and have resisted American pressures for such action, although the greatly increased cost of fighting the guerrilla movement has forced them to dip into their reserve accumulations in the last couple of years. They have also opposed a revision of the exchange rate, fearing that an increase in counterpart piasters might lead to a reduction in American aid.

The American and Vietnamese governments have, in the second place, different aims when it comes to spending the American aid. The Vietnamese would naturally like to have full discretion in this matter, while the Americans are interested in ensuring that the aid is used effectively and for its intended purposes. They are also highly sensitive to Congressional and public outcries that the American taxpayer's money is being wasted. This American concern has led to elaborate procedures for approving counterpart expenditures and supervising their use that the Vietnamese find extremely annoying. Ngo Dinh Nhu has gone so far as to recommend that the American economic aid mission withdraw entirely from the development of aid projects and concern itself only with their implementation.[24] The Vietnamese dislike of American influence in their economic decisions has also been an important factor in their unwillingness to devalue the

[24] "On the Much-Debated 'Interview' of Counsellor Ngo Dinh Nhu," *Times of Vietnam,* June 7, 1958.

piaster. Devaluation would increase the proportion of Vietnamese expenditures from the counterpart fund, over which the United States has joint control. By doubling the cost of imported goods, it would require a lowering of import taxes, over which the Vietnamese have full control. When the United States pressed them to revise their exchange rate in late 1961, the Vietnamese instead replaced a patchwork of import taxes with a uniform tax of 25 piasters on American-financed imports.[25] They have also rebuffed American attempts to gain influence over revenues produced by taxes on American imports. The United States has failed in its attempts to have these proceeds, which constitute about 90 per cent of all of Vietnam's import revenues, deposited in the counterpart fund or even subjected to American audit.[26]

The concern of the American aid mission in Vietnam over stateside criticism, especially from Congress, has been a third source of American-Vietnamese economic conflict. The mission's reluctant participation in the highlands development program was influenced by fears of what Congress might say. The mission was particularly worried about Vietnamese use of American-aid funds and equipment. When one development center that was being used as a political detention camp rose up against its military guards, the possibility of a Congressional investigation was a source of extreme anxiety to the American advisors. The sensitivity of American aid officials to Congressional criticism has resulted in long delays and complex administrative clearances in the implementing of aid projects. It has made the economic aid mission seek publicity for its good works, to the extent of objecting to the U.S. Information Agency in Saigon's policy of playing down American contributions to Vietnamese government programs in the newsreels it makes for Vietnamese movie houses. And it has led to criticisms from the Vietnamese — Ngo Dinh Nhu once accused the economic aid mission as being "always afraid of reproaches from the American Congress."[27]

The differing economic beliefs of the United States and Vietnam have produced their share of friction in the relations between the two governments. Although the United States pushed the Vietnamese into embarking on a land redistribution program, it refused to provide the $30,000,000 needed to pay off the landowners. (It did however pro-

[25] "Ten Decree-Laws to Reorganize Vietnam's Economic and Financial Structure," *News from Vietnam* (Embassy of Vietnam, Washington), February 8, 1962, pp. 3–4.

[26] Senate Committee on Foreign Relations, *Situation in Vietnam, Hearings, December 7 and 8, 1959,* pp. 238, 241.

[27] *Times of Vietnam,* June 7, 1958.

vide $4 million for the administrative costs of the program). It appears that the United States was unwilling to support the appropriation of private property openly. Similarly, the American government was long opposed to aiding public-controlled industrial development. This policy was particularly noticeable during the Eisenhower administration, and was the cause of considerable strain in Vietnamese-American relations. It gradually gave way before Vietnamese insistence upon at least mixed public-private ownership of new industries.

Finally, the friction has sometimes been based not on differences in economic belief but on differences in economic interest. A prime example is the American legal requirement that where possible at least one-half the gross tonnage of commercial and related American aid be transported by American commercial vessels. Similarly, the generous American policy of permitting Vietnamese importers to buy U.S.-financed commodities in a Free World competitive market was superseded in 1961 by a "Buy American" policy that excluded purchases from most of Vietnam's non-American suppliers. Both policies have considerably increased the costs of Vietnamese imports. American interests have seen to it that the commercial aid program does not finance industrial food processing equipment which might increase Vietnam's potential for exporting commodities in competition with certain American food surpluses. Until 1959, when the administrative — not Congressional — restriction was removed, no American economic aid or technical assistance could go to Vietnamese rice production because the United States was concerned about its own rice surplus. Before then American-supported agricultural projects benefiting Vietnam's rice farmers had to be conducted under other pretenses.[28]

In their approaches to the problem of security, too, the American and Vietnamese governments have differed. One major difference has been in the emphasis they give it. If the United States has made security a key objective, the Vietnamese government has gone yet further. For example, in the highlands development program the American economic aid mission was dismayed by the lack of careful planning by the Vietnamese authorities. Settlement sites were selected with little regard to soil fertility or water resources; the land allotments seemed too small to sustain the settlers; and the whole program was pushed with alarming speed while the Americans were still wondering whether it was economically feasible. The Vietnamese, however, saw the program primarily in military, not economic, terms. The

[28] See John D. Montgomery, *The Politics of Foreign Aid* (New York: Praeger, 1962), pp. 128–33, for various advantages given to American business interests by United States economic policies.

development centers were designed to form a human wall against Communist North Vietnam, and President Diem himself selected many of the sites in flights over the area or from military maps.[29]

Likewise, to the Vietnamese government, security has been more a military matter than it has been to its American ally, as can be seen in the drawn-out dispute over the Civil Guard force. The police advisers of the Michigan State University Group recommended in 1955 that the 50,000-man Civil Guard be reduced one-half and be trained, equipped, and assigned to strictly police duties. In their eyes it was a rural police organization which should not live apart in military posts but among the villagers it would protect. The Vietnamese government, on the other hand, rejected this concept; it wanted, in effect, 50,000 auxiliary military troops. Thus, one equipment list presented to the Americans included armored vehicles, bazookas, artillery, landing craft, and helicopters. The strategic hamlet program is a more recent example of the different approaches of the two governments in security matters. Both governments have agreed on the need to make the hamlets secure against external attack, but have disagreed on the handling of the people within them. The Vietnamese have tended to regard the strategic hamlets as a device for controlling their residents while the Americans have wanted to give the inhabitants social and economic benefits and a strong voice in hamlet affairs.

Probably the greatest tensions in American-Vietnamese relations in the area of security derive from the special concerns of each partner. The United States obviously cannot base its anti-Communist policies solely on the requirements of Vietnamese security, and the Ngo Dinh Diem government has been acutely concerned with its own security in addition to that of the country itself. America's other concerns are illustrated by the attempt of high-level American officials in 1957 to get President Diem to modify his policy of forcing Vietnamese nationality on the large Chinese community in Vietnam. This policy had strained Vietnam's relations with Taiwan and the United States intervened on behalf of the Nationalist Chinese and in the interest of maintaining the solidarity of the anti-Communist coalition that fringes the Chinese mainland. President Diem responded by telling the American ambassador to Vietnam that while Vietnam's Chinese residents posed no serious problem so long as the United States supported the Taiwan government, he could not be sure this support would continue. Since loss of United States support would mean the elimination of a Nationalist China, which would establish Communist China's claims over Vietnam's Chinese population, he felt his move necessary in anticipation of future danger.

[29] See *ibid.,* pp. 72–83.

Indeed, the Vietnamese government has been nagged constantly by doubts about the dependability of the United States in the Cold War. It was disturbed by American acceptance of the Communist wall in Berlin, by American failure to take direct action to eliminate Castro in Cuba, by American aid to neutralist and Communist states — the Vietnamese have no dealings at all with the Communist bloc. The American backdown in Laos in 1961 was particularly unsettling to the Vietnamese. Instead of direct intervention in the civil fighting there, the United States chose a political settlement that forced the Laotian anti-Communists to accept an end to hostilities and a tripartite government in which they were outnumbered by Communist and neutralist representatives. The Vietnamese fear that they may be abandoned by the United States as a dispensable bargaining counter in the Cold War, and a not insignificant part of the task of American leaders has been to assure them of the fidelity of American intentions. A major purpose of Vice-President Johnson's trip to Vietnam and other Far East countries in the spring of 1961 was to calm the Vietnamese fears excited by the Cuban fiasco and the Laos disengagement then taking place. The fears, however, remain and, furthermore, have some basis in reality. In early 1963, for example, four members of the Senate Foreign Relations Committee questioned whether "an ever-deepening total involvement of the United States on the Southeast Asian mainland" was the only or the best way to cope with the Communist Chinese threat to long-range American security. What made this senatorial doubt, expressed in a written report, especially ominous to Vietnam was that the group's chairman was Mike Mansfield, the majority leader of the Senate and an early and influential supporter of the Ngo Dinh Diem government.[30]

While the United States might find that it was to its interest to make an arrangement with Communism detrimental to Vietnamese security interests, as it did in Laos, the Vietnamese do not seem to have a similar option. Those occupying the highest places in the Vietnamese government, at any rate, seem to be committed to a rigid anti-Communist policy for the foreseeable future, however much they may chafe at their situation. They are anti-Communist by conviction (many are Catholics), by the memory of the treatment they or their families received from the Communists in the past, by economic interest, by their individual records of hostility to Communism. They are in the situation of the Nationalist Chinese and the South Koreans: They are

[30] Senate Committee on Foreign Relations, *Vietnam and Southeast Asia, Report of Senators Mike Mansfield, J. Caleb Boggs, Claiborne Pell, Benjamin A. Smith* (Washington, 1963).

America's allies in the Cold War, but there is always the possibility that they will become its pawns as well.

The other major strain in American-Vietnamese relations respecting security has stemmed from the concern of the Ngo Dinh Diem regime with its own tenure. Put differently, the regime has equated the security of the nation with its own safety. But the regime's self-concern has resulted in policies that, at least in the short run, have impeded effective countering of the Communist threat and set United States and Vietnamese authorities at odds. The Americans have been understandably less sensitive to the implications measures they have considered rational from the standpoint of security have for the safety of Diem's regime. Thus, the two governments have conflicted on Diem's use of personal loyalty as the main criterion in military appointments and promotions, his frequent shifting of capable military officers to less useful but safer posts (for the regime), his tight control over military strategy and operations, his continual political interference — and that of his close associates — in the military chain of command. One reason Diem wanted a strong Civil Guard in 1954 and 1955 was as a counterforce to the Army, whose loyalty was then in serious doubt. In late 1954, Diem and J. Lawton Collins, the special American ambassador to Vietnam, were in dispute over a successor to General Nguyen Van Hinh, who had just been ousted as chief of staff of the army. Diem was reported as opposing General Nguyen Van Vy, Collins' candidate, because Vy was "insufficiently submissive," while Collins apparently feared that army morale would suffer if Diem's choice, General Le Van Ty, were given the post.[31] Similarly, the Michigan State University Group tried unsuccessfully for several years to prod the Vietnamese President into clearly demarcating the jurisdictions of the various Vietnamese police and security services and wanted the Civil Guard freed from the control of the province chiefs. It seems clear that Diem saw safety for his regime in the conflicts produced by overlapping jurisdictions and, in particular, did not want the Civil Guard placed under strong central direction. The province chiefs are too many and too isolated from one another to pose a threat to the President, and he has used them not only to fragment the line of command of the police and security services but of the army as well.

American-Vietnamese conflicts originating in differing attitudes and policies concerning political freedom have been of two kinds. One is based on what may be described as the promptings of the American diplomatic conscience. The American ambassador's criticism of skullduggery in the 1959 National Assembly elections, mentioned earlier,

[31] *New York Times,* December 5, 1954, p. 5.

is an example. This same ambassador once gave President Diem his uncomplimentary views on the doings of the Personalist Labor Party and its leader, Ngo Dinh Nhu, and different high-level American diplomatic personnel have from time to time urged their Vietnamese counterparts to temper their authoritarian behavior. The sum of these efforts has not been great, nor has their impact; they have been expressions of American concern with the course of political development in Vietnam rather than the expressions of a determined American policy.

A second kind of conflict over democracy has not concerned the freedoms of the Vietnamese at the hands of their government, but those of the Americans in Saigon. The American Embassy there has interceded in conflicts between American journalists and the Vietnamese government a number of times, not always successfully, in an effort to uphold the principle of freedom of the press against Vietnamese desires to expel those who had written critically about the regime. The relations between the Michigan State University Group and the Vietnamese government raised the democracy-for-Americans issue in several contexts. There was, for one thing, the academic freedom issue. For instance, the University subscribed to a number of American and other foreign journals for the library it developed for the National Institute of Administration. Some of these periodicals occasionally carried stories critical of the Vietnamese government or otherwise conflicted with the government's propaganda line. The Institute's leadership was not sure how it should cope with this unwanted material; it was evidently too embarrassed to raise the matter directly with its American colleagues. The predicament was resolved by more or less surreptitious removal of offending issues of the *New York Times, Figaro,* and other publications. Similar embarrassments were caused by some of the studies that Michigan State academic personnel produced for the Vietnamese government. The General Directorate of Information and Press was understandably irritated by a local-government study that reflected poorly on the government's informational activities and reproduced Communist propaganda documents.[32] The Presidency itself reacted when a propaganda broadcast by Radio Hanoi called its attention to a critical analysis by a Michigan State professor of economic development in Vietnam,[33] and it insisted that the University Group call back all distributed copies of the study and turn

[32] John D. Donoghue and Vo Hong Phuc, *My Thuan: The Study of a Delta Village in South Vietnam* (Saigon: Michigan State University Vietnam Advisory Group, May, 1961.)

[33] Frank C. Child, *Essays on Economic Growth, Capital Formation, and Public Policy in Vietnam* (Saigon: Michigan State University Vietnam Advisory Group, May, 1961).

them, with the supply on hand, over to the Vietnamese government. To ensure that future University studies directed to a Vietnamese audience would be suitable as to content, the Vietnamese required that they be submitted either to the National Institute of Administration or the General Directorate of Information and Press for prior approval.

The Vietnamese government also viewed with disfavor the relationships of some of the Michigan State professors with members of the Vietnamese nationalist opposition, though it never interfered with them.[34] Likewise, it quite naturally resented the open criticisms some professors made of the regime in the cafes and other places of Saigon, and in one instance demanded the removal of a too-articulate member of the Michigan State Group. In these concerns, it should be noted, the Vietnamese government behaved not too differently from the official American agencies in Saigon. The U.S. Information Service library did not carry books likely to offend the Vietnamese authorities, and willingly removed those that did. The American economic aid mission felt that the Michigan State Group should conform to *its* economic line — one director argued that the Group should actively promote this line whatever its own views, and one of the Group's economic specialists was reprimanded for departing from it in his personal conversations with the Vice-President of Vietnam. The Michigan State specialist had expressed doubts that financial reform demanded devaluation of the piaster. Likewise, the American Embassy from time to time has cautioned American personnel against associating with Vietnamese oppositionists and has sometimes prohibited such associations. As one American professor teaching under State Department auspices at the University of Saigon reported it, the Political Counsellor at the American Embassy informed him that "the Ambassador . . . wants no association with the intellectual opposition to the Diem regime by U.S. officials — and that includes Smith-Mundt professors."[35]

The democracy-for-Americans conflict between the Vietnamese government and Michigan State University came to a head with the American publication in 1960 and 1961 of several journal articles by University faculty members who had returned from service in Vietnam. None of the articles was flattering, and President Diem was particularly incensed by those which recommended that he dissolve his

[34] The Vietnamese government did however expel a visiting American professor at the University of Saigon whose opposition contacts included persons implicated in an attempt on President Diem's life. See the *New York Times,* May 26, 1962, p. 2; *ibid.,* May 27, 1962, p. 13; and Stanley Millet, "Terror in Vietnam," *Harper's,* September, 1962, pp. 32–39.

[35] Luther A. Allen, "South Vietnam: The Issue Is Freedom," *The Nation,* March 17, 1962, p. 234.

family oligarchy[36] and predicted the overthrow of his regime.[37] The Vietnamese leader apparently could not understand why those whom, he said, he had regarded as his friends should treat him thus, nor why Michigan State University was unable to control the writings of its faculty. Coming on top of other strains, some of them mentioned earlier, this barrage of criticism convinced Diem that he did not want the University Group around after its contract expired on June 30, 1962.[38]

To summarize at this point, the American government has pursued several objectives in its Vietnamese policy, the overriding one being military security. The Vietnamese government has shared the American preoccupation with security, but this has not eliminated from their relationship important conflicts of views and interests. In the following pages we shall examine how some of these conflicts between the two governments have been resolved.

My-Diem: The Bargaining Relationship

The North Vietnamese government and its National Liberation Front almost invariably refer to the South Vietnamese government as the *My-Diem* — American-Diem — regime. The epithet implies that the United States controls the Ngo Dinh Diem regime and one need not be a Marxist to find a certain plausibility in the charge. The United States has provided a staggering proportion of South Vietnam's military, economic, and financial resources since 1954. Without American aid an independent South Vietnam could not have survived; without American political support it is highly doubtful that Ngo Dinh Diem could have kept himself in power.

Diem's political dependence on the United States deserves special attention. It is generally believed by the Vietnamese that Diem is America's man and that the American government would not deal with any group that ousted him. The United States provided some evidence for this belief as early as the fall of 1954, at the time of Diem's conflict with his army leaders. In October of that year Senator Mike Mansfield issued a report, which was highly influential in Washington circles, recommending that "in the event that the Diem government falls . . . I believe that the United States should consider an

---

[36] Adrian Jaffe and Milton C. Taylor, "A Crumbling Bastion: Flattery and Lies Won't Save Vietnam," *New Republic,* June 19, 1961, pp. 17–20. While Jaffe was also on the Michigan State University faculty, his service in Vietnam was not connected with the University's program there.

[37] Frank C. Child, "Vietnam — The Eleventh Hour," *New Republic,* December 4, 1961, pp. 14–16.

[38] See the *New York Times,* February 21, 1962, p. 8.

immediate suspension of all aid to Vietnam and the French Union forces there. . . ."[39] That Mansfield's view reflected official American policy was made clear the following month when President Eisenhower's special ambassador to Vietnam, J. Lawton Collins, arrived in Saigon to take up his duties. Collins announced that the United States was not interested in "training or otherwise aiding a Vietnamese army that does not give complete and implicit obedience to its premier."[40] The Chief of Staff of the Vietnamese army, General Nguyen Van Hinh, who had headed the military opposition to Diem, allowed himself to be packed off to France two days after Collins' announcement. Hinh asserted to a foreign correspondent, "I had only to lift my telephone and the *coup d'état* would have been over. . . . But the Americans let me know that if that happened, dollar help would be cut off."[41]

In May, 1955, Ngo Dinh Nhu asked if the United States would support Diem's plan to oust Bao Dai as Chief of State, and apparently got what he requested.[42] In March, 1956, Secretary of State Dulles backed the Vietnamese government's refusal to consent to the reunification elections stipulated by the Geneva Agreements.[43] And throughout the early period of the Diem government's existence the United States Information Service participated in an intensive propaganda campaign to build up the prestige of the Vietnamese leader. In fact, the Vietnamese government's propaganda agency, an American official has said, was practically run by American information specialists until 1957.[44] Recent assurances of American support of Ngo Dinh Diem occurred in February, 1962. In mid-February the American ambassador to Vietnam reminded Diem's nationalist opponents that the United States fully supported the Diem regime, and called upon the opposition to cooperate with it.[45] And when two Vietnamese air force planes attacked the Presidential Palace later that month, President Kennedy quickly cabled his relief that President Diem had been spared injury, in order "to provide him with the greatest possible

[39] Senator Mike Mansfield, Senate Committee on Foreign Relations, *Report on Indochina, October 15, 1954,* (Washington, 1954), p. 14.

[40] *New York Times,* November 17, 1954, p. 14. See also *ibid.,* November 18, 1954, p. 3.

[41] Quoted by Peter Schmid, "Free Indochina Fights against Time," *Commentary,* January, 1955, p. 28.

[42] *New York Times,* May 7, 1955, p. 1; *ibid.,* May 12, 1955, pp. 1–2.

[43] *Ibid.,* March 15, 1956, p. 12.

[44] Testimony of Ambassador Elbridge Durbrow, Senate Committee on Foreign Relations, *Situation in Vietnam, Hearings, July 30 and 31, 1959,* p. 184.

[45] "Address by Ambassador Frederick E. Nolting, Jr., before the Saigon Rotary Club, Feb. 15, 1962," *Vietnam Press* (English edition), February 16, 1962 (morning issue), pp. D-3, D-4.

political backing in the event that the rebel pilots might enjoy any sympathies in South Vietnam."[46]

Thus, the Vietnamese leadership has been heavily indebted to the United States for its material and political backing. Its dependence, moreover, is quite irreversible, for it cannot threaten to evade its obligations by coming to terms with the Communist bloc or by slipping into unaligned neutralism.

Considering this dependence, it is surprising that the Ngo Dinh Diem regime has been able to keep control of so many of its decisions. The Communists — and some others[47] — to the contrary, the United States does not call the tune in Vietnam. Indeed, the number of things the United States has failed to get is impressive. It has not accomplished a devaluation of the piaster. Revenues from American-aid imports still remain under full Vietnamese control. The Vietnamese government's Chinese policy was carried out despite American remonstrances. The intervention of the American ambassador did not give Phan Quang Dan the National Assembly seat to which he was elected, nor did it keep the Michigan State University Group in Vietnam after June, 1962. Some differences between the two governments have, of course, been resolved through compromise, but it is striking how much the United States (and how little the Vietnamese government) has given up in reaching these adjustments. The dispute over whether the orientation of the Civil Guard should be civil or military ended with Washington acceding to the basic position of the Vietnamese. The dispute over the land development program ended with the United States renewing its support (after a temporary withdrawal) essentially on the Vietnamese government's terms. It would be fair to say that in most disagreements the Vietnamese have largely if not entirely had their own way.

How has the Vietnamese government managed to fare so well in dealing with its powerful ally? There are several explanations. For one thing, Vietnam is not entirely dependent upon the United States for carrying out programs of national development. If the United States government refuses to support a particular program or attaches unwanted conditions to its support, the Vietnamese can often get help from other countries. The Japanese, for example, willingly provided the money, equipment, and personnel for the Da Nhim hydroelectric project after the American government turned the Vietnamese down; the Germans similarly helped to establish a medical faculty at the Uni-

[46] *New York Times,* February 28, 1962, p. 2.

[47] For example, Bernard Fall, in *Revue française de science politique,* p. 554, erroneously believed that "The National School of Administration of Vietnam has passed entirely under the control of Michigan State University."

versity of Hue; and other countries have also been willing to substitute their aid for that of the United States where the costs have not been too high. Also, the Vietnamese have sometimes undertaken projects solely with their own funds when the United States refused to cooperate. Self-financing is, of course, made possible, or at least easier, by the circumstance that America supports so many other Vietnamese public expenditures. Indeed, the United States has at times facilitated Vietnamese execution of projects that it has opposed. In 1958, for example, American authorities withheld the piaster equivalent of $5 million (at the official rate of exchange) from the land development program because they objected to the way the program was being carried out, but then permitted the Vietnamese government to transfer to the program an equivalent amount of American aid that had been earmarked for the Vietnamese military budget.

A second reason for Vietnamese success in dealing with the United States has been the ability of the Vietnamese to exploit shifts and divisions in American policy. A case in point was the Vietnamese reaction to visits by Vice-President Lyndon Johnson and an economic study mission headed by Professor Eugene Staley of Stanford University to Saigon in the spring and early summer of 1961. Johnson assured the Vietnamese of full American support for the Diem government and an increase in American aid. The Staley group recommended American support for a variety of economic and security projects strongly desired by the Vietnamese leadership. Prior to the Johnson visit, American officials in Saigon had thought the Vietnamese had reached the point of seriously discussing devaluation of the piaster; after the visit the Vietnamese abruptly refused to discuss the matter at all. The Johnson and Staley visits also changed the Vietnamese government's attitude toward its domestic critics. Following the attempted *coup d'état* of November, 1960, the government, feeling the need for a public outlet for critical expression, created a National Union Front. This organization gained a fair amount of attention through the public meetings it called during the spring and early summer of 1961, and then it suddenly sank into oblivion. According to reliable reports, Ngo Dinh Nhu let some of the pro-government representatives on the Front's executive committee know that he and the President felt the Front was no longer needed since the American government had now given its unconditional support to the Vietnamese leadership.[48]

It has sometimes been difficult for American agencies in Saigon to present a united front to the Vietnamese in cases of dispute. The opposition of the American economic aid mission to the land develop-

[48] This information is based on personal interviews with members of the National Union Front's executive committee in August, 1961.

ment program was counteracted by the American ambassador's support of the program for political reasons. Some of the Michigan State University police advisers believed that President Diem resisted their position on the Civil Guard issue because he received covert encouragement from the American military advisory group for his own military conception of the Civil Guard. And even when the American agencies in Saigon have maintained a united front, the Vietnamese have occasionally been able to win out by taking their case to Washington. The atomic-reactor controversy illustrates the use of the diplomatic end-run in American-Vietnamese relations. The Vietnamese government wanted a reactor both for prestige purposes and as a means of inducing Vietnamese scientists living in France to return home. American officials in Saigon felt that Vietnamese resources and American money could be more profitably used for other purposes. Unknown to the American agencies in Saigon, the Vietnamese raised the question in the United States with State Department and Atomic Energy Commission officials in early 1959 and reached an agreement in mid-summer. The United States met the Vietnamese desire for an atomic reactor to be located at Dalat.

A third reason for Vietnamese success in bargaining with the United States has been the restraint of the American partner. The American government has frequently expressed its respect for Vietnamese sovereignty and has viewed its role in Vietnam as advisory only: American officials may suggest and recommend policies to the Vietnamese, but the latter are free to accept, modify, or reject American proposals. It must be added that the Vietnamese government has taken special pains to keep American officials in their proper advisory role. Vietnamese army officers have been told by their government that they should not enter into close off-duty relations with American military advisers, and civil officials are generally careful not to gain the reputation of being too pro-American. At least one high Vietnamese administrator, not very well thought of by President Diem, has probably kept his position mainly because American officials have persistently asked the President to get rid of him. The visit of a Congressional subcommittee to Saigon in late 1959 for the purpose of holding hearings on the American aid program sharply illustrates the Vietnamese determination to prevent Americans from meddling in their affairs. President Diem, wrongly believing that the Congressmen were coming to inquire into the operations of his government, sent no one to welcome the group on its arrival, and directed four of his Cabinet members to cancel their acceptance of invitations to a dinner honoring the distinguished visitors.[49]

---

[49] *Congressional Record,* House of Representatives, 86th Cong., 2nd Sess., 1960, p. 8385–88. Diem finally agreed to receive the Congressmen on the

Respect for Vietnamese sovereignty has indeed induced the United States to act with moderation in its dealings with the Vietnamese government, but this is not the main reason why the United States has been reluctant to add coercion to advice. In Laos, for example, it was willing in 1962 to suspend payments to the army to compel the pro-Western faction in Laotian politics to accept a coalition government that included pro-Communists and neutralists. Even in Vietnam the United States could not possibly divorce advice from coercion unless it were to grant its aid in lump sums at levels stipulated by the Vietnamese. Furthermore, the United States has, in its political support of the Diem regime and other ways discussed in this chapter and elsewhere, exceeded its purely advisory capacity.

The truth is that the United States has generally acted with restraint in disputes with the Vietnamese government over what it considered issues of secondary importance, and with firmness over issues of major concern. Two kinds of issues have fallen into the latter category. First have been matters affecting domestic American interests, especially those arousing political concern at home. An example is the recent conflict between Vietnamese and American authorities over the local costs for operating the strategic hamlet program, including transportation of American aid to protected rural areas and the maintenance of necessary roads. The United States had authorized a cash transfer of $10 million of American aid in the fall of 1962 to permit the purchase of Vietnamese piasters for meeting these expenses, but it refused to permit additional cash transfers. There had been Congressional criticism that the Vietnamese were relying too much on American financing of their counter-guerrilla operations; besides, the Kennedy Administration disapproved of cash transfers because they added directly to the American balance-of-payments deficit. The Vietnamese resisted paying for the local costs of the hamlet program but, confronted with an unyielding American attitude, finally capitulated in May, 1963, and agreed to supply the funds through deficit financing.[50] It may also be noted that the Buy-American requirement of the commercial import program, instituted in 1961 despite strong Vietnamese objections (because it raised the cost of import commodities), serves to return to the United States in the form of Vietnamese purchases most of the dollar aid that the American government allocates to the import program.

---

last day of their stay and allowed his Cabinet members to reaccept the dinner invitations after the American ambassador and American chief military advisor convinced him that the subcommittee was committing no trespass upon Vietnamese sovereignty.

[50] *New York Times,* May 10, 1963, pp. 1, 6.

Secondly, the United States has been willing to deal firmly with the Vietnamese government when it has felt its main interest in Vietnam — the containment of Communist expansion — to be in jeopardy. In late 1954 American policy-makers feared that the mounting tension between Diem and leaders of the political-religious sects and other groups would undermine South Vietnam's fragile political structure. In consequence, strong pressure was brought upon Diem to bring his nationalist rivals into the government, and Ambassador Collins reportedly warned him of the possible loss of American backing if he failed to do so.[51] By April, 1955, American concern had become so acute that Collins "advocated replacing Diem with someone more acceptable to the sects and France."[52] Diem resolved American doubts about his leadership by his quick military victory over the sects, and the United States put thoughts of getting rid of him aside. There is some evidence that the American government once again considered taking steps to replace Diem during the 1961 low point in the guerrilla war, but decided that the hazard was too great. It did, however, seek important concessions from him in return for the increased support he needed to fight the guerrillas. The American demands, presented in November, 1961, were based on recommendations made by a study mission headed by General Maxwell Taylor which had visited Vietnam the previous month. According to published stories, the United States wanted Diem to decentralize his administration, particularly his own control over the army, and demanded better coordination of the government's multiple and chaotic intelligence activities and greater political freedom for the Vietnamese people.[53] The United States, it was reported, sought "democratic reforms" and major economic changes, and was persuading Diem "to give young and capable aides a voice in his government and army and to halt persecution of persons branded as opponents."[54]

The course and outcome of the 1961 negotiations tell much about the bargaining relations between the American and Vietnamese governments. The Vietnamese government's public reaction to American pressure was a series of stories in Vietnamese newspapers inspired, according to informed sources, by Ngo Dinh Nhu. The stories criticized American "imperialist" designs upon Vietnam and wondered if Vietnam should not reconsider its relationship with the United States.

[51] *Ibid.*, October 13, 1954, p. 3; December 5, 1954, p. 5.

[52] Wells C. Klein and Marjorie Weiner, "Vietnam," in George McT. Kahin (editor), *Governments and Politics of Southeast Asia* (Ithaca: Cornell University Press, 1959), p. 340. See also C. L. Sulzberger in the *New York Times,* April 18, 1955, p. 22.

[53] *New York Times,* November 27, 1961, p. 1; Agence France Presse despatch from Saigon, November 24, 1961.

[54] *New York Times,* December 1, 1961, p. 1.

On December 1, the *New York Times* reported that Washington was considering the temporary recall of its ambassador if President Diem continued to resist American wishes. On December 6 the *Times* observed that progress was being made in the negotiations. On December 7 the *Washington Post* reported that the two governments had reached a "general agreement" on a course of action. The results of the negotiations began to emerge about the middle of December and were partially reported in an official communiqué in early January, 1962.[55] The Vietnamese gained from the negotiations almost everything they wanted: an increase in the commercial import program and an acceleration of direct military aid. In return, they agreed to establish a national advisory council, its members to be chosen by President Diem, and similar councils at the province level with members appointed by the province chiefs they were to advise. Diem promised to share responsibility for military strategy with American military officers and vaguely agreed to improve the Vietnamese government's use of financial resources. There was no mention of important economic, administrative, or political reforms; in fact, the two governments agreed that the exchange rate for the piaster would remain unchanged.[56] Robert Trumbull correctly assessed the results of the negotiations for the *New York Times* when he reported that "Ngo has prevailed once more. . . . Little has emerged, at least openly, from the discussions except for a set of assurances by Ngo that steps will be taken to make his Administration more 'efficient.' "[57]

It is not surprising that the United States obtained so little from the 1961 negotiations. Even while these were in progress, the Vietnamese knew that the Kennedy Administration had decided to increase its aid to Vietnam, and that military equipment was then en route.[58] The main accomplishment of the United States in the negotiations was to gain some influence over Vietnamese military operations. It should be noted that it had made its demands for political and economic reforms for military reasons, and that the concessions granted were really only face-saving gestures except in the military sphere.

Because the United States has been primarily concerned with secu-

[55] "Joint Communiqué by the U.S. and South Vietnam," *ibid.*, January 5, 1962, p. 2.

[56] See, for example, *ibid.*, December 17, 1961, pp. 1, 27; and January 5, 1962, pp. 1–2; and the *Los Angeles Times,* January 5, 1962, pp. 1, 9.

[57] " 'Mandarin' Who Rules South Vietnam," *New York Times Magazine,* January 7, 1962, p. 87.

[58] The *New York Times,* November 17, 1961, pp. 1, 12, for example, announced that President Kennedy had decided to strengthen South Vietnam's ability to withstand the Communist assault at a November 15 meeting with the National Security Council.

rity, it has been willing to give in to the Vietnamese government on most other issues. And because it has viewed security largely in military terms, it has in the past misunderstood both the political nature of Communist guerrilla war and the importance of political reform as a means of countering the Communist challenge to Vietnam. As early as 1951, the State Department's explanation of Viet Minh strength was that "the Viet Minh Communist rebels . . . are supplied, trained, and advised by Communist China," a gross exaggeration of Chinese aid to the Viet Minh at that time. "There is," the State Department then reported, "strong and growing evidence that the war-weary people under Ho's domination are dissatisfied with Viet Minh rule, with its unceasing exactions of manpower and rice."[59] American officials knew, of course, back in 1957 and 1958 that Communist groups were active in the Vietnamese countryside, but the threat was not considered serious because it was not presented under a military guise. Even in 1959, when the countryside was slipping rapidly from the control of the Vietnamese government, American officials were far from alarmed. The deputy chief of the American military advisory mission then reported that "the Viet Minh guerrillas . . . were gradually nibbled away until they ceased to become a major menace to the government."[60] The American ambassador shared his view. "The [Vietnamese] government," he told a Senate Committee in July of that year, "is becoming more and more effective in curbing these terrorist acts . . . [and] the internal situation has been brought from chaos to basic stability."[61] These evaluations were apparently accepted by responsible officials in Washington.[62] It is ironic that the Vietnamese press was during this period running a series of articles on the growing Communist strength in rural Vietnam. One story, for example, entitled, "Rural People Call for Help," reported that "Now more than ever before security in the rural areas is seriously threatened."[63]

What American officials failed to grasp in 1959 was that Communist political activity and terrorism were the visible signs of a deteriorating

---

[59] Department of State, Office of Public Affairs, "Indochina: The War in Vietnam, Cambodia, and Laos," *Background,* August, 1953, pp. 2, 6.

[60] Report of Major General Samuel L. Myers, cited in Senate Committee on Foreign Relations, *Situation in Vietnam, Hearings, July 30 and 31, 1959,* p. 171.

[61] Testimony of Ambassador Elbridge Durbrow, *ibid.,* p. 9.

[62] See, for example, Senate Committee on Foreign Relations, *United States Aid Program in Vietnam, Report,* p. 1: "By any measure, Vietnam has made great progress under President Ngo Dinh Diem in the improvement of internal security. . . ."

[63] Article in *Nguoi Viet Tu Do,* reprinted in USOM, *Saigon Daily News Round-Up,* May 14, 1959, p. 6.

security situation. American miscalculation of the Communist threat continued well into 1961. High-level Embassy officials in Saigon were then claiming to see improvements in what was in fact a deepening military crisis for the Vietnamese government.[64] A perceptible change in the official American attitude toward the security situation, and toward the Ngo Dinh Diem regime, occurred only after the visit of the Taylor mission in October, 1961. It is only a slight exaggeration to say that high-level American authorities in Vietnam realized how badly things were going only when they received the new line from Washington.

Given the American shortcomings in understanding the nature of the Communist threat, it is natural that the United States should become concerned with its security interest in Vietnam only when that threat had taken overt military form. It is likewise natural that it should, until crisis struck, have been satisfied with the leadership of Ngo Dinh Diem however much it may have wished he were more democratic. Diem has satisfied the requirements of a policy based on military security: he has been personally honest, militantly anti-Communist, and, it appeared, well in control of things. Diem became America's indispensable man; the United States has considered him the only alternative to Communism in Vietnam.[65] Needless to add, the willing dependence of the United States upon Diem has given him a great advantage in his dealings with his major ally. American officials have been reluctant to press their demands against his opposition, and Diem on the other hand has felt safe in rejecting American demands. His greatest asset, according to what one American official has told me, is his ability to say no and to stand by his decision. True, sometimes prolonged deadlocks between Diem and the United States have deprived him of needed aid, with attendant dangers for Vietnamese security, but he has usually been able to force the American government to accede to his terms because of its security interests. Also, he has known that the United States was basically committed to him, though he has been concerned lest the Americans shift their attention to another leader.[66] The Vietnamese President understands

[64] This is based on my own interviews with Embassy officials, including the ambassador, as well as information received by Amercian journalists in Saigon.

[65] This view was expressed to me by two ambassadors to Vietnam and a number of other American officials.

[66] The Vietnamese government is hypersensitive to the possibility that the Americans might withdraw their support from Diem. Following the paratrooper revolt of November, 1960, a high Vietnamese official charged that the *coup* officers had been pushed into rebellion "by colonialist and imperialist hands." (*Times of Vietnam*, November 15, 1960.) A leaflet

very clearly how to hold the American government to its Vietnamese commitments. If Ngo Dinh Diem is, as the Vietnamese Communists charge, a puppet in the *My-Diem* relationship, he has been a puppet who pulls the strings.

Conclusion

The dominant American objective in Vietnam has been, at least since 1950, the containment of Communism. Thus, its key concern has been with security, which has been expressed largely in military terms and through a regime which has been implacably anti-Communist. The goals of economic self-sufficiency and representative government have been secondary to this overriding objective. The United States has devoted the bulk of its financial and diplomatic efforts to ensuring the military security of Vietnam, to the extent of firmly entrenching the Diem government in power; it has been especially reluctant to use its great power to pressure President Diem to relax his authoritarian rule. In its absorption with the military aspect of security, the United States has underestimated both the political nature of Communist guerrilla warfare and the inadequacies of the Diem regime in countering this threat. The problem for American policy is not whether to intervene in Vietnam's domestic political scene for, whether American officials realize it or not, the United States is a major factor in the internal balance of power in Vietnam; the problem rather is how to use this power wisely.

---

distributed by the government-created People's Committee against Communist Rebels was more explicit, claiming that the rebellious officers had "gotten the support of a group of American, French, and British colonialists and imperialists."

SELECTED BIBLIOGRAPHY

The best single reference source on Vietnam is Roy Jumper, *Bibliography on the Political and Administrative History of Vietnam, 1802–1962; Selected and Annotated* (Saigon: Michigan State University Vietnam Advisory Group, June, 1962). Mimeographed.

1. HISTORICAL (PRE-1954)

Anh Van and Jacqueline Roussel. *Mouvements Nationaux et lutte de classes au Viet-Nam.* Marxisme et Colonies, Publications de la IVe Internationale; Paris: Imprimerie Réaumur, 1947.

Buttinger, Joseph. *The Smaller Dragon; A Political History of Vietnam.* New York: Praeger, 1958.

Cady, John F. *The Roots of French Imperialism in Eastern Asia.* Ithaca, New York: Cornell University Press, 1954.

Chesneaux, Jean. *Contribution à l'historire de la nation vietnamienne.* Paris: Éditions Sociales, 1955.

Devillers, Philippe. "Vietnamese Nationalism and French Policies," in William L. Holland (ed.), *Asian Nationalism and the West.* New York: Macmillan, 1953.

Devillers, Philippe. *Histoire du Viet-Nam de 1940 à 1952.* Paris: Éditions du Seuil, 1952.

Fall, Bernard B. *Street Without Joy: Indochina at War, 1946–1954.* Harrisburg, Pa.; Stackpole, 1961.

Gourdon, Henri. *L'Indochine.* Paris: Librairie Larousse, 1951.

Hammer, Ellen J. *The Struggle for Indochina.* Stanford: Stanford University Press, 1954.

Huard, Pierre, and Maurice Durand. *Connaissance du Viet-Nam.* Paris: Imprimerie Nationale, 1954.

Le Thanh Khoi. *Le Viet-Nam, histoire et civilisation.* Paris: Éditions de Minuit, 1955.

Lacouture, Jean. "Ho Chi Minh et la tradition révolutionnaire française," in *Cinq hommes et la France.* Paris: Éditions du Seuil, 1961, pp. 11–108.

Lacouture, Jean, and Philippe Devillers. *La fin d'une guerre: Indochine 1954.* Paris: Éditions du Seuil, 1960.

Lancaster, Donald. *The Emancipation of French Indochina.* London: Oxford University Press, 1961.

Mus, Paul. *Viet-Nam; Sociologie d'une guerre.* Paris: Éditions du Seuil, 1952.

Savani, A. M. *Visage et images du Sud-Vietnam.* Saigon: Imprimerie Française d'Outre-Mer, 1955.

Taboulet, Georges. *La geste française en Indochine; Histoire par les textes de la France en Indochine des origines à 1914.* 2 vols. Paris: Adrien-Maisonneuve, 1955–1956.

Thompson, Virginia. *French Indochina.* London: George Allen and Unwin, Ltd., 1937.

2. GENERAL

Cole, Allan B., and others (eds.). *Conflict in Indochina and International Repercussions; A Documentary History, 1945–1955.* Ithaca, New York: Cornell University Press, 1956.

Corley, Francis J. "Vietnam since Geneva," *Thought* (Fordham University Quarterly), XXXIII (1958–1959), 515–68.

Donoghue, John D., and Vo Hong Phuc. *My Thuan: The Study of a Delta Village in South Vietnam.* Saigon: Michigan State University Vietnam Advisory Group, May, 1961. Mimeographed.

Dorsey, John T., Jr. "South Vietnam in Perspective," *Far Eastern Survey,* XXVII (December, 1958), 177–82.

Fall, Bernard B. "South Vietnam's Internal Problems," *Pacific Affairs,* XXXI (September, 1958), 241–60.

Fall, Bernard B. *Le Viet-Minh: La République Démocratique du Viet-Nam, 1954–1960.* Paris: Librairie Armand Colin, 1960.

Fishel, Wesley R. (ed.). *Problems of Freedom: South Vietnam since Independence.* Glencoe, Ill.: Free Press; East Lansing, Mich.: Bureau of Social and Political Research, Michigan State University, 1961.

Honey, P. J. (ed.). *North Vietnam Today: Profile of a Communist Satellite.* New York: Praeger, 1962.

Lindholm, Richard W. (ed.). *Vietnam: The First Five Years.* East Lansing, Michigan: Michigan State University Press, 1959.

Montgomery, John D. *The Politics of Foreign Aid.* New York: Praeger, 1962.

"Reports from Asia and Europe on Southeast Asia," *Atlas,* April, 1961, pp. 12–19.

Tongas, Gérard. *J'ai vécu dans l'enfer communiste au Nord Viet-Nam.* Paris: Nouvelles Éditions Debresse, 1960.

United States Congress. Senate. Committee on Foreign Relations. *Vietnam and Southeast Asia; Report of Senators Mike Mansfield, J. Caleb Boggs, Claiborne Pell, Benjamin A. Smith.* 86th Cong., 1st Sess. Washington: Government Printing Office, 1963.

Vietnam: Articles and Editorials from The New Republic, 1955–1962. (Washington: The New Republic, n.d.).

Weiner, Marjorie, and Wells C. Klein. "Vietnam," in George McT. Kahin (ed.), *Governments and Politics of Southeast Asia.* Ithaca, New York: Cornell University Press, 1959, pp. 315–417.

3. ADMINISTRATIVE

Allen, Luther A., and Pham Ngoc An. *A Vietnamese District Chief in Action.* Saigon: Michigan State University Vietnam Advisory Group, 1961. Mimeographed.

Finkle, Jason L. *A Profile of NIA Students.* Saigon: Michigan State University Vietnam Advisory Group, May, 1961. Mimeographed.

Finkle, Jason L., and Tran Van Dinh. *Provincial Government in Vietnam: A Study of Vinh Long Province.* Saigon: Michigan State University Vietnam Advisory Group and Republic of Vietnam, National Institute of Administration, August, 1961. Mimeographed.

Truong Ngoc Giau and Lloyd W. Woodruff. *My Thuan: Administrative and Financial Aspects of a Village in South Vietnam.* Saigon: Republic of Vietnam, National Institute of Administration and Michigan State University Vietnam Advisory Group, 1961. Mimeographed.

Grant, J. A. C. "The Vietnam Constitution of 1956." *American Political Science Review,* LII (June, 1958), 437–63.

Jumper, Roy. "Mandarin Bureaucracy and Politics in South Vietnam." *Pacific Affairs,* XXX (March, 1957), 47–58.

Jumper, Roy. "Problems of Public Administration in South Vietnam," *Far Eastern Survey,* XXVI (December, 1957), 183–90.

Lam Le Trinh. "Village Councils — Yesterday and Today," *Viet-My* (Saigon: The Journal of the Vietnamese-American Association), Part I (August, 1958), pp. 36–44; Part II (September, 1958), pp. 59–70.

Montgomery, John D., and the NIA Case Development Seminar. *Cases in Vietnamese Administration.* Saigon: Michigan State University Vietnam Advisory Group, 1959.

Murphy, Marvin. "Budget Reform in the Republic of Vietnam," *Revue internationale des sciences administratives,* XXVI (1960), 357–63.

Republic of Vietnam. *Constitution* (and *Rules of the National Assembly*). Saigon, 1956.

Republic of Vietnam. National Institute of Administration, Research and Documentation Division. *Government Organization Manual, 1957–58.* Saigon, 1958.

Rose, Dale L., assisted by Vu Van Hoc. *The Vietnamese Civil Service System.* Saigon: Michigan State University Vietnam Advisory Group, 1961. Mimeographed.

Scigliano, Robert, and Wayne W. Snyder. "The Budget Process in South Vietnam." *Pacific Affairs,* XXXIII (March, 1960), 48–60.

Woodruff, Lloyd W. *Local Administration in Vietnam — Its Future Development.* Saigon: Michigan State University Vietnam Advisory Group, 1961. Mimeographed.

Woodruff, Lloyd W. *Local Finance in South Vietnam: A Study of 25 Villages in the Two Southern Regions.* Saigon: Michigan State University Vietnam Advisory Group, 1961. Mimeographed.

Woodruff, Lloyd W. *The Study of a Vietnamese Rural Community: Administrative Activity.* 2 vols. Saigon: Michigan State University Vietnam Advisory Group, 1960. Mimeographed.

Zasloff, Joseph J., and Nguyen Khac Nhan. *A Study of Administration in Binh Minh District.* Saigon: Michigan State University Vietnam Advisory Group and Republic of Vietnam, National Institute of Administration, 1961. Mimeographed.

4. POLITICAL AND MILITARY

Fishel, Wesley R. "Vietnam's Democratic One-Man Rule," *New Leader,* November 2, 1959, pp. 10–13.

Honey, P. J. "The Problem of Democracy in Vietnam," *World Today,* XVI (February, 1960), 71–79.

International Commission for Supervision and Control in Vietnam. *Interim and Special Reports.* London: H.M. Stationery Office. Published about once a year.

Jumper, Roy. "The Communist Challenge to South Vietnam," *Far Eastern Survey,* XXV (November, 1956), 161–68.

Nguyen Tuyet Mai. "Electioneering: Vietnamese Style," *Asian Survey,* II (November, 1962), 11–18.

Nguyen Khac Nhan. "Policy of Key Rural Agrovilles," *Asian Culture* (Saigon), III (July-December, 1961), 29–49.

Republic of Vietnam. *The Problem of Reunification of Vietnam.* Saigon: Ministry of Information, 1958.

Schmid, Peter. "Free Indochina Fights against Time," *Commentary,* January, 1955, pp. 18–29.

Scigliano, Robert. "The Electoral Process in South Vietnam: Politics in an Underdeveloped State," *Midwest Journal of Political Science,* IV (May, 1960), 138–61.

Scigliano, Robert. "Political Parties in South Vietnam under the Republic," *Pacific Affairs,* XXXIII (December, 1960), 327–46.

United States Congress. Senate. Committee on Foreign Relations. *Report on Indochina; Report of Mike Mansfield on Study Mission to Vietnam, Cambodia, Laos.* 83rd Cong., 2d Sess. Washington: Government Printing Office, October 15, 1954.

United States Department of State. Office of Public Service, Bureau of Public Affairs. *A Threat to the Peace: North Vietnam's Effort to Conquer South Vietnam.* 2 parts. Washington: Government Printing Office, 1961.

Zasloff, Joseph. "Rural Resettlement in South Vietnam: The Agroville Program," *Pacific Affairs,* XXXV (Winter, 1962–63), 327–40.

5. SOCIAL AND ECONOMIC

Buu, Hoan. "Vietnam: Economic Consequences of the Geneva Peace," *Far Eastern Economic Review,* December 11, 1958, pp. 753–57; "Vietnam: Structure of a Dependent Economy," *ibid.,* December 18, 1958, pp. 789–90, 793–94, 797–98; "Impact of Military Expenditure on the South Vietnamese Economy," *ibid.,* December 25, 1958, pp. 839–43.

Child, Frank C. *Essays on Economic Growth, Capital Formation, and Public Policy in Vietnam.* Saigon: Michigan State University Vietnam Advisory Group, May, 1961. Mimeographed.

Cole, David C. *Financing Provincial and Local Government in the Republic of Vietnam.* Doctoral dissertation, University of Michigan, 1959.

Gittinger, J. Price. *Studies on Land Tenure in Vietnam: Terminal Report.* Saigon: United States Operations Mission to Vietnam, 1959.

Gittinger, J. Price. "United States Policy toward Agrarian Reform in Underdeveloped Nations," *Land Economics,* XXXVII (August, 1961), 195–205.

Hammer, Ellen J. "Progress Report on Southern Vietnam." *Pacific Affairs,* (September, 1957), 221–35.

Hendry, James B. "Land Tenure in South Vietnam," *Economic Development and Cultural Change,* IX (October, 1960), 27–44.

Hendry, James B., assisted by Nguyen Van Thuan. *The Study of a Vietnamese Rural Community: Economic Activity.* Saigon: Michigan State University Vietnam Advisory Group, December, 1959. Mimeographed.

Hickey, Gerald C. *The Study of a Vietnamese Rural Community: Sociology.* Saigon: Michigan State University Vietnam Advisory Group, 1960. Mimeographed.

Hotham, David. "U.S. Aid to Vietnam — A Balance Sheet," *The Reporter,* September 16, 1957, pp. 30–33.

Scigliano, Robert. "They Work for Americans: A Study of the National Staff of an American Overseas Agency," *American Sociological Review,* XXV (October, 1960), 695–704.

Taylor, Milton C. "South Vietnam: Lavish Aid, Limited Progress." *Pacific Affairs,* XXXIV (September, 1961), 242–56.

Taylor, Milton C. *The Taxation of Income in Vietnam.* Saigon: Michigan State University Vietnam Advisory Group, 1959. Mimeographed.

Trued, M. N. "South Vietnam's Industrial Development Center," *Pacific Affairs*, XXXIII (September, 1960), 250–67.

United States Agency for International Development. Statistics and Reports Division. *U.S. Foreign Assistance and Assistance from International Organizations, July 1, 1945–June 30, 1962.* Revised; Washington, April 24, 1963.

United States Congress. House of Representatives. Committee on Foreign Affairs, Subcommittee for Review of the Mutual Security Programs. *Staff Report on Field Survey of Selected Projects in Vietnam and Korea.* 86th Cong., 1st Sess. Washington: Government Printing Office, May 14, 1959.

United States Congress. House of Representatives. Committee on Foreign Affairs, Subcommittee on the Far East and the Pacific. *Current Situation in the Far East, Hearings, July 27, August 3, 11, 14, 1959.* 86th Cong., 1st Sess. Washington: Government Printing Office, 1959.

United States Congress. Senate. Committee on Foreign Relations, Subcommittee on State Department Organization and Public Affairs. *Situation in Vietnam, Hearings, July 30 and 31, 1959.* 86th Cong., 1st Sess. Washington: Government Printing Office, 1959.

United States Congress. Senate. Committee on Foreign Relations, Subcommittee on State Department Organization and Public Affairs. *Situation in Vietnam, Hearings, December 7 and 8, 1959.* 86th Cong., 1st Sess. Washington: Government Printing Office, 1960.

United States Congress. Senate. Committee on Foreign Relations, Subcommittee on State Department Organization and Public Affairs. *United States Aid Program in Vietnam, Report.* 86th Cong., 2nd Sess. Washington: Government Printing Office, February 26, 1960.

United States Operations Mission to Vietnam. *Annual Report.* Saigon: Published at end of each fiscal year.

United States Operations Mission to Vietnam. Program Office, Research and Statistics Section. *Annual Statistical Bulletin.* Saigon: Published annually.

Wurfel, David. "Agrarian Reform in the Republic of Vietnam." *Far Eastern Survey*, XXVI (June, 1957), 81–92.

INDEX

Adloff, Richard, 74n
Administration, pre-French, 7–8; colonial period, 8–12; structure, 31–34; colonial influences, 34–35, 36–39, 48–51, 62–64; administrative class, 49–50; attrition of administrators, 67–68
Agrarian reform, *see* land reform
Agriculture, 104–105, 107
Agrovilles, 171–72, 178–80
Allen, Luther A., 32n, 45n, 205n, 218
Annam, *see* regions
Alsop, Joseph, 134, 150
American, *see* United States
Anh Van, 74n, 217
Anti-Communism, denunciation campaign, 167–69; negativism, 185–86
Army, size, 47; condition, 162, 183–84; political interference, 185

Bao Dai, 11, 22–23
Binh Xuyen, 18–24, 89
Bloc for Liberty and Progress (Caravelle Group), 84–85, 88
Bui Van Luong, 64n, 133n
Buss, Claude A., 105n
Buttinger, Joseph, 4n, 7n, 217
Buu Hoan, 101n, 102n, 220
Buy-American policy, 109–110, 200

Cady, John F., 217
Cambodia, and Geneva Agreements, 131–32; Associate State, 191; alleged Communist bases, 143
Cambodians in Vietnam, 4
Cao Dai, 18–24, 74, 84, 86–87, 89
Caravelle Group, *see* Bloc for Liberty and Progress
Catholics, 57–58, 76; percentage of population, 53–54; influence, 53–55
Centralization of power, in post-1954 Vietnam, 55–56; by Ngo Dinh Diem, 56–57

Chau, Nguyen Huu, *see* Nguyen Huu Chau
Chesneaux, Jean, 217
Child, Frank C., 116n, 119n, 204n, 206n, 220
China and Vietnam, early history, 6–7; Communist China, 131–32, 148–49, 150; Nationalist China, 201
Chinese in Vietnam, 4–5, 118–19, 201
Citizens Assembly, 79
Civil Guard, 138–40, 160, 161; size, 47; as internal security force, 163–67, 184, 201, 208
Civil service, 47–50; surplus of personnel, 48; Western orientation, 48–49; loyalty, 50–51
Cochinchina, *see* regions
Cole, Allan B., 23n, 134n, 190n, 217
Cole, David C., 220
Communists, political activities, 80–81, 92; harassment of elections, 95–97; interference with economic development, 103, 107, 109, 113–14, 117–18, 123–24; theory of guerrilla war, 135–37; decision to overthrow regime, 137; propaganda themes, 137–38; size of forces in South, 141–42, 143, 145; influence in rural areas, 142; appeal in South, 157–59
Communist China, *see* China and Vietnam
Community action programs, 169
Confucian principles, in economic development, 111
Conner, Judson J., 163n
Constitution, drafting, 26–27; institutions established, 28–29; and security situation, 171–72; and trade unions, 177
Corley, Francis J., 218
Coups d'état, attempted, 187–89, 207–208, 209, 215–16
Courts, 29, 35–36, 171
Cuong De, Prince, 71–72